Contents

Part 3: Confronting the Most Common Concerns

How God Uses Wives
to Shape the Souls
of Their Husbands

SACRED INFLUENCE

GARY THOMAS

BEST-SELLING AUTHOR OF *SACRED MARRIAGE*

ZONDERVAN.com/
AUTHORTRACKER
follow your favorite authors

We want to hear from you. Please send your comments about this book
to us in care of zreview@zondervan.com. Thank you.

ZONDERVAN

Sacred Influence
Copyright © 2006 by Gary L. Thomas

This title is also available as a Zondervan ebook.
Visit www.zondervan.com/ebooks.

This title is also available in a Zondervan audio edition.
Visit www.zondervan.fm.

Requests for information should be addressed to:
Zondervan, Grand Rapids, Michigan 49530

Library of Congress Cataloging-in-Publication Data

Thomas, Gary (Gary Lee) –
    Sacred influence : what a man needs from his wife to be the husband she wants /
Gary L. Thomas.
       p. cm.
    Includes bibliographical references.
    ISBN-10: 0-310-27768-X
    ISBN-13: 978-0-310-27768-2
    1. Wives – Religious life. 2. Influence (Psychology) – Religious aspects – Christianity. 3.
Husbands – Psychology. 4. Marriage – Religious Aspects – Christianity.
    I. Title.
    BV4528.15.T56 2006
    248.8'435 – dc22   2005023927

Interior design: Michelle Espinoza

Printed in the United States of America

13 14 15 16 17 18 /DCI/ 29 28 27 26 25 24 23 22 21 20 19 18 17 16

To Drs. Steve and Rebecca Wilke.
"The pleasantness of one's friend springs from his earnest counsel"
(Proverbs 27:9).

From Lisa Thomas

Dear Readers,

Thanks for picking up this book! I hope and pray that you will choose to read it. If you're like me, you have a pile of really good and helpful books waiting to be read, and sometimes it's hard to prioritize them. I truly believe that Gary has something worthwhile to say in this book; I know your marriage will be blessed if you do read it.

Gary wrote this book partly in response to the many emails and questions received from women who had heard him speak or who had read his other books. He heard their frustration, pain, and sometimes anger at husbands who just didn't seem to be getting it. Because of this, he deals with real-life stuff, addressing issues that women like you and me are dealing with. He doesn't offer "five easy steps" that are guaranteed to transform your situation, but he tries to help women gain a better understanding of how men tick and catch a glimpse of the spiritual dynamics at work within your marriage. I hope you'll see his brotherly love as he walks you through the process of your own marital journey.

I'm often asked if Gary really lives what he writes, and my answer is always a resounding yes! Because he is a man of integrity, I can wholeheartedly recommend his books. And just in case you're wondering, yes, he did ask my permission to use every story involving me. It is our hope and prayer that our vulnerability will be used by God to bless others. Like any couple, we don't have a perfect marriage, but it's a marriage I thank God for every day. I can't imagine another life, and if our journey can, in any way, inspire your own, I'm pleased to share it with you. May you be encouraged.

Enjoy!

Lisa Thomas

Acknowledgments

There are so many people to thank.

First, thank you to those who agreed to let your stories inspire others. Many of you chose to remain anonymous, so I'll respect your privacy. You know who you are, and I am deeply grateful for the courage it took to open up your lives for the benefit of others.

Second, my "four therapists" who provided their expert analysis (and the specific, relevant education I lack in this regard) and who helped shaped this book accordingly: Dr. Melody Rhode, Leslie Vernick, Dr. Mitch Whitman, and Dr. Steve Wilke. Thank you for being so generous with your understanding and patient with my lack of it.

Then to the readers: Donna Burgess, Cheryl Scruggs, Jo Franz, Lisa Fetters, Dina Horne (who actually read through an early draft in the waning days of her political campaign and just before she left town on a missions trip), and Nicole Whitacre. Bless you for your input, your encouragement, and the very helpful comments.

I especially want to thank Mary Kay Smith and Dr. Rebecca Wilke, who have both previewed several of my books. Thank you for loving me and this work in progress enough to speak the hard word when it needed to be spoken and for challenging me, consistently and persistently, to go deeper. You both are true friends.

None of the aforementioned may fully agree with all that is said in the book you now hold, but I believe everything is that much closer to the truth — and much better said — because of their service.

I also want to thank John Sloan at Zondervan, who had his hands full trying to redirect an initially scattered manuscript. This hasn't been the easiest book, has it? My appreciation goes to Dirk Buursma, for his word management and encouragement; and especially to Jen Abbas, whose enthusiasm and fresh energy lifted me up enormously in the latter days of this whole process.

My wife has been no less than a saint throughout this ordeal — she has read, reread, and listened to me think out loud more than any wife should ever have to endure over a lifetime. She has done far more than merely "influence" this man — God has used her to reshape him. I love you, Lisa.

Introduction:
God Hears and Sees

My friend Nina walked up to me after church one time. "Matt and Riley are sick," she said. "They want me to rent them something to watch, but I don't know what to get them."

"That's easy," I said. "*Band of Brothers*. They'll love it."

"I haven't heard of that."

Just then, my teenage son — who also happens to be one of Riley's best friends — showed up. "Graham, Nina needs a movie for Matt and Riley to watch while they get better. I suggested *Band of Brothers*. What do you think?"

"Yeah, that's a good one," Graham said. "They love war movies."

This was just one small incident in my life that Nina may not even remember — but it helped to cement the idea for this book. When a wife wants to rent a good movie for her husband and son, whom is she likely to ask? Hopefully, it won't be someone who thinks it just doesn't get any better than *Breakfast at Tiffany's*.

She's probably going to ask another guy.

And when you want to know how you, as a wife, can encourage your husband to become more involved at home, grow in his Christian walk, or lose some bad habits — like looking at pornography or losing his temper — doesn't it also make sense that you might benefit from a man's perspective?

Many excellent books have been written by women to encourage other women in their marriages. Stormie Omartian, Linda Dillow, Dr. Laura, and many others have blessed women with wise advice and well-written books. But as you study your man, might it not also be helpful to get a guy's perspective on how to move another guy? My publisher and I thought it long past the time for you to hear from a brother in Christ who can give you some male insights into your husband's thoughts and feelings.

God's Heart

As I began the writing process, one morning in particular gave me an entirely new enthusiasm for this book. While praying, I began to get a sense of God's heart for what I believe he wants to do in these pages. I realized that if I could truly understand God's heart for his daughters, if I could but glimpse the passion he feels for you and the tears he cries when you cry — how he feels each slight that you feel and how he hates the condescending tone with which you often get addressed — then I might begin to realize why God would care about a book like this and why he might put it in my mind to write it. He doesn't want to leave you alone in relationships that bring you less than what he designed.

In fact, God sees and hears everything taking place in your life and relationships. He knows the many wives who suffer in loveless marriages. He knows how men tend to look down on women and act condescendingly toward their wives. He knows that men can provide great strength, nurture, comfort, and security, but also that they can be frustrating, terrifying, demanding, and selfish. He sees the women who feel trapped in difficult marriages, as well as those who enjoy relatively good marriages with men who still occasionally act selfish, thoughtless, or distant.

But he also knows the holy ways in which a woman can profoundly move a man!

That's good, since my wife and I have heard more horror stories than we can count:

- the man with eight children, his wife pregnant with number nine, who says he wants to quit work, go back to college, earn another degree, and make a career change;
- the husband who becomes more obsessed about achieving a single-digit handicap in golf than about the emotional state of his children;
- the man who models risky and immoral behavior in front of his children, including substance abuse, violation of the law for financial gain, and the like;
- the man more eager to build a huge congregation than to nurture and care for the family who waits for him at home;
- the man who complains that his wife is "cold" in bed but who is himself mechanical, selfish, and in a rush during intimate moments.

These, of course, are the extreme cases. Far more often, a husband remains involved, caring, and even sacrificial — but still, you might wish you knew how to help redirect your man down an even better path.

I'll be up-front with you: you can't *change* a man. But you *can* influence him or move him — a far subtler art. And that's what we're going to discuss in this book.

Hope for the Hurting

I believe God has heard your prayers, and I *know* he sees your pain. I further believe that, since he designed marriage, you should look first to him about how you can best encourage, inspire, challenge, and appropriately influence the man you married. God wants you to feel loved, to be noticed, and to be cherished. He didn't create you and cast you adrift on a sea of happenstance or circumstance. He has watched you every day, and he is watching you even now, catching the tear you might be shedding this very moment at the thought of a God so involved in your life that he put your thoughts on paper for you to read.

But be forewarned! Your husband isn't the only imperfect person in your relationship. You also contribute sin every day. We are all sinners, and you can be sure that God desires to work on your own heart every bit as much as he desires to have greater influence in your husband's life. In keeping with this perspective, this book will present some serious challenges for *you* to be moved as well — closer to God and closer to your husband.

As you make your way through these pages, I long for you to see God's care and concern between every line. He truly loves you. He really is intimately familiar with your situation. He wants to give you guidance on how a woman can create a sacred influence. It may surprise you to learn about the many biblical personalities you may have read right over — such as the widow of Zarephath — not realizing the powerful lessons their lives offer. I also pray that you'll see how contemporary women like Catherine, Diana, Pat, and Jo found a way to lovingly redirect their husbands at crucial crossroads.

You can do more than wring your hands and hope for the best. You can learn to inspire your husband, profoundly influence him, encourage him, and eventually help him to move in the right direction. One day in the not-too-distant future, I pray that you'll wake up in bed, look at the man lying next to you, and finally experience *hope*. A woman who commits herself to God and who learns to act with his wisdom is a fully empowered woman who is embarking on an exciting and life-changing journey. I trust in the reality of God's presence in our lives. It may sound like a cliché, but it's still a biblical truth: *With God, all things are possible.*

Let's get started.

Part 1

Your Marriage Makeover Begins with *You*

Chapter 1

The Glory of a Godly Woman

Understanding Who You Are in Christ

I laughed out loud when I saw it. While waiting in line at a grocery store, I read the cover of a leading women's magazine and just *had* to write down the title of one of its articles: "Why so many smart, good women put up with snarly, dreadful men."

You know what made me laugh? I can't even *imagine* a leading men's magazine — say, *GQ* or *Esquire* — with an article titled "Why so many honorable, decent men put up with conniving, manipulative women." It would never happen. Nor will you ever see books titled *Men Who Love Too Much* or *The Men-Haters and the Men Who Love Them.*

There's a good reason for this. Historically, neurologically, socially, and even biblically, I believe one can make the case that women tend to be more invested in their relationships and marriages than are men. As my friend Dr. Melody Rhode, a psychologist and marriage and family therapist, puts it, "Women are bent to their husbands; we just are." This reality has its roots in the very first family.

Back in Genesis 3, following the fall, God tells Eve, "Your desire will be for your husband" (verse 16). Respected Old Testament commentators Keil and Delitzsch suggest that the Hebrew language here evokes a "desire bordering on disease."[1] It comes from a root word connoting a "violent craving" for something.

Some women exhibit more of this than others. I recently listened to a talk program in which a woman described how her husband had carried on a secret affair for more than four years. The husband had acted cruelly on many fronts. He had introduced his mistress to his wife, for example, and in his wife's absence he had brought the mistress home. In fact, he even took his mistress into his wife's bed. The illicit relationship ended only when the mistress died.

But do you know what most surprised me about the call? The wife seemed more concerned about losing this despicable man than she did about facing a life without him! Even though he had disrespected her as deeply as possible, trampled on their marital intimacy, and offended their marriage bed, she felt more afraid of waking up without him than of waking up next to him. In fact, she really wanted to find out more about the mistress! What did she look like? What kind of personality did she have? What did her husband see in her?

Contrast this with a recent question-and-answer article in *Sports Illustrated*, in which a number of professional male athletes were asked if they would ever take back a "runaway bride," a woman who left them at the altar and embarrassed them in front of their family and friends. Not a single athlete said he would. One of the men responded so vehemently and colorfully that I can't even print his answer in this book.

Why the discrepancy? In some cases, it may indeed be that women are more spiritually and emotionally mature, willing to forgive for the sake of the family and larger considerations. But in other cases, it might be less noble than that. Some women never rise above a sinful propensity to define themselves according to their likability — or acceptance — by men. Unfortunately, some men seem to have an ultrasensitive spiritual radar that picks up on this. They somehow intuit a woman's spiritual neediness and will exploit it for their own ends.

Because of Christ's work and the conquering power of the Holy Spirit, however, Christian women can be set free from such psychological dependency and destruction. Listen to a passage from 1 Corinthians 7, as rendered by Eugene Peterson in *The Message*: "And don't be wishing you were someplace else or with someone else. Where you are right now is God's place for you. Live and obey and love and believe right there. God, not your marital status, defines your life" (verse 17).

Did you catch that last line? *God, not your marital status, defines your life.*

Is this true of you? The more it is, the more success you will have in moving your man, because weak women usually forfeit their influence.

Look at this from a very practical perspective: do you care much about what a person for whom you have little respect thinks of you? Probably not. So then, how is such a person going to influence you? When their opinion doesn't matter, they may communicate clearly, honestly, and practically — but you're still not going to listen to them. In the same way, if your husband doesn't respect you, if you have sinfully put his acceptance of you over your identity as a daughter of God, then how will you ever influence him for the better?

Now let's put a positive spin on this. If someone you really respect, greatly admire, and enjoy spending time with comes to you with a concern, aren't you going to give their words extra thought? Aren't you at least going to consider that they may have a point, and that you need to pay attention?

Of course you are.

This explains why the type of woman who moves her man is a woman who also *impresses* her man. I heard one husband gush about his wife's business acumen, while another raved about his wife's intelligence. Yet a third man went on and on about his wife's spiritual maturity and her ability to understand the Bible. A reserved, introverted husband spoke with great admiration about his wife's ability to make friends, while another man described in detail his wife's most recent athletic accomplishment.

You may not have realized this, but husbands *like* to brag about their wives. They may not say it to you, but they notice your strengths and take pride in them. But far more important than your business savvy or social skills is your spiritual core. This is what will give you the strength and respect that are so necessary for being a godly change agent in your marriage. And it will bless your husband immensely. According to 1 Timothy 3:11, a man's qualification for spiritual office includes being married to a woman "worthy of respect."

The first step toward influencing your man is becoming such a woman — the unique person God created you to be, in all your glory.

Truly understanding the radical and liberating nature of Jesus' message concerning women will help you become such a person. In this next section, I'd like to move those of you who define yourself based on the fall ("I'm worthy because men like me") to defining yourself based on your relationship to God ("I matter because I'm made in the image of God, am loved by God, and am regularly empowered by God to make a difference in this world").

World Shapers

The Bible affirms women in a way that was quite radical for the time in which it was written. The Old Testament stepped outside its cultural milieu to insist that women mirror God's own character and image just as fully as do their male counterparts: "So God created man in his own image, in the image of God he created him; male and female he created them" (Genesis 1:27). Right from the start, we learn that women and men *together* mirror the image of God. Males, by themselves, are not up to the task; since God is above gender, males alone (or females alone) fail to adequately represent his character and image.

While the apostle Paul does ascribe a certain significance to the man's being created first, if you look at the line of creation, females are the culmination! Everything keeps getting more sophisticated, more intricate, until finally a woman appears — and only then does God rest.

Just as tellingly, the admonition to act on this world, shape this world, and even to rule over this world is given to women just as much as it is to men: "God blessed *them* [the man *and* the woman] and said to *them*, 'Be fruitful and increase in number; fill the earth and subdue it. Rule over the fish of the sea and the birds of the air and over every living creature that moves on the ground'" (Genesis 1:28, emphasis added).

Women are not told to sit passively on the sidelines and cheer for their husbands as the men run the show. On the contrary, from the very beginning women share God's command for humans to rule, subdue, and manage this earth. They are co-regents.

Some ancient theologians tried to amend this somewhat by blaming Eve for the fall, thus implying that women are spiritually weaker; but the Bible itself is far fairer to women. While it acknowledges Eve's complicity in the fall, it also trumpets Eve's redemptive role in the future. The Genesis account doesn't end with Eve (and Adam) eating the fruit. God prophesies that though the serpent "won" this round, his certain and annihilating defeat would come *through the woman*. Keil and Delitzsch put it this way:

> If then, the promise [to crush the head of the serpent] culminates in Christ, the fact that the victory over the serpent is promised to the posterity of the woman, not of the man, acquires this deeper significance, that as it was through the woman that the craft of the devil brought sin and death into the world, so it is also through the woman that the grace of God will give to the fallen human race the conqueror of sin, of death, and of the devil.[2]

Jesus, Friend of Women

This strong, affirming view of women continues into the very first book of the New Testament, with the inclusion of women in the genealogy of the Messiah (a literary act that breaks with the tradition of the first century). Yes, there is Abraham and David and Joseph — but there is also Rahab, Ruth, Mary, and even a reference to Bathsheba. Who would expect such a thing from a very patriarchal and even misogynistic culture? It took *both* men and women to set up the human events that led to the birth of the Messiah. God chose women of diverse personality and status — including some women with less than pristine purity — to build the human line that ushered in the Savior of the world.

Just as significantly, Jesus came into this world through a woman. Not a single male had anything to do with the conception or birth of our Lord. Instead, God chose a woman to accomplish the miracle of the incarnation.

While the notion that we have to tear down men to lift up women is destructive and unhelpful, it is nevertheless amazing to realize how often the men who surrounded Jesus simply didn't get it, while the women did. One time, a Pharisee was having dinner with Jesus when a prostitute came in and washed our Lord's feet with her tears, drying them with her hair (Luke 7:36–50). This act appalled the Pharisee, but Jesus said (I'm paraphrasing and amplifying here), "You just don't get it! She understands who I am, while you, even with all your learning, remain blinded to my place and glory."

In addition to the clueless Pharisees, the male disciples of Jesus also occasionally revealed thick skulls. One time a woman poured costly perfume all over Jesus' head (Mark 14:3–9). Some of the disciples said to themselves, "What a waste!" while Jesus thought, "Finally, here's someone who really gets who I am." In fact, Jesus declared that this woman's action would be remembered wherever his gospel would be preached. Not one person out of a hundred can name all twelve disciples, but most people have heard of this bold woman.

Jesus also elevated women in his teaching. In Mark 10:11, Jesus astonishes his disciples when he tells them, "Anyone who divorces his wife and marries another woman commits adultery against her." Why was this astonishing? According to rabbinic law, a man could commit adultery against another married *man* by sleeping with that man's wife, and a wife could commit adultery against *her husband* by sleeping with another man; but no provision stipulated how a husband could commit adultery against his wife.[3] According to one commentator, Jesus "is expressing a reaction against the frequently low esteem of women, even in Judaism.... This sharp intensifying of the concept of adultery had the effect of elevating the status of the wife to the same dignity as her husband."[4] Jesus was telling those first-century men, "Your wife has equal value in God's sight. It is possible for you to sin against her every bit as much as it is possible for her to sin against you."

And let's look at Jesus' death. While one male disciple betrayed our Lord and ten others cowered behind locked doors, some very courageous women (and just one male disciple) dared to watch Jesus' final minutes on this earth. Mark goes out of his way to emphasize the scene at the foot of the cross: "Some women were watching from a distance. Among them were Mary Magdalene, Mary the mother of James the younger and of Joses, and Salome. In Galilee these women had followed him and cared for his needs. *Many other women who had come up with him to Jerusalem were also there*" (Mark 15:40–41, emphasis added). In Jesus' most trying moments, he was supported by many women and one man. Modern readers might read right over this narrative fact — but in the early history of the church, this was a startling truth and a challenge to any false view of male superiority.

But perhaps the boldest statement came after Jesus died and was raised from the dead. According to ancient Pharisaic law, a woman's testimony was inadmissible in a tribunal as too untrustworthy. Only men could give witness. So when Jesus rose from the dead — the most important event that has ever occurred or ever will occur — who was present to give witness and testimony? Women! Jesus pointedly uses women, whose testimony could not be heard in contemporary courts of law, to proclaim his glorious resurrection.

This elevation of women at all points — in theological pronouncements, historical accounts, and practical teaching — should really astonish us, given the male-oriented culture in which the Bible took shape. Thousands of years before *feminism* had become a word, God repeatedly stood up for women, giving them a prominent place in the story of all stories.

Let the words of the Bible wash away any mistaken cultural notions you may hold that inaccurately depict God's view of women.

The Bible presents a woman as a strong image bearer of God, able to stand against the world, powerfully influencing men and culture (witness the case of Deborah in the Bible or Teresa of Avila in history) as she lives the life God created her to live. Despite the negative messages you may have received — whether from your family, church, or culture — you need to

- understand the glory of being a woman made in God's image;
- experience the strength you have as the recipient of his Holy Spirit;
- and find refuge in the worth and purpose you have as his daughter.

Through this mighty spiritual core you can influence the world — including your husband. *God, not your marital status or the condition of your marriage, defines your life.*

You may have thought that biblical submission sentences you to a second-tier status, that you must be your husband's doormat and allow him to walk all over you without ever raising your voice as you quietly pray in the corner. Such an outdated view comes from the culture, not the Bible.

Don't think I am promoting a radical feminist agenda here! In fact, I believe it is important to affirm differences in gender roles (we'll talk more about this later). Men and women *aren't* the same — but they *are* equal in God's eyes, and there is a unique glory in both genders.

I believe you owe it to the God who created you — and to yourself, to the husband who married you, and to any kids you've given birth to — to become the woman he designed you to be, in all your glory, power, strength, and wisdom.

When Marriage Becomes Idolatry

While some women define themselves on the basis of how one man (or men in general) views them and accepts them, as a *Christian* woman you have the opportunity to define yourself in relation to your Creator — not in defiance of your husband but in a way that

will complement your marriage and bless your husband. It will unleash in you the glory of being a godly woman.

Let's apply some simple theology here. Who does the Bible say is
your refuge — God, or your husband? Deuteronomy 33:27 provides
the answer: "The eternal God is your refuge, and underneath are the
everlasting arms."

In whom does your hope lie? Your husband's continuing affection? First Peter 1:21 says, "Your faith and hope are in God."

Where will you find your security? Your husband's ability to
earn a living and his commitment to stay married to you? Philippians 4:19 answers, "My God will meet all your needs according to
his glorious riches in Christ Jesus."

Where will you find supreme acceptance that will never fade or
falter for all the days of your life? "As a bridegroom rejoices over his
bride," replies Isaiah 62:5, "so will your God rejoice over you."

If you're trying to find your primary refuge in your husband,
if you've centered your hope on him, if your security depends on
his approval, and if you will do almost anything to gain his acceptance — then you've just given to a man what rightfully belongs to
God alone.

And that means you've turned marriage into idol worship.

When you do that, both you and your husband lose. You can't
love a false idol long term. You just can't. You may worship it for
a while, but eventually that idol's limitations will show and you'll
become bitter and resentful. Just as surely as a block of wood can't
speak wisdom, so a human man can't love you as God created you
to be loved. And what happens when an idol disappoints you? Ah,
that's the type of experience that gives birth to the cliché, "Hell hath
no fury like a woman scorned."

In addition, how will you ever find the courage to confront
someone whose acceptance so determines your sense of well-being
that you believe you can't exist without him? How will you ever
take the risk to say what needs to be said if you think your future
depends on your husband's favor toward you?

Your future depends on God, not on a fallen man. Your security rests with your caring Creator's providence, not with your

husband's paycheck. Your acceptance as a person became secure when God adopted you, not when your husband proposed to you. If you truly want to love, motivate, and influence your husband, your first step must be to connect — and to stay connected — with God. Find your refuge, security, comfort, strength, and hope in him.

This line of thinking is neither academic nor theoretical. Statistics show that most women will die as widows. Women, by and large, live longer than men. Since most women marry men as old as or older than they are, the math isn't all that hard to figure out. *If you die while still married to your spouse, you'll be in the minority.* Sooner or later, you're probably going to have to live without your husband.

This means the day will likely come when you will need strength, courage, and character like you've never had before. You'll have to stand on your own. So then, why not develop that strength, courage, and character *now*, while your husband is still living and you're not beside yourself with grief? Why not bless this world with the example of a woman defined by God, living a life that reveres God, twenty or thirty years sooner than widowhood forces it on you?

Before I address the practical issues of how to influence your husband, I encourage you to reevaluate and affirm your biblical standing as a woman. More often than not, this will be a process — perhaps you'll have to pray over the Bible verses in this chapter until they become real to you. But you *must not* accept any identity that gives you less than the Bible offers you. Before you run the race, you have to train. Before you can influence someone, you must become spiritually strong enough to stand up to your husband's "functional fixedness."

We'll discuss this, and much more, in the next chapter.

Chapter 2

The Strength of a Godly Woman

Becoming Strong Enough to Address Your Husband's "Functional Fixedness"

D r. Melody Rhode often uses a psychoneurological term to describe a man's reluctance to change: *functional fixedness*. Men don't normally change if what they've been doing seems to be working for them. When a woman allows her husband to treat her with disrespect, he has no motivation to change — and so it's unlikely he ever will.

Melody notes, "There's a simple question I ask wounded women who seek help to endure belittling or degrading treatment from their man: 'Why does your husband treat you badly?' Answer: *because he can.*" This is not, in any way, to blame a woman for the abuse but to develop a new blueprint for a different future.

Melody continues. "If what he's doing is working for him, why change? He needs a compelling reason to change, and it needs to be more compelling than your unhappiness or private misery with the situation."

I would think that a God-fearing man would be motivated to change simply by understanding that his actions hurt you. But I'm also a realist. Some of you may be married to a man who doesn't much care if his actions hurt you, as long as he gets what he wants. In such cases, allowing the behavior to continue while complaining about it won't change anything. It's not *your* pain that motivates him but *his* pain. You have to be willing to create an environment in which the status quo becomes more painful than the experience of positive change.

Here's the trap I've seen too many wives fall into: a woman keeps expressing to her husband how he is doing something (or *not* doing something) that is hurting her. Even after several such conversations, he doesn't change — or he'll change for a few days and then go back to his old habits, at which point the wife complains again. Still, no long-term change. The wife reads a book or attends a seminar and decides she needs to find a better way to communicate so she can get her message across, but even after this, there's no permanent change. Her error is assuming that she's not getting through. In point of fact, she *is* getting through to her husband — he may fully understand and be completely aware of her pain, but he's not motivated by *her* pain. If he likes the marriage as it is, he'll put up with an occasionally disagreeable conversation now and then.

In such cases, spouses need to make a serious evaluation. There was a point in "Jenny's" marriage when she realized, based on her and her husband's parents' health history, that she and "Mike" could be married for sixty years. At the time, Jenny had been married for just fifteen years, but that left, potentially, another forty-five years of being together — which also meant another forty-five years of a situation that Jenny wasn't sure she could live with.

"There is no scenario in my life plan in which I want divorce — none," Jenny told me. "At the end of my life, my fervent hope and determination is to be, unreservedly, a one-man woman. But I also know enough not to overestimate my patience. I could put up with some disappointments at the time, but was I willing to live with this for another forty-five years?

"At that point, I felt I needed to be more honest about some struggles and more up-front about making a change. It created some discomfort for a season as I stopped pretending that everything was OK — but was a season of discomfort worth changing the course of our marriage for the next forty-five years? Without question!"

Without nagging and without petty recriminations (withholding sex, the silent treatment, a critical spirit, and so forth), Jenny gently but forcefully made her husband see that as long as he acted the way he did, their marriage was going to suffer in specific ways — ways that affected *him*. It was only when Mike started feeling his own pain that he was shaken out of his functional fixedness enough to change his behavior.

I believe Jenny makes an important point: be wary of over-estimating your willingness to live with a glaring hurt or a gaping need. Don't pretend that Satan won't exploit it or that you won't be tempted by another man who happens to be strongest exactly where your husband is weakest. If, like Jenny, your ideal life plan leaves no room for divorce, you must honestly accept your weaknesses and be willing to create a climate in which your spouse will be motivated by his pain. This is a courageous and healthy movement toward your spouse and toward preserving and strengthening your marriage, and it is an act of commitment, not rebellion.

All this requires a very specific application based on your spouse's personality, so I can't give you "five steps to overcome functional fixedness" here — but you'll receive plenty of ideas and suggestions as we touch on various topics throughout this book. At this point, it's enough to say that if merely communicating your hurt isn't solving the problem, you're most likely dealing with a case of functional fixedness, and you'll need to be strong to address that issue.

Some women fall into the trap of failing to speak up for fear of losing their man; they don't want to "rock the boat," even though it appears that the boat is headed toward a waterfall. But this passive acceptance makes it *more* likely that the husband will stray; he won't respect his wife for putting up with his poor behavior, and this attitude will only reinforce his disrespectful behavior. Sadly, many women think their husband's anger is the great enemy of their security, but, in fact, weakness and the corresponding relational boredom pose a far more potent threat.

If you can stand strong and secure in your identity and in your relationship with Christ, courageously making it clear how you will and will not be treated, you will be amazed to see how the respect you show for yourself rubs off on your husband.

Things Must Change

Here's the male insider's view, right at the start: you have more influence over your husband than you realize. When you are a woman of respect, the last thing your husband wants is to lose you. If he thinks he can have you *and* his aberrant behavior, he'll take both. But if the day comes when he knows you won't simply turn a blind eye to what he's doing, when he thinks he might even lose you if he continues down the path he's walking, he's going to be shaken out of his functional fixedness and at least consider making changes.

Your reactions and opinions matter greatly — far more than you may realize. In a later chapter, I'll discuss how *desperately* men want their wives' affirmation. When a woman stands up and says, "This *will* affect our relationship and my view of you," most men will at least start listening. You'll notice as you read this book that many of the women who moved their husbands toward holiness came to a point where they decided that things could not and would not stay the same. They stopped "playing the game" and made it clear to their husbands that they were determined to stand strong in the Lord.

As noted earlier, too many women have given up this power to influence their husbands because they fear being left alone. "If I say, 'No more,' he may leave me. Then what?"

Consider this: what if he stays and then grows in the Lord because of it?

Has your past acquiescence ever changed *anything*? If not, why should it change anything in the future? God's provision and strength will help you face the consequences of obedience. God won't leave you alone, regardless of what happens. God, not your marital status, defines your life.

Embrace this freedom and the glory of being a strong woman who is alive to God! God has given you the power to influence your man. But even if your man should leave, God will give you the grace and power to cope. Once you fully understand your status before God, you need never again live at the mercy of a man's approval. Understand the power you have, and utilize that famous "mystery" of a man with a woman (Ephesians 5:31–33).

Dr. Melody Rhode sees the threat of a husband's losing his wife as perhaps the greatest possible motivator for a husband. Of course, we have to place this within the context of a covenantal, committed marriage. The Bible is very specific and very limiting regarding what constitutes an acceptable divorce. Discontentment, seeming incompatibility, and mere displeasure *don't* qualify! Melody points out, "A woman's power needs to be surrendered to God and used for his purposes, not our own."

She also stresses, however, that most women, because of our culture, don't realize the power they have to move their husbands. "They feel powerless because of their sex," she observes, "and this has resulted in a lot of pent-up anger, frustration, and even desperation." As your brother in Christ, I'm encouraging you to be bold, courageous, and strong. Use the natural and very real spiritual influence and role that God has designed for you to move the man in your life.

Be Bold

The first thing so many women in the Bible had to be told was to stop being afraid, to become bold. When Hagar was abandoned by her husband and exiled to what looked like her and her son's slow starvation and death, God's angel encouraged her, "Do not be afraid" (Genesis 21:17). When the women who had been faithful to Jesus were beside themselves with grief, wondering what had happened to the body of their precious Jesus, an angel admonished them, "Do not be afraid" (Matthew 28:5).

I know I may sound as though I'm encouraging you toward risky action, but the "safe" path is sometimes a slow drift toward destruction. One of my favorite Christian philosophers, Elton Trueblood, put it so well:

The person who never goes out on a limb will never, it is true, have the limb cut off while he is on it, but neither will he reach the best fruit. The best fruit which human life offers seems to come only within the reach of those who face life boldly ... with no excessive concern over possible failure and personal danger. The good life is always the gambler's choice, and comes to those who take sides. Neutrality is seldom a virtue.[1]

Fear gives birth to paralysis — and sometimes inaction is our greatest enemy. Marriages can slowly die from years of apathy. I've seen many relationships wilt from unhealthy patterns that one or both partners refused to address. The most damaging thing you can do in an unhealthy relationship is *nothing*. FedEx CEO Frederick Smith observes, "Too many think inaction is the least risky path. Sometimes action is the most conservative and safest path. Not doing anything is exceedingly dangerous. Before Pearl Harbor, they put all the airplanes in the middle of the airfield thinking saboteurs were the biggest risk, not a carrier-borne attack. They were undone by cautiousness, not bravado."[2]

If you always play it safe in your marriage, you're going to end up in some ruts. What I believe will give you the most boldness and courage to address issues that need to change is, first, understanding who you are in Christ and, second, letting God, not your marital status, define your life. Armed with that acceptance, security, and empowerment, you become a mighty force for good. You can then claim the power of Moses' words in Deuteronomy 31:8: "The LORD himself goes before you and will be with you; he will never leave you nor forsake you. Do not be afraid; do not be discouraged."

Fear and discouragement create stagnancy and persistent disappointment in marriage. If you've had your fill of those, why not try God's path of faith and boldness?

Hope Is *Not* a Strategy

One of the things I've been trying to do in these opening pages is to awaken in you a capability not often expressed to Christian women.

Our culture in general — even Christian culture — is on a long slide toward passivity that completely goes against who God made us to be.

Let me be blunt: *hope is not a strategy*. Merely "wishing" that your husband would change, merely "wanting" your marriage to be different, won't do anything. The problem is that some Christians spiritualize wishing — we call it "praying." Please understand, I'm not knocking prayer; I'm challenging a *misconception* about prayer, namely, that we can merely voice our displeasure and expect our world and our relationships to be transformed. True biblical prayer is about much, much more than that. It involves receiving our marching orders and then *acting* on them.

A good marriage doesn't happen by accident, and a good marriage isn't maintained by accident. I've never written a book by accident, and you can't build a business by accident. These endeavors require deliberate choices and much perseverance. When you start acting instead of merely wishing, when you begin taking initiative instead of simply feeling sorry for yourself, you become an active woman, and active women mirror the active God who made them.

Active God, Active Women

Genesis 1 provides our initial glimpse of who God is. The first thing God wants us to know is that he is an extraordinarily *active* God. In Genesis 1 there are *thirty-eight* active verbs describing what God does: he creates, he speaks, he separates, he calls, he blesses, he gives, and much more — all in just *one* chapter.

Then — and this is key — he tells the woman and the man *to do the same*: "God blessed them [male and female] and said to them, 'Be fruitful and increase in number; fill the earth and subdue it. Rule over the fish of the sea and the birds of the air and over every living creature that moves on the ground'" (Genesis 1:28).

God made you, as a woman, to rule in this world, to subdue it, to act according to his image. Sin begins with sluggishness, despair, and despondency. People give up on their marriages, give up on prayer, give up on their churches, give up on their kids, and eventually even give up on themselves. They say, "It's no use," and start to sulk instead of painstakingly remaking their marriage — simply because their first (or even tenth) attempt failed.

This may sound like a hard word, but readers of my previous books know I'm not one to shy away from that. *Your marriage is what you make it.* The relationship you have is the direct result of what you've put into it, and in many cases, a marriage can rise only to the level of your courage. Initial romantic intensity is unearned; it seems to fall on us out of nowhere. But marriage has to be built stone by stone. We have to make deliberate choices; we have to be active and confront the weaknesses we see in ourselves and in each other.

A Quick Test

Before you proceed to the next chapter, please take a quick test. On a scale of 1 to 10, how strong do you think you are? An answer of "1" would denote a fearful woman who lets everyone run over her and who never speaks up — for herself or for anyone else. Five would be a woman who is willing to occasionally speak up for others but not for herself. Ten would be a strong woman who stands courageously with God to become a change agent in her home, her church, and her world.

The second question to ponder is this: how can God use one of the current challenges in your marriage to move you from a "3" to a "5," or from a "7" to a "9"?

Finally, the test ends with this; it requires a simple yes or no answer: Will you allow God to make you stronger by courageously addressing the issues in your marriage and by persevering through the fallout as he guides you?

It's my firm belief that the current challenges in your marriage may well be God's vehicle for you to become the strong woman he created you to be.

Chapter 3

"Be Worthy of Me"

How God Uses the Weaknesses of Others to Help Us Grow

Bestselling author and historian David McCullough stumbled across a startling letter by John Adams, written to his wife, Abigail, in the heat of the Revolutionary War: "We can't guarantee success in this war, but we can do something better. We can deserve it."

Later, McCullough read another letter, this one by George Washington, which uses the exact same line. He traced the words to a play called *Cato*. This line summarizes the spirit behind the birth of our country, and it can help modern women reform their marriages. McCullough explains, "That line in the Adams letter is saying that how the war turns out is in the hands of God. We can't control that, but we can control how we behave. We can deserve success."[1]

The same principle is true for you in your marriage. You can't guarantee how everything will turn out; you definitely can't control another human being. But you *can* "deserve" success. You can act in such a way that transformation is most likely.

I want you to think about something: What if your husband's faults are God's tools to shape you? What if the very thing that most bugs you about your man constitutes God's plan to teach you something new? Are you willing to accept that your marriage makeover — the process of moving a man — might begin with you?

"Be Worthy of Me"

Napoleon Bonaparte's astounding military success found a rival only in his raging ego. In one letter he chastised his wife, "I insist you have more strength. I am told you are always crying. For shame, that is very bad! ... Be worthy of me and develop a stronger character. Make a proper show in Paris. ... If you are always weeping I shall think you have no courage or character. I do not like cowards. An empress should have heart."[2]

While Napoleon's condescension both nauseates and offends us, I think he stumbles onto an interesting turn of phrase: "Be worthy of me." This should be the goal of every husband and wife — a man aspiring to be "worthy" of his wife, and a wife aspiring to be "worthy" of her husband.

In our self-esteem-obsessed culture, telling someone he or she needs to become "worthy" sounds anathema, but there's biblical precedence for this. Jesus says that anyone who fails to take up his cross is not worthy of him (Matthew 10:38). Paul asks the Romans to receive Phoebe "in a way worthy of the saints" (Romans 16:2). He urges the Ephesians to live a life "worthy of the calling you have received" (4:1). Saints are urged to be worthy, or commended for being worthy, in Philippians 1:27; Colossians 1:10; 1 Thessalonians 2:12; 2 Thessalonians 1:11; 3 John 6; and Revelation 3:4.

This is a clarion call for us to seriously develop deep spiritual roots, to keep cultivating relational skills. We need to search the Scriptures, grow in wisdom, keep praying, and keep developing spiritual insight. With Christ in us and the Holy Spirit transforming us, we really have no excuse for continuing immaturity.

The apostle Paul charged Timothy to fully develop the gifts God gave him, and then he wrote, "Be diligent in these matters; give yourself wholly to them, so that everyone may see your progress" (1 Timothy 4:15). Paul wants Timothy to know, "You're not perfect, but people should see *progress* in your life. In five years you should be wiser, stronger, and more mature in character than you are now."

My wife married a very immature twenty-two-year-old. I sincerely hope that her husband is now more mature, more loving, and less selfish than he was back then. And I pray fervently that in another ten years, her husband will have become that much more mature, that much more loving, that much kinder and wiser and selfless.

This growth won't happen by accident, of course. It won't occur unless I am — to use Paul's words — "diligent in these matters," unless I "watch [my] life and doctrine closely" (1 Timothy 4:16), "persevering" in them. If I won't grow, my wife may well grow past me. I can't give Lisa a perfect husband, but I certainly don't want to give her a spiritually lazy one. I want to become "worthy" of her. I may never fully get there, but it won't be for lack of trying. I'll never be as thin as I once was, and I'll never have the hair I did back then, but I can become a man whose character far outshines that of the twenty-two-year-old she married.

You see, when you grow in character, when you sink your spiritual roots deep, when you learn to hear God's voice and build your mind with his wisdom, when you allow his Holy Spirit to transform your character and reshape your heart — then you can make your husband fall in love with you over and over again, and he'll be all the more motivated to maintain your respect and affection. Nothing compares to being married to a godly woman — *nothing*. And nothing gets more tiresome more quickly than living with a narcissist or a weak wife or a fearful one.

Your husband chose you as you were and accepts you as you are — but you can bless him with the woman you want to become. Will you do that? Will you honor his faith in you by becoming a woman he could only dream about?

Painful Perseverance

The reason it's so important for you to concentrate on your own growth is so that you can avoid the sin of pride, which constantly tempts us to focus on changing our spouses while neglecting our own weaknesses. Jesus warned against this with startlingly strong words: "Why do you look at the speck of sawdust in your brother's eye and pay no attention to the plank in your own eye? How can you say to your brother, 'Brother, let me take the speck out of your eye,' when you yourself fail to see the plank in your own eye? You hypocrite, first take the plank out of your eye, and then you will see clearly to remove the speck from your brother's eye" (Luke 6:41–42).

Making over your marriage *begins with you*. For me to suggest anything else would be to deny everything I've ever written. I'm not saying it's wrong to desire more from your husband. I'm not denying that you might enjoy your marriage more if your husband would drop some bad habits and pay more attention to you. I *am* saying that if you use this book to focus on changing your husband in such a way that you neglect to grow yourself, all I've done is inspire another Pharisee, not the godly woman God seeks.

Let's agree to keep this perspective in mind throughout the book.

How is God using the reality of living with an imperfect man to teach you how to grow in patience and understanding? How is God using your marriage to an irritable man to teach you how to love angry people? How is God using your husband's sexual desires, your husband's vocational insecurities, or perhaps your husband's lack of social skills to teach you how to deny yourself, take up your cross, and follow him?

How is he using your marriage to teach you how to love?

When you find yourself in a difficult marriage, or in a basically good marriage with one particular issue that grates on you, you can be sure that God wants to mature you as you face this problem *with strength, courage, dignity, and biblical wisdom.* God could, of course, speak the word and your problem would be solved — voilà! But that's not how God usually works. He allows us to face issues that may terrify us and make us feel completely inadequate — he may even walk us through our deepest fears — so that we can grow in him.

The Bible is adamant about this. Spiritual growth takes place by persevering through difficult times:

- "We also rejoice in our sufferings, because we know that suffering produces perseverance; perseverance, character; and character, hope. And hope does not disappoint us" (Romans 5:3–5).

- "Consider it pure joy, my brothers, whenever you face trials of many kinds, because you know that the testing of your faith develops perseverance. Perseverance must finish its work so that you may be mature and complete, not lacking anything" (James 1:2–4).
- "These [trials] have come so that your faith — of greater worth than gold, which perishes even though refined by fire — may be proved genuine and may result in praise, glory and honor when Jesus Christ is revealed" (1 Peter 1:7).

Most of us will never confront the physical persecution these verses were directly addressing, but we do face spiritual and relational trials with the same effect. God can use your marriage to make you a stronger, wiser, and more complete woman — provided you don't run from the challenges that being married to your husband represents.

The Equation of Change

Your marriage isn't just a number on a scale of 1 to 10; it's a mathematical equation: $x + y = z$. Your husband may be the x — a number you absolutely can't change. But if you change the y (that's you), you influence the overall result of your marriage: $x + 2y = q$. That's at once both the beauty (change is always possible, even if only unilaterally) and the frustration (the nature of that change is limited and not guaranteed) of human relationships. It's also why this book focuses on how a woman can *influence* a man, not on how a woman can *change* a man.

It is entirely natural and healthy to dream big things for your husband, but that's very different from selfishly *demanding* those things.[3] When you dream something in a positive way, you offer yourself to God as an instrument of love, change, and spiritual transformation. When you demand that someone change for your sake, you're literally trying to bend the world around your comfort, your needs, and your happiness. That's pride, arrogance, and self-centeredness — and God will never bless *that*.

So let's lay out our expectations right at the outset. What do you dream for your man? Maybe you want your husband to stop drinking, to pay more attention to the kids, to pray with you, or to read with you. Or perhaps you want him to stop giving free rein to his temper, to quit looking at pornography, or to be more of a spiritual leader. Chances are pretty good you want your husband to be more relationally aware and involved.

These are good dreams! Any man would get a tremendous blessing if just one of them were to come to pass. But please keep this in mind: your eternal standing before God does *not* depend on the success of any of these endeavors.

The good news is that you and God are in this together. He knew, even before he created you, who you'd marry. And he will continue to give you the tools you need to become the person he's called you to be and to do the work he's created you to do within your current relationship. God would *never* leave you alone in any situation: "He will never leave you nor forsake you" (Deuteronomy 31:6). Even if you married a non-Christian, God's grace is sufficient for you. You cannot dig a hole so deep that it cuts you off from God's provision, care, and life-giving strength. Yes, our choices may result in unpleasant consequences, but even then, God helps us to endure.

That's the message I want to communicate: you and God are in this together, and he's beginning your marriage makeover *with you*. Let him transform you as you seek to move your husband. While you may never achieve the results you have in mind, you can — without question — change the equation of your marriage by remodeling yourself. It begins with understanding, perhaps for the first time, the glory of being a godly woman and acting with the strength of a godly woman who understands she was created in the image of God, forgiven of her sins through the work of Jesus Christ, and gifted and empowered by God's Holy Spirit to live the life God has called her to live.

You may have picked up this book simply to find out how you can motivate or even transform your husband. I'm here to tell you that as noble as this cause may be, it's too small for you. God made you to remake *the world*. Your home is where it starts. By courageously facing up to the challenges that every marriage faces, and by letting God change *you* in the process, something wonderful takes place — the formation of a new woman, fully alive to God, who can take the lessons she learns at home and apply them everywhere else.

"We can't guarantee success in this war, but we can do something better. We can deserve it."

Part 2

Creating the Climate
for Change

Chapter 4

The Widow at Zarephath

Understanding a Man's Deepest Thirst

Was there ever a more desperate woman? In a land laid waste by famine, with no food anywhere, the mother looked at the remaining flour and oil and realized she had enough for one last meal.

This scene played out nearly three thousand years ago, long before supermarkets overflowed with food and before convenience stores and fast-food restaurants on every street corner promised quick remedies for growling stomachs. Back then, during a famine and drought, no food meant, literally, *no food*. Every apple had been picked; every potato had been dug up. Even the bark had been stripped off the trees. Anything that could possibly be consumed had been, leaving death as the last certainty.

Imagine you are this widow. You've endured the trauma of watching your husband die — and now you face the awful prospect of watching your son slowly waste away from starvation.

Just then, a strange man enters your life, claiming to be God's prophet. He asks you to make him a meal. When you reply that you're running out of flour and oil, with just enough to make one last meal for you and your son, he assures you that if you'll bake him the last loaf, your jar of flour will never run out and your jug of oil will never run dry.

What do you have to lose? So you do what he says and then watch in amazement as his words prove true. For months on end, that tiny pile of flour and that small jug of oil continue to replenish themselves. At first, you opened that jar and jug with great trepidation. You wanted to believe you were living a miracle, but your mind fought the idea all the way: "Maybe the flour was just stuck to the sides of the jar; maybe the oil likewise just ran down the sides and gathered at the bottom — " Gradually, after a few days, you realize that only one explanation makes sense: God is miraculously providing for you through this prophet named Elijah. No natural phenomenon can explain what you're experiencing.

Over time, you're no longer surprised when you open up the jar and the jug. In fact, though it goes against all reason, you would be more surprised if those receptacles were empty than full. The replenishing has happened so often that it no longer seems like a miracle. It's just the way things are.

But then tragedy strikes and shakes you from your complacency.

Your son becomes seriously ill from a disease that bears no connection to hunger. After a painful battle, he succumbs to the sickness and dies.

Now you are furious with the man of God who has kept you from starvation. What good did it do you to be spared an early death from hunger, only to watch your son die from disease? You confront Elijah and tell him exactly what you think of him and how you wish you had never laid eyes on him.

Elijah takes your son into a back room, out of your sight. A short while later, you can't believe your eyes — your once-dead son walks straight into your arms! You've never felt joy like this — and in a spontaneous gush of praise, you cry out, "Now I know that you are a man of God and that the word of the LORD from your mouth is the truth" (1 Kings 17:24).

Suddenly it gets very quiet. You realize you've just insulted the man who saved your son. *Now* you know that he is a man of God and that God speaks through him? Only *now* you believe him? What have you been eating for the last several months? From where do you think that flour kept coming? Who told you, against all reason, that the oil would keep flowing? And yet, still, it takes *this* for you to believe his words?

What happened to the widow so long ago continues to happen in many marriages today. Elijah's miraculous provision for this woman became commonplace. What once seemed like an extraordinary occurrence — flour and oil that never ran out — soon became a common blessing, so expected that it ceased to be noticed, much less appreciated. After a week or so, it was just the way things were.

Sadly, many women view their husbands in this very way. Their spouses' strong points become so familiar that the women no longer see them, much less appreciate them. But when one weakness rears its ugly head, all else gets blotted from memory.

Husbands, of course, pick up on this. In a poll of a thousand men, just 10 percent of husbands — only one out of ten — believe their wives love them more than they love their wives. We think we're much happier with you than you are with us.[1]

Blinded to the Blessing

On the first anniversary of the 9/11 attacks, Lisa and I watched several interviews with women widowed as a result of those attacks. "What has changed most about your perspective in the past year?" one interviewer asked. The first widow to respond said, "The thing I can't stand is when I hear wives complain about their husbands." Every woman nodded her head, and then another widow added, "It would make my day if I walked into the master bathroom and saw the toilet seat left up."

Their words have a profound ring. The little things we allow to annoy us seem trivial compared to the loss of blessings once taken for granted. In the face of their enormous loss, these women no longer cared about the little irritations; instead, they had to face the big, black hole of all that their husbands had done for them, suddenly sucked out of their lives forever.

❧

"Sarah" lives on the East Coast. (For various reasons, I've made this a composite story.) She attended one of my "Sacred Marriage" conferences and had gathered with several women in a small group between sessions. One wife started boasting about the beautiful backyard rock garden her husband had built over a three-day weekend. Sarah seemed unusually quiet until she finally held up her hand and said, "Please, stop! My husband spent all last weekend on the couch, watching a golf tournament. I don't need to hear about how your husband spent those days working in the yard!"

Later, I spoke with Sarah one-on-one.

"How large is your house?" I asked.

"A little over two thousand square feet," she said. "And it has a nice yard."

"Wow, that sounds great, especially with three small children. You must feel fortunate to be there."

"I guess so," she said.

"Where do you work?" I asked.

"Oh, I don't work," Sarah replied. "My husband makes enough for me to stay at home with the kids."

"That's fantastic!" I told her. "Do you realize that 65 percent of the women in your situation have to work outside the home, whether they want to or not? You're one in three as far as being able to choose to stay home. That's gotta feel good."

"I guess so," she said.

I steered the conversation to the Monday following her husband's lazy weekend. Unknown to Sarah, I had spoken with her husband, so I knew what had taken place on Monday. "Jim" took their son out to do a little batting practice; the young boy was preparing to start his first T-ball season and was eager to get some tips from his dad. Later that afternoon, Jim took their daughters to a movie. On the way home, he called Sarah and asked if he could get anything for her at the grocery store.

After Sarah recounted all this, I asked her, "Do you have any idea what a single mom would say if, for just one day, a man came over and took her son out for some 'guy time,' teaching him how to hit a baseball, or if he gave her a break by taking her daughters out in the afternoon and then called to see if he could pick up anything for her at the store on the way home? She'd feel like she had died and gone to heaven! She'd go to bed praying, 'Thank you, Lord, for one day when it wasn't all on my shoulders.'"

I watched as a light switched on in Sarah's face. She glided over to Jim and kissed him on the forehead.

"What was that for?" he asked.

"For being you," Sarah replied.

Sarah had forgotten Jim's "common blessings." Minutes before, she remained blind to what her husband did by focusing only on what he hadn't done on one weekend. Now, she saw him in a new light.

I recently had the privilege of ministering in South Africa. Our hosts took my son and me to Soweto, a famous housing area home to the Mandelas and Bishop Desmond Tutu. Amid some nice homes lay a vast landscape of makeshift dwellings, cobbled together with scrap materials. We stopped at one place, and small children ran up to meet us, holding out their hands for free candy. Off in the distance, I saw a young mother carrying a five-gallon bucket to the group water spigot. Her neighborhood had no electricity and only a few shared faucets. Our eyes met fleetingly. While she could only imagine to what I would return, for me, there was no imagining. I could *see* how she lived. And I wished I could give every Western wife a glimpse of what this woman faces every day. You might not live like a movie star, but then again, you probably don't have to walk a couple of blocks through muddy alleys to gather your daily water.

When did you last thank your husband for helping to make your style of life possible?

Loving the Less Than Perfect

It is the rare wife indeed who compares herself to a young mother in Soweto. Most will feel tempted to compare themselves to someone who has it just a little (or even a lot) "better." They're like Sarah, the wife of the golf-watching husband, who fell into the same trap as did the widow at Zarephath. Though Elijah had proven himself time and again, once a new problem arose, the widow suddenly couldn't see all that Elijah had done. She could see only what he *hadn't* done.

I admit that if I were talking to Jim, I'd challenge him to consider whether spending most of the weekend watching golf is the best use of time for a young husband and father. Jim certainly overdid it. Even so, it wasn't fair of Sarah to look at Jim only in regard to this one lost weekend. Jim had provided a beautiful home. He earned enough money so Sarah could stay at home with her kids, as she wanted to. He was involved in his children's lives. Jim wasn't a perfect man, but there was plenty to be thankful for. As my friend Lisa Fetters says, "Wives need to look at the big picture, not isolated incidents."

To move a man, you have to learn to appreciate him for who he is and for what he has done. I've talked to wives who, in the abstract, know their husbands can't be perfect; but in reality, they resent the fact that they're not. As author and marriage counselor Leslie Vernick states, "They're looking for their Prince Charming. When he turns out to be just a regular guy, they're disappointed."[2]

James 3:2 has revolutionized the way I look at family life: "We all stumble in many ways." Notice the words "all" and "many." No spouse avoids this reality. We *all*—including your husband — stumble in *many* ways. To live with a man is to live with someone who is certain to let you down — not just once or twice, but in many ways. Even Dr. James Dobson and Pastor Rick Warren stumble in *many* ways. That "Mr. Perfect Husband" you see so graciously open the door for his wife every Sunday, who always seems so kind and thoughtful and who provides a wonderful income? Somewhere, in some concrete expression, that man stumbles in many ways. If you were to divorce your husband and spend five years interviewing potential second husbands, if you gave them psychological tests and interviewed their closest friends and family members, if you found a man who seemed to match you emotionally and spiritually and recreationally — you'd still end up with a husband who would stumble in many ways.

Only one perfect man ever walked this earth, and he never married. Since every wife is married to an imperfect man, every wife will have legitimate disappointments in her marriage. Are you going to define your husband by these disappointments, or will you pray that God will open your eyes to the common blessings that your husband provides and to which you often become blinded?

Think about this carefully and honestly: as soon as you marry a real man, you're going to have to learn to let go of certain expectations. A real man *will* be a sinner. A real man *will* have rough edges. A real man comes with real weaknesses and with gaps in his knowledge or ability. If you don't want to be married to a real man — or if you're going to resent the unpleasant fact that your husband is real, not perfect — then don't get married. When you marry a real person, you're going to be sinned against; you're going to be disappointed; you're going to be frustrated. That's real life.

My wife and I once met a woman married to a marvelous handyman, the type of guy who can fix anything. If he builds a tree house for his children, it has working doors and windows. He keeps his wife's SUV in perfect running condition. Nothing in their house stays broken for longer than forty-eight hours. But he isn't particularly "deep," in his wife's view. He doesn't favor long, soulful talks. He's a good listener, but you won't hear him sharing a lot of personal feelings. And he never cracks open a book.

My wife immediately liked the sound of this man because she lives with the constant frustration of having a mechanical klutz for a husband. She has to endure toilets that keep running, doors that stick, and projects that get put off until we save up enough money to pay a professional to do them. When I try to fix something, the problem invariably gets worse, costing us even more to fix it in the long run.

And yet this other wife made it pretty clear that she wished her husband would be available to talk things out. She wondered aloud to my wife what it would be like to be married to a writer who deals with concepts and who regularly talks to people and who likes to discuss books with his wife. I'm pretty sure my wife may have felt tempted to wonder whether this woman had a much better thing going, particularly when Lisa had to get up in the middle of the night (for the umpteenth time) to jiggle the handle on the toilet to get the water to stop running!

No husband comes in a perfect package. No husband can do it all. Your job as a wife is to fight to stay sensitive to your husband's strengths. Resist the temptation to compare his weaknesses to another husband's strengths, while forgetting your husband's strengths and that other husband's weaknesses. Don't resent your husband for being less than perfect; he can't be anything else.

Disappointment Detectors

Why is this perspective crucial if you are going to provide a sacred influence? Husbands detect disappointment with uncanny accuracy. Because we so deeply value affirmation, whenever we don't get it, it feels like living with one long, loud, psychic scream. And we tend to react like this: "If I can't please her by trying my hardest, then why should I try at all?" I'm not saying we *should* react this way; I'm just saying that's how we usually *do* react.

If you want to move your husband in a positive direction, then you need to appreciate him from your heart.

In her book *Capture His Heart*, Lysa TerKeurst tells of boarding a shuttle bus at the airport, where she met a sixty-year-old man who said something very simple but astonishing. Lysa commented that people must love to see the shuttle bus pull up, because it means they're going home. The driver laughed. "Yeah, everyone is excited to see me pull up to the curb. That's why I like my job so much. People get on the bus and smile so big. They've just been waiting for me, and when I finally arrive, they are happy I'm here. I've often wished I had a video camera to tape people as they get on my bus with the smiling faces and glad-to-see-ya comments. I'd love for my wife to see a tape like that. That's the way I've always wanted her to look when I come home from work."[3]

That's the way I've always wanted her to look when I come home from work.

I doubt there's a guy alive who doesn't feel this way. Whether we're a shuttle bus driver, a CEO, a world-class athlete, or an assistant manager at a grocery store, it does something to a man's heart when his wife and kids look happy to see him. I know — sometimes with our surly moods and our air of entitlement, we can make it very difficult for you to feel happy to see us. But that's what we need.

My friend Dave Deur, a pastor at Central Wesleyan Church in Holland, Michigan, taught a class on marriage, during which he asked all the men to list five ways they love to be loved. Virtually *all* the lists included acts or words of appreciation — and many men listed affirmation several times, using different words. I was struck by how many men used at least two (or often even three) of their five answers to describe affirmation. In fact, one man's list of five things could all be summarized as affirmation!

So you see, that shuttle driver who just wants his wife's face to light up when she sees him isn't unusual; he's typical. Rule number one for influencing your man is this: *stop taking your husband for granted*. He wants to feel noticed, special, and appreciated. That puts him in a "moldable" mood. When he feels he is taken for granted, he becomes defensive and resentful of the mere suggestion of change.

Leslie Vernick, author of *How to Act Right When Your Spouse Acts Wrong*, once asked a husband in a counseling situation what he would most like from his wife. He responded, "There was a guy at work who was clumsy and never did the job quite right. None of us guys thought much of him, but when his wife came in one day, she looked at him like he could do no wrong. All of us guys were jealous of him from then on, because we knew he wasn't perfect, but his wife treated him like he was. I would love for my wife to look at me like that."

Spiritual Acceptance

Without feeling appreciated, admired, and genuinely respected, your husband probably will never change. If you notice a lot of tension in your home; if you notice a high level of frustration and anger in your husband's life; if you sense a discouragement leading to passivity (where he underachieves); if you notice an "escapist" mentality, where he spends his free time playing computer games or watching sports, escaping the home with excessive recreation — then, more times than not, you're looking at a man who doesn't feel loved, appreciated, and respected. He's a man who is *coping*, not truly living. And men who merely cope never change; they just pass time.

Affirmation is more than a man's desire — much more. Acceptance and encouragement are biblical requirements:

- "Accept one another, then, just as Christ accepted you, in order to bring praise to God" (Romans 15:7).
- "Encourage one another and build each other up" (1 Thessalonians 5:11).
- "Encourage one another daily" (Hebrews 3:13).

Even if your husband never changes; even if every bad habit, every neglected responsibility, every annoying character trait, stays exactly the same — then, for your own spiritual health, you need to learn how to love this man *as he is*. Too many books and articles ignore this point. Your first step — the primary one — is to love, accept, and even honor your imperfect husband.

Now, some of you may think this sounds contradictory to what I've said in previous chapters. Yet when applied, the two truths — confronting your husband and affirming him — can complement each other. When you show respect and affirmation toward your man, it's amazing how vulnerable that imperfect husband will be to change. Dan Allender's story provides a compelling example of this.

"You're a Good Man"

In his excellent book *How Children Raise Parents*, Dr. Dan Allender describes how his young son lost his nerve on a ski slope. When the boy asked Dan to carry him down, Dan refused, so the boy fell down and began to cry and kick his feet. Dan grew irritated with his son and demanded that he ski down. As Dan raised his voice in anger, his wife, Becky, suggested he go on ahead and let her handle it.

Dan did so but then watched as his son refused Becky's entreaties. That did it for Dan; he walked back up the slope, fuming all the while, and met Becky with the words, "Move. Your way didn't work. I'll get him down my way."[4]

You're about to witness the incredible and profound power that a strong, godly woman represents. I'll let Dan take it from here:

> *Becky stood her ground.*
>
> *My wife looked at me with kindness and strength. When I finally reached her, her head slowly turned from side to side and she said, "No."*
>
> *There was a moment of silence, and she said, "I know you've been shamed by many men who meant the world to you. And I know that is not what you want to do to your son." It was all she had to say. A myriad faces flashed in my memory; and I felt again the raw experience of being humiliated and shamed by men who really did matter to me. It silenced my anger and I began to cry. My wife put her hand on my heart and said, "You're a good man." She turned away and in one fluid, graceful movement, she skied down the icy slope.[5]*

Even while Dan acted at his worst, his wife called him to his best, using affirmation. She stood up to him, but she also touched him in his anger and firmly but gently reminded him, "You're a good man."

When Dan reached his son, he was a much-changed man. That's the power women have — one magnanimous gesture and one aptly spoken phrase can work wonders. Since Dan's son had seen and heard everything, Dan opted for the direct approach.

> *"Andrew, you saw my face as I was coming up the slope, didn't you?"*
>
> *He quivered. "Yes."*
>
> *"And you saw how angry I was, didn't you?"*
>
> *"Yesss."*
>
> *"And you were afraid, weren't you?"*
>
> *"Yes, yesss."*
>
> *"And you knew I'd make you pay if Mommy had not been so strong and loving and stood in my way and protected you."*

At this point his eyes were bristling with tears, and his cheeks were shivering with fear. I looked at him, put my hands on his cheeks, and said, "Andrew, I was wrong. Mommy loved me well and loved you well too. She invited me to see what I had become and what I did not want to be. Andrew, I'm sorry for being so angry. Please forgive me."

The gift my son gave is incalculable. He put his hand on my heart as he had seen my wife do and he said with tears, "Daddy, Mommy is right. You are a good man."[6]

Can you see the good in your husband, even when he's at his worst? Can you pause long enough to see the hurt behind the heat, and call him to his best? If you can learn to do that, you *will* move your man — directly into God's arms.

Chapter 5

The Zarephath Legacy

How You Can Learn to Appreciate
an Imperfect Man

When Bobby Kennedy became the U.S. attorney general, the leaders of the civil rights movement despaired. Bobby was Irish and, according to one leader at the time, "famously not interested in the civil rights movement. We knew we were in deep trouble. We were crestfallen, in despair, talking to Martin [Luther King Jr.], moaning and groaning about the turn of events, when Dr. King slammed his hand down and ordered us to stop the [complaining]. 'Enough of this,' he said. 'Is there nobody here who's got something good to say about Bobby Kennedy?' We said, 'Martin, that's what we're telling ya! There is no one. There is nothing good to say about him. The guy's an Irish Catholic conservative [expletive], he's bad news.'"[1]

Maybe at times you've felt this way about your husband. You see so many negatives, so many challenges and prejudices and bad habits to overcome, that you honestly can't think of one good thing to say about him. As long as you stay in this place, you'll never move him. You'll never influence him.

Martin Luther King Jr. understood this, profoundly so. He looked at his fellow leaders and said, "Well, then, let's call this meeting to a close. We will re-adjourn when somebody has found one thing redeeming to say about Bobby Kennedy, *because that, my friends, is the door through which our movement will pass.*"[2]

King then ended the meeting, insisting that there wouldn't be anything more to do until somebody came up with something good to say about Bobby Kennedy. In his view, there was no way they could move this man toward their position until they found one redeeming thing to say about him. That one thing would be the door of redemption, the door of influence, the door of change.

King's plan worked. They discovered that Bobby was close to his bishop, and they worked through this bishop so effectively that, according to the same leader who once could not find a single positive thing to say about Kennedy, "there was no greater friend to the civil rights movement [than Bobby Kennedy]. There was no one we owed more of our progress to than that man."[3]

Their greatest nightmare turned into their greatest dream.

This incredible triumph was built on the power of recognizing one or two strengths, building on them, and finding the road for their movement through that. You'll move your husband in the same way. When you find yourself in despair, overcome by negativity toward the man you married, remember the words of Martin Luther King Jr.: "We will re-adjourn when somebody has found one thing redeeming to say about Bobby Kennedy, because that, my friends, is the door through which our movement will pass."

You're Not Alone

Though every wife has married a man with a unique background and gifts and personality, every wife has one thing in common: her husband is an imperfect man. No woman has a spouse who never gives her reason for legitimate complaint. You may, indeed, have more to complain about than others; but every wife can find something that could stand improvement — otherwise, you wouldn't be reading this book!

This presents you with a spiritual challenge. You will have to fight the natural human tendency to obsess over your husband's weaknesses. When I urge you to affirm your husband's strengths,

I'm not minimizing his many weaknesses; I'm just encouraging you to make the *daily* spiritual choice of focusing on qualities for which you feel thankful. The time will come when you can address the weaknesses — *after* you've established a firm foundation of love and encouragement. For now, you must make a conscious choice to give thanks for his strengths.

I have found Philippians 4:8 as relevant for marriage as it is for life: "Whatever is true, whatever is noble, whatever is right, whatever is pure, whatever is lovely, whatever is admirable — if anything is excellent or praiseworthy — think about such things."

Obsessing over your husband's weaknesses won't make them go away. You may have done that for years — and if so, what has it gotten you, besides more of the same? Leslie Vernick warns, "Regularly thinking negatively about your husband *increases* your dissatisfaction with him and your marriage." Affirming your husband's strengths, however, will likely reinforce and build up those areas you cherish and motivate him to pursue excellence of character in others.

Guys rise to praise. When someone compliments us, we want to keep that person's positive opinion intact. We love how it feels when our wives respect us; we get a rush like nothing else when we hear her praise or see that look of awe in her eyes — and we will all but travel the ends of the earth to keep it coming.

Isn't this approach, based in God's Word, at least worth a try?

To make this realistic, you have to keep in mind that no man is ever "on" all the time. This explains why your husband can be so thoughtful, caring, and attentive one day, and so aloof, harsh, and critical the next. You have to give your husband room to be a less-than-perfect human, to have bad days, "off" days, and "average" days. The spiritual challenge comes from the fact that you are likely more apt to define your husband by his bad days than you are to accept the good days as the norm. Hold on to the good; begin to define him by the good; thank him (and God) for the good — and thereby *reinforce* the good.

The rest of this chapter will provide practical spiritual exercises to help you learn how to appreciate an imperfect man. My prayer is that it will guide you away from taking your husband for granted and toward becoming intensely and consistently grateful for the man God has given you as a companion in this journey of life.

Nurture Instead of Condemn

In my boyhood days, our family had a pet toy poodle that loved to chase cars. One fateful afternoon, she finally caught one and got seriously injured. My dad ran out to the road to retrieve the dog — and our family pet became a monster. Frenzied with fear and pain, that poodle kept biting my dad as he gathered her into his arms. He had rushed to help her, to try to bring her healing, but the pain so overwhelmed her that she could only bite the very hands trying to nurture her.

Your husband can be like that. Even if he had extraordinary parents, he most likely still brings some element of woundedness into your marriage. Maybe his siblings teased him. Maybe a former girlfriend broke his heart. Maybe he had a cold and calculating mother. The possibilities are endless — except that he comes to you as a hurting man. Maybe you even married a *deeply* wounded man. Unfortunately, hurting men bite; sometimes, like our dog, they bite the very hands that try to bring healing.

Before a casual relationship morphs into a permanent commitment, many women see a hurting man and think, "I want to help him." But something about marriage often turns that around and makes her say, "Why does he have to *be* that way?" The man's needs once elicited feelings of nurture and compassion; now these same hurts tempt his wife toward bitterness and regret.

Before you get married is the time to make a character-based judgment ("Do I really want to live with this man's wounds?"). Once the ceremony has ended, God challenges you to maintain an attitude of concern and nurture instead of one of resentment and frustration.

Can you maintain a soft heart over past hurts, patiently praying for long-term change? Or will you freeze him in his incapacities with judgment, resentment, condemnation, and criticism? Can you maintain a *nurturing* attitude instead of a judgmental one?

Give Your Husband the Benefit of the Doubt

Some wives can literally stew in their disappointment about their husbands' relational shortcomings — "Why won't he help me?" "Why won't he talk to me about this?" "Why doesn't he seem to care?" — all the while failing to realize that their husbands may not know what to do. Many women accuse their husbands of being uncaring or unloving when, in fact, he may just be incompetent! He's not *trying* to be stubborn, uncaring, or unfeeling; he just honestly doesn't know what you need or what he's supposed to do.

Norma Smalley, wife of Christian author Gary Smalley, found this to be true about the people in her married couple's small group:

> Women often feel that if their husbands loved them, the men would know what they are thinking and what they need. This simply isn't true. As wives, we need to learn to speak our husbands' language; we need to be direct in our communication and tell them what we want them to do. When we want them to listen to us and not give us advice, we need to tell them so. When we want their help on something, we need to ask them directly. [4]

My brother once frustrated his wife even while trying to please her. The kids had run out of toothpaste, so he went to the store and purchased something he thought his kids would love — Star Wars toothpaste gel. His daughters squealed with delight, but his wife hated it. "Have you ever tried to clean up that blue gunk?" she pointed out. "It's terrible, and it sticks everywhere!" Thankfully, she understood this as a case of good intentions gone bad.

Sadly, far too many wives refuse to give their husbands this benefit of the doubt. They assume he doesn't care or, worse, that he's trying to make their lives more difficult, when the reality may be that he just doesn't have a clue. My sister-in-law could choose one of two ways to look at the toothpaste fiasco: either my brother cared enough to make the trip to buy the toothpaste (despite his poor choice), or he intentionally made his wife's life more difficult by purchasing a brand that creates a cleaning nightmare.

How you choose to view your husband's actions will largely determine whether you feel pleased with him or furious with him.

May I slay a very destructive myth? Perhaps you think that the more your husband loves you, the better he'll become at reading your mind. That's a romantic but *highly* unrealistic, and even destructive, notion. It can create havoc in a marriage, and it hinders mature communication by keeping you from being direct, while at the same time tempting you toward resentment when your husband proves utterly incapable of telepathy.

Let me suggest a much healthier strategy. Instead of resenting your husband's occasional insensitivity, based at least partially (remember — you're giving him the benefit of the doubt) on cluelessness, try to address him in a straightforward manner. Be direct instead of hoping he'll "guess" what you need. His seeming reluctance to help may well result from his having no idea what you want. My friend Donna Burgess told me that, early on in her marriage, she said to her husband, "Honey, the lightbulb is out" — and her husband thought she was making an observation, while she thought she was making a request of him to change it.

Consider some other examples:

- "Honey, I'd really love it if you would rub my feet for ten minutes. I've had a hard day."
- "I'm feeling very discouraged today. Will you please listen to me talk for the next half hour? I don't want advice, but I do want you to understand. I need some strong shoulders right now."
- "Boy, it's been an exhausting day at work. I was kind of hoping we could have sex tonight, but it'll really help if you'll finish up these dishes while I sit down for a moment."

I've seen too many women want these things but never directly make their requests. They think, "If you loved me, you'd know what I want." But the truth is, if he loves you, he'll listen to your concern and act accordingly. Love is a commitment and a policy — *not* telepathy! It is far healthier to be direct and ask for help than to hope he "guesses" what you need. Most of us guys aren't nearly as clued in to you as you are to us. So help us connect. Please, just ask — directly, concretely, and regularly.

Respect the Position Even When You Disagree with the Person

The Bible calls wives to respect their husbands: "The wife must respect her husband" (Ephesians 5:33). It doesn't say wives should respect *perfect* husbands or even *godly* husbands. It says that husbands — no qualifier — should be respected.

Respect, in some instances, comes with the position, not with the person. The apostle Paul insulted a man by using bold language ("you whitewashed wall!") but then apologized after he learned he had been speaking to a high priest: "Brothers, I did not realize that he was the high priest; for it is written, 'Do not speak evil about the ruler of your people'" (Acts 23:3–5).

Your husband, *because he is a husband*, deserves respect. You may disagree with his judgment; you may object to the way he handles things — but according to the Bible, his position alone calls you to give him proper respect. If you withhold this respect, your husband may very well stop hearing you.

Give Him the Same Grace That God Gives You

Elyse Fitzpatrick, a counselor, once told her small group about how God had moved her from a legalistic, works-oriented faith to a "grace-filled, peaceful existence with my merciful heavenly Father."

"The pressure is off me," she told them. "Don't get me wrong; it's not that I'm not pursuing holiness. It's just that I know that my Father will get me where He wants me to be and that even my failures serve, in some way, to glorify Him. My relationship with God is growing to be all about His grace, His mercy, His power."

Then Elyse's friend "astounded" her by responding, "That must be such a blessing for your husband, Elyse. To be walking in that kind of grace must enable you to be so patient and so grace-filled with Phil. To know that God is working in him just as He's working in you must make your marriage so sweet and your husband so pleased. It must be great for him to know that the pressure is off for him too."

The reason this friend "astounded" Elyse is because Elyse rarely made the connection her friend made. "I scarcely ever extended to Phil the grace I enjoyed with the Lord. Instead, I was frequently more like the man in Jesus' parable, who, after he was forgiven a great debt, went out and beat his fellow slave because he owed him some paltry sum."[5]

It takes great spiritual maturity to love mercy, to offer grace, to give someone the same spiritual benefits we ourselves have received from our heavenly Father. Get in touch with how much God has done for you — how he has seen every wicked act you've ever committed; heard every syllable of gossip; noticed every malicious, ugly, and hateful thought — and still, he loves you. Even more, he adores you. And he's forgiven you.

Now comes the hard part: will you give your husband what God has given you?

Form Your Heart through Prayer

Practice praying positive prayers for your husband. Find the five or six things he does really well — or even just one or two! — and try to tire God out by thanking him for giving you a husband with these qualities. Follow up your prayers with comments or even greeting cards that thank your husband personally for who he is.

I've practiced this with my wife — with amazing results. One morning, I awoke early and immediately sensed my frustration from the previous evening. We had an issue in our relationship that we had talked to death over the previous two decades. Lisa acknowledged her need to grow in this area, but events of the previous weeks had convinced me that nothing had changed.

I felt resentful, and in my resentful mood, I can slip into what I call "brain suck." I start building my case. Like a lawyer, I recall every slight, every conversation, and prove to my imaginary jury how wrong my wife is and how right I am.

Suddenly, I remembered the widow of Zarephath. I decided to apply the truth from this passage, so I mentioned something about Lisa's personality for which I felt very thankful. That reminded me of something else, which reminded me of something else, which reminded me of yet another quality. After about fifteen minutes, I literally started laughing. I saw so much to be thankful for that it seemed preposterous that I should waste time fretting over this single issue.

Prayers of thankfulness literally form our soul. They very effectively groom our affections. Leslie Vernick explains this from a counseling perspective: "Cognitive therapists know that what we think about directly affects our emotions. If we think on negative things, nursing bad attitudes or critical spirits, our emotions take a downward spiral. Conversely, if we think on things that are good, true, right, things that we are thankful for, then our emotions can be uplifted."

Make liberal use of this powerful tool. We have to give it time. One session of thankfulness will not fully soften a rock-hard heart. But over time, thankfulness makes a steady and persistent friend of affection.

Drop Unrealistic Expectations

I found one of the wisest tidbits on marriage I've come across in a long time when I read the words of Patricia Palau, wife of the famous evangelist Luis Palau. Patricia says she knew, even before marrying Luis, that her husband intended to zealously fulfill God's call to reach the lost: "God wants everyone to be saved (1 Timothy 2:4), and there have been times when I thought my husband was determined to do his best to reach the last four billion lost souls for Jesus Christ."[6] Because of Luis's call, Patricia faced certain difficulties that would drive some women crazy: "extensive travel, lengthy separations, and mothering four boys alone at least a third of the time." Add to this an uncertain income and living in three countries during the first few years of their marriage, and you might expect to find a resentful, bitter wife.

Not if you talk to Patricia.

Here's that bit of wisdom I said was coming: "We expected things to be different from the norm. We also knew up front that we couldn't meet each other's needs 100 percent. That realization protected us from disappointments that result from unrealistic expectations."[7]

Your husband will not meet 100 percent of your needs. He probably won't even meet 80 percent. If you expect him to, you're going to become frustrated, bitter, resentful, and angry. God didn't set up marriage to meet 100 percent of your needs! Your beef isn't with your husband; it's with the one who created marriage! When you ask more of your marriage than God designed it to give, you have only yourself to blame for your frustration.

You may be tempted to reply, "But *my* expectations are legitimate, and he's not meeting those!"

Just know this: that's what *every* angry and disappointed woman says. I'm not saying this to scold you or to deny the hurt you're feeling but simply to open your eyes to the hard, but ultimately nourishing, truth. I want you to find satisfaction rather than live in constant frustration.

Patricia discovered that accepting the role of the cross in her life helps her check her own desires. Listen once more to this wise woman:

> Perhaps some things are improved by a lack of inward focus. Instead of focusing on our marriage or our desires, Luis and I have focused on the call of God on our lives. We have lived for a cause that's bigger than both of us. And after forty years, we like each other, get along well, and have fulfilled one another as much as is possible.
>
> Our fulfillment is doing the will of God. Our heart prayer is, *Not my will, Lord, but Yours.* This focus kept me from saying, "I deserve more help than this" when Luis has been gone for two weeks, leaving me with four little boys. I didn't think, *I can't believe Luis has to leave again so soon*, two or three weeks after his last trip. For me, the Lord's command to "take up your cross and follow Me" has meant letting Luis go while I take care of things at home. No, it isn't "fair," but it brings life — eternal life — to others. And I gain peace, contentment, and satisfaction.[8]

Patricia's attitude works just as well for wives married to hardware salesmen as it does for wives married to evangelists or pastors. Patricia surrendered to *God's will*, whatever it was. Raising children, supporting a husband, staying involved in your church — all of these activities can constitute a call "bigger than both of us," even if such a call will never get celebrated in a history book.

Regardless of your life situation, the Christian life does require a cross. Your cross may look different from Patricia's, but you *will* have a cross to bear. Resentment and bitterness will make each splinter of that cross feel like a sharp, ragged nail. A yielding, surrendered attitude may not make the cross soft, but it will make it sweeter; and at the end of your life, it may even seem precious.

When, as a mature woman married for more than four decades, Patricia testifies that she has gained "peace, contentment, and satisfaction," she means she has found what virtually every woman wants — and yet very few women find. Why? Because so many women look at the cross as their enemy instead of as their truest friend. Peace? Contentment? Satisfaction? From a woman who raised four boys with an often absent husband? Who went through *two years* of chemotherapy? How can this be? Patricia understands something the world mocks: "In the end, nothing makes us 'feel' as good as does obedience to Him."[9]

If you don't die to unrealistic expectations and if you refuse the cross, you'll find yourself at constant war with your husband instead of at peace. You'll feel frustrated instead of contented, and disappointed instead of satisfied. Why? We often forget that *both* partners in a marriage have their expectations, and sometimes these expectations conflict.

Martie Stowell, married to Dr. Joseph Stowell (former president of Moody Bible Institute), found this to be true in her own marriage:

> When Joe and I became engaged, I had a set of assumptions about how our married life would be. One of those was that Joe would be home most evenings and we'd spend hours together talking, sharing activities, and dreaming together,

just like we did when we were dating. But those expectations didn't materialize. After we were married, Joe juggled seminary, a part-time job, and a ministry assignment in addition to his commitment to me as his wife. He often came home late and I would be upset about having to spend the evening without him after working hard all day at my frustrating job. I felt Joe was breaking some unspoken promise about spending time with me. But you see, that was the problem: I never spoke with him about my expectations. In my mind he was breaking a promise, but in his mind he was simply fulfilling his responsibilities.[10]

Eventually, Martie talked to Joe about her desires, and the two of them worked out an arrangement to spend some evenings together. Because of his calling as a Christian leader, Joe is not home every night as Martie once dreamed he'd be; but also because of his calling as a Christian husband, he is home more evenings than he probably envisioned as a single man. Neither received all they wanted, but both bowed to something bigger than themselves. That's why I say that harmony, joy, and peace will never grace a home ruled by expectations instead of by the cross.

In her book *It's My Turn*, Ruth Bell Graham gets pretty blunt in this regard:

> I pity the married couple who expect too much from one another. It is a foolish woman who expects her husband to be to her what only Jesus Christ can be: always ready to forgive, totally understanding, unendingly patient, invariably tender and loving, unfailing in every area, anticipating every need, and making more than adequate provision. Such expectations put a man under an impossible strain.[11]

Your Husband Isn't a Church

This fallen world will unfailingly disappoint us; that's why we need each other. You have a natural desire to know and to be known, to love and to be loved, to care and to be cared for. That's why God doesn't call us only into marriage; he calls us into community. Your husband may be a wonderful, godly man, *but he's not a church!*

Your husband cannot possibly be all things to you. You are responsible to get certain things that you need for your own personal development — and emotional and spiritual health — outside the marriage. If you've blown off your support system — your female friends, your hobbies, your recreation, your spiritual friendships — hoping your husband could replace all of these while also meeting all your relational needs, then you're setting up yourself (and your marriage) for disappointment and failure. No husband, by himself, is enough; you still need others, and it's *your* responsibility to cultivate those other relationships.

Could someone else help fill some of that aching void of disappointment you feel with your husband? For instance, maybe you wish your husband would pray with you more about your family. While you're working on that, why not find another woman and pray with her about your families? If your husband feels too tired or simply doesn't want to go to those weekly Bible studies with you, ask a female friend. Maybe your husband is more of a couch potato than a running partner; so find a woman who will run a few miles with you.

If you get some of these understandable and natural desires met outside your marriage, you will become less likely to resent your husband for what he doesn't do and more likely to recognize what he *does* do. Keep reminding yourself, *My husband is a man, not a church, and it's not fair to ask him to be all things to me.*

It all goes back to God, and not your marital status, defining your life. You have all you need as God's daughter to live a meaningful, productive, and fulfilling life. Such a life is best lived in the context of a church community. That's where we get built up, and that's where we find opportunities to serve.

Ask God to Change *You*

As soon as you begin offering prayers of thankfulness for your husband, be sure of this: the enemy of your soul and the would-be destroyer of your marriage will remind you of where your husband falls short. You can count on it.

You'll find yourself growing resentful: "Why should I thank God that my husband works hard during the day but when he comes home he won't even talk to me at night?" "Why should I thank God that my husband has always been faithful to me — when he doesn't earn enough money for us to buy a house and I have to work overtime more than I want to?"

You need to respond to this temptation with a healthy spiritual exercise: as soon as you recall your husband's weaknesses — the very second those poor qualities come to mind — start asking God to help *you* with specific weaknesses of your own. That's right — as backward as it may sound, respond to temptations to judge your husband by praying for God to change *you*. Go into prayer armed with two lists: your husband's strengths and your weaknesses.

Lest you think I'm blaming women for everything, let me say that I do the same thing: I go into prayer armed with my wife's strengths and my weaknesses. I think *both* husbands and wives should do this; but since this book is directed at wives, I'm emphasizing your response, not your husband's.

Let me be brutally honest here: a husband married to a disappointed wife loses most of his motivation to improve his bad habits. Why do you think your husband worked so hard before you got married? Because he loved the way you adored him. He wanted to catch your attention, to impress you. And when he saw that you *did* notice and *did* appreciate him, it made him want to please you even more. *He felt motivated to move by the way you adored him.*

The relational cancer of blatant disappointment will eat away any motivation for further change. Before you try to move your man, sit back, enjoy him, appreciate him, and thank God for him. Before you begin to think about what he needs to change, make an exhaustive inventory about what you want to stay the same. Then thank God for that — and thank your husband too.

Get Fresh Eyes

"Greg's" greatest failure as a husband occurred more than a decade and a half ago. Despite working as hard as he could in a small ministry, money grew scarce. Greg's wife, "Anne," was shocked at how incompetent he seemed in comparison to her own father when it came to practical things. They had a young baby, so Anne expected more and more of Greg; yet he needed to spend many of his evenings in ministry.

Greg gained considerable esteem from his work outside the home. Many people praised him, thanked him, and affirmed him for how they perceived God had used him in their lives. Yet at home, he always felt like the husband who didn't earn enough money or couldn't fix things or was always too tired.

Do you see the diabolical trap being laid?

Greg freely acknowledged himself as a less-than-stellar husband. He was still in his twenties, self-centered, and hadn't learned how to love or appreciate a woman. In hindsight, he completely understands how his wife became so frustrated with him.

Then Greg began working with a woman who shared the same vision for the ministry he had. Initially, he felt no physical attraction to this woman, so he let down his guard. But after a few months of working together, Greg went "over the line" emotionally. Scared of his thoughts, he foolishly went to the woman (when he should have approached another man in the ministry), explaining in a roundabout way that the two of them shouldn't spend any more time together.

The other woman wasn't stupid. When Greg talked about how important his family was to him and how he didn't want to endanger that, she could read between the lines.

"So you mean — ," she said, not finishing her statement, but both of them knew full well what she meant. The truth felt too shocking for two Christians to mention.

"I can't believe this," she said. "You're just so perfect — "

Those four words, "You're just so perfect," felt like the most potent drug Greg had ever known. Feeling unappreciated, disrespected, and taken for granted at home — and then hearing someone utter something so enthrallingly uplifting — literally sent him soaring.

The relationship soon became a mess. Greg decided he could work through the attraction on his own, but, of course, he couldn't. The relationship never became physical, but the emotional infidelity caused tremendous hurt. If not for the strong advice and correction of some godly men, as well as some noble choices made by the other woman, God only knows what might have happened.

Without a doubt, Greg blundered badly. His wife's perceived neglect did not drive him to this failure, nor does he blame the other woman. Greg freely admits his fault.

I tell his story in the hope that its painful lesson might encourage other wives. You see, the *same Greg* disappointed one woman and enthralled another. One woman saw him with tired eyes, while the other saw him with fresh eyes. One looked at him through frustrated expectations; one saw him with unlimited possibilities.

With what set of eyes are you gazing at your husband? *Keep in mind, you're not the only one looking at him.* That's not a threat; it's just a statement of reality.

I've talked to a number of influential men who seem surprisingly unappreciated by their spouses. Because these wives see their husbands' domestic limits, they remain blind to their accomplishments and public esteem, so they give them less encouragement at home than they receive in the marketplace — a dangerous mix, to be sure. A wise wife sometimes sits back and readjusts her view of the man she married and thus gives him his due esteem.

Let me put it another way: maybe your husband is "just" an assistant manager or even an associate pastor. While this might not seem like much to you, others still look up to your husband with respect and even affection — those your husband has hired or trained, as well as customers or church members who have come to rely on his leadership and skills. When a husband feels more respected and appreciated at work than he does at home, a precarious situation erupts. Eventually, his heart may gravitate to the place where he feels most cherished.

Working wives may face this temptation even more than stay-at-home moms, in large part because you may be among the almost 33 percent of women who earn more than their husbands.[12] Ginny Graves writes wisely about this:

> Many women are angry and exhausted after spending long days at the office, then doing the bulk of the "women's

work" at home. And if they have children, they often yearn for more free time and less stress — and wish their partners would take on more of the financial burden, a desire that often goes unfulfilled because many men can't find higher-paying work.[13]

In the midst of living with this kind of frustration, it can be easy to forget the things that first drew you to your man: his sense of humor, his thoughtfulness, his spiritual depth, or any number of other strengths. Though you may become blind to these qualities, that doesn't mean everyone else will. Respect is a spiritual obligation and discipline. Give your husband his due!

Linda Dillow writes about the time she spoke on the college campus where her husband worked. After the introduction, an eighteen-year-old said, "Oh, are you Jody Dillow's wife? I think he's wonderful!" Linda writes, "The last sentence was said with a sort of swoon. She went on to talk about my husband as if he were Tarzan, Albert Einstein, and Billy Graham all in one. I barely made it through my message that afternoon. All the way home I thought about the way this girl saw my husband. It jolted me to look at him through another woman's eyes!"[14]

How can you begin to appreciate an imperfect man? Ask God for fresh eyes.

Immeasurable Worth

In the twelfth century, the vast wealth of Weinsberg Castle lay in peril.[15] Enemy forces besieged the stone fortress and threatened the riches that lay within. The inhabitants stood no chance of defending themselves against such a great horde, and the opposing forces demanded a full and complete surrender. If the occupants would agree to give up their wealth and the men would give up their lives, the women and children would be spared.

After consultation, the women of Weinsberg Castle asked for one provision: they asked to leave with as many possessions as they could carry. If the opposing forces would agree to this one request, the men inside would lay down their arms and hand over the castle's riches.

Fully aware of the wealth of riches loaded within the castle, the enemy forces agreed. After all, how much could these women take?

Finally, the castle gates opened, and the sight that emerged elicited tears from even the most calloused soldiers. Every woman carried her husband on her back.

How many of those rescued men were perfect? Not one. But every one of those imperfect men meant more to their wives than anything they owned.

Where is *your* greatest wealth?

Chapter 6

The Helper

Embracing the High Call of Marriage

When Grant Fishbook decided to leave his position at a church, a few people didn't like his reasons, so they created their own and started slandering him. They called into question Grant's character and integrity, which only added to the misery he already felt. Discouraged, Grant was working at an eight-dollar-an-hour job, crawling under houses and trying to figure out how to pay his mortgage and feed his family while still listening to God's voice for the future.

Grant still believed God had called him to ministry, so the disappointment of recent events, the frustration of working at a less-than-satisfying job, the uncertainty of the future, and the sudden financial crisis all threatened to bury him with discouragement.

But Grant has a wife — a godly and strong wife — who stepped in. Laurel saw the disappointment in her husband's face, but she never stopped believing in him. In the midst of his discouragement, she became his protector rather than his accuser.

One day, Grant walked into the house and overheard Laurel talking on the telephone; because Grant entered the room from behind her, Laurel wasn't aware of his arrival. But this is what Grant

77

heard: "No, you *can't* talk to my husband. You don't get to him unless you go through me. And if you find a way to go around me, you'd better remember something: that's my husband, and I am his wife."

Today, Grant pastors the largest evangelical church in Whatcom County, Washington (where I live). On a recent Easter morning, over five thousand people showed up to celebrate the resurrection at Christ the King. And Grant would be the first to tell you that the reason he can do what he does is based in part on what Laurel did back then. At that time, he was a fragile man supported by a strong wife; but with Laurel's support, Grant has become a spiritual leader for an entire region.

This is exactly what God intended marriage to do.

The Spiritual Weight of Marital Roles

When God said, "It is not good for the man to be alone. I will make a helper suitable for him" (Genesis 2:18), he wasn't talking to himself — he was talking to *us*. He was letting us in on the Trinity's design for human marriage. God designed the wife to help her husband.

This theme appears throughout Scripture. The book of Proverbs proclaims the truth of a woman's helpful influence:

- "A wife of noble character is her husband's crown, but a disgraceful wife is like decay in his bones" (12:4).
- "The wise woman builds her house, but with her own hands the foolish one tears hers down" (14:1).
- "Her husband has full confidence in her and lacks nothing of value" (31:11).

Paul assumes marital "helping" to be a transferable, teachable skill; he urges a young pastor named Titus to ensure that older women properly "train" the younger women how to love — help — their husbands (see Titus 2:3–4).

This, of course, raises that most contentious of issues — biblical submission. The phrase itself can be (and has been) so misconstrued that much harm has been done in arguing both for it and against it. So let's be clear on several things.

First, the Bible does *not* teach the subjugation of women to men. The Bible does not prohibit women from serving as government leaders or CEOs or from working outside of the home. The Bible addresses roles of a husband and wife and various roles within the church, not the relationships between neighbors or coworkers.

Second, submission, properly defined, does not mean "inferior." We are all one in Christ in such a way that you could even say there exists complete sexual equality (see Galatians 3:28). God cherishes women every bit as much as he cherishes men. Women can be every bit as capable, if not more so, than men.

Third, "helper" isn't an *exclusive* title for a wife. I am called to be a husband — a servant-martyr with regard to my wife — but that doesn't mean I don't have other roles God has called me to as well. I've sometimes heard biblical submission taught in such a way that it seems as though a woman's *only* role in life is to please and help her husband. Neither the author of Genesis nor the apostle Paul teaches that. "Helping" may be *a* defining role to which God calls married women, but it's not *the* defining role.

Finally, the context of submission is *mutual*. Right before Paul instructs wives to submit to their husbands (Ephesians 5:22), he tells all of us to "submit to one another out of reverence for Christ" (verse 21). The wife's submission to her husband gets placed in the context of a marriage in which a husband is called to be like Christ — laying down his life on her behalf, putting her first, serving her, caring for her, always loving her in the same sacrificial, lay-down-your-life manner in which Christ loves the church (verse 25).

Paul describes an idealistic view of a simultaneous commitment to the other's welfare. I don't mean to use "idealistic" in a negative way — certainly every marriage should strive for it. But I also think Paul would be the first to object if he heard women being urged to submit, while condescending and dictatorial husbands heard no corresponding challenge to love in the manner of Christ. The church must not teach the submission of wives *apart from* the sacrificial love and servanthood required of husbands. This doesn't mean a husband's lack of sacrificial love *cancels* a wife's call to submission, but it does make applying this principle a little trickier.

When a man is condescending and dictatorial toward his wife, when he treats her like hired help, when he requires her to dole out sexual favors on demand — the *last* place he should look to justify his lifestyle is the Bible. His actions and attitudes offend God's revealed will and written Word. This is *not* marriage as God designed it, and it is not what Genesis, Proverbs, and Paul teach regarding the roles of husband and wife.

What, then, *are* these roles?

Complements

The formal theological terms for the two primary views of gender roles within marriage are *egalitarian* and *complementarian*.* The egalitarian view sees no such thing as gender roles in marriage. Every couple should make their own decisions about who does what best and then divide up the responsibilities as they base their marriage on individual strengths and weaknesses. In this view, the only God-ordained difference between a husband and a wife is, so to speak, their plumbing.

In the complementarian model, God has given the husband a role of loving servant-leadership. The Bible describes the husband's role more as one of *responsibility* than as one of *privilege*, however. While New Testament women ministered and even taught, Paul clearly expected men to lead the way at home and in church. This is what many — myself included — believe the Bible teaches in Genesis 3:16; 1 Corinthians 11:3; Ephesians 5:22–32; Colossians 3:18–19; and 1 Timothy 2:12–14, among other passages.

The complementarian view seems to square better with recent findings in neuroscience about how the male and female brains work. Because of the way guys are wired, a wife's submission appears to be the most effective doorway to influence her husband. Linda Dillow suggests, "Submission is your only hope of changing your husband. Your husband will change as you allow him to be head of his home and as you are submissive to him. He will not change by your nagging, belittling, suggesting, reminding, or mothering."[1]

*Some scholars break these two labels into additional distinctions.

If your husband senses that you are trying to "take over," he'll get defensive, not malleable. He'll fight for his turf without even trying to understand you. *He won't hear you if he doesn't feel as though you support him.*

If you agree that Scripture teaches the complementarian model, you also have to accept that your husband doesn't have to *earn* his role. The catch is that submission, from a biblical perspective, is determined, not by the worthiness of the person to whom we submit, but by the worthiness of the person who calls us to submit: "Submit to one another *out of reverence for Christ*" (Ephesians 5:21, emphasis added).

It's worth pointing out that Jesus "submitted" ("was obedient," Luke 2:51) to his parents, not because they were somehow more worthy than he (since he never ceased being the Son of God), but because this is what his heavenly Father asked of him — to fulfill the legitimate roles of parent and child.

We can assume that when the Bible teaches submission, God knew full well that wives would have to watch their husbands fail and make mistakes. Thankfully, this verse also presents some boundaries. If you submit "out of reverence for Christ," you are never obligated — *ever* — to do anything that would offend Christ.

I'll admit that it's not easy to submit to an imperfect person. That's why I stress evaluating the character of a future mate when I talk to singles and college students. Feelings fade, but character hangs around. If you're choosing someone for life, it's foolish to let feelings override concerns about character.

But hey, from the guy's perspective, if you think submission is tough, try being the one who's supposed to *love you like Christ loves the church*! We husbands have our own challenges. There's a reason I'm on the road as often as I am — my activity allows Lisa to stay home, where she has always wanted to be (and she told me so before we got married). There's a reason I try to pray every day, "Lord, how do I love my wife today like she has never been loved and never will be loved?" Just as Christ remains focused and active in his love for us, so he calls me to remain focused and active in my love for Lisa.

Lisa and I have found that by following the complementarian model, based on our understanding of Scripture, we have managed to create a mutually supportive home that affirms each other's calling in Christ. My role as a spiritual leader doesn't mean I "rule the roost" with an iron fist; nor does it mean I concern myself with "men's work" while Lisa concerns herself with "women's work." On any given Sunday morning rush hour in our home, you'd be far more likely to find me ironing Lisa's clothes than Lisa ironing mine. Lisa handles all our financial transactions, tax returns, and the like because she's better at those things than I am.

The spiritual weight of fulfilling my role as a leader who sacrifices and serves and looks out for the good of his family matures me as a man in Christ. It confronts my laziness, my self-centeredness, and my accursed male autonomy. Lisa's calling as a helper keeps her from pride, self-centeredness, and frivolous living. Lisa was still a few weeks shy of turning twenty when we got married, and I was a very immature twenty-two-year-old — but the tasks of denying ourselves, learning to love, and creating a family together have resulted in an incredibly satisfying and soul-stretching journey. For both of us, marriage and family life have been essential components that move us further along toward spiritual maturity. To the world at large, it may seem as though we've given up a lot — my "freedom," Lisa's "self-actualization" — but what we've received in return is worth far more: "Whoever loses his life for [Jesus] will save it" (Luke 9:24).

Regardless of which view you adopt on marital roles, the author of Genesis and the apostle Paul are both pretty explicit that the wife should, at least, see herself as a "helper" — which, when you think about it, is quite similar to being a "mover."

Something to Give

Sadly, some have written off this biblical teaching because they believe it is demeaning to describe women as "helpers" for men. But if that is so, does the Bible also demean God when it describes him as *our* helper?

- "My father's God was my helper" (Exodus 18:4).
- "He [the LORD] is your shield and helper" (Deuteronomy 33:29).
- "You [God] are the helper of the fatherless" (Psalm 10:14).
- "You have been my helper" (Psalm 27:9).
- "The LORD is with me; he is my helper" (Psalm 118:7).

Genesis pictures a man created with an acute vulnerability. He is clearly not self-sufficient; he needs someone to come alongside him, to live this life with him. Adam, and every man after him, was, as Derek Kidner notes, "made for fellowship, not power: he will not live until he loves, giving himself away to another on his own level. So the woman is presented wholly as his partner and counterpart; nothing is yet said of her as childbearer. She is valued for herself alone."[2]

If you have entered into God's invention called marriage, your role is to be your husband's helper. This does not diminish you any more than the Bible diminishes God by calling him our helper. In fact, being able to help assumes, in one sense, that you have something the person you are helping lacks. If you cease to think of yourself as your husband's helper, the marriage will suffer, because that's the way God designed marriage to work.

You should not enter marriage and then entertain "single" thoughts. That is, you shouldn't become a wife and then act as though you're still single. The marriage vows of many of us included the line "forsaking all others." This goes beyond sexual fidelity to include "single" thinking. We agreed to forsake our me-first, single-oriented worldview and committed ourselves to building a *couple*. To be married to a man is to help him; that's the biblical model. Helping can take different forms, but it always serves the other person's good. In willingly assuming the role of wife, you pledge to spend a good deal of effort and time on the welfare of your *husband*.

I stress the word "husband" because contemporary life tempts women to focus everywhere else: your job, your home, even your children. Carolyn Mahaney reminds wives, "Notice ... that we were created to be our husband's helper, not our children's mother. Certainly we are to love, care for, and nurture our children, but this love is to flow out of a lifestyle that is first and foremost committed to helping our husbands. Our husbands should always remain first in our hearts and in our care."[3]

How often do you give thought to this role of helper? How often do you wake up and think, "How can I help my husband today?" When you repeatedly ask this question, you're living in marriage as God designed it. When you allow selfishness to reign ("How come my husband isn't helping *me*?"), you're living in marriage as Satan polluted it.

Lest you think I'm being unfair, please know that when I speak to men, I tell them that we should entertain these daily thoughts: "How can I care for my wife today? How can I serve her? How can I lay down my life on her behalf, as Christ laid down his life for me?"

But since I'm talking to you and not your husband, it's my duty to put this responsibility at your feet. You may feel greatly tempted to picture your marriage as broken — or less than it could be — because of something wrong with or lacking in your husband. The first step is to take a self-inventory, beginning with this fundamental question: "How can I begin helping my husband today?" Once you start putting this into practice, you are on the way to creating a climate more conducive to fostering change in your husband.

Marriage won't work if the wife neglects this duty. If the wife lacks this attitude, it doesn't matter if she married the most perfect man on earth; her relationship with him will suffer, because she was designed (and the relationship she has entered into is designed for her) to be a helper.

The Way Men Are

Even some feminists have discovered the wisdom behind biblical submission (though most would *never* use that phrase). Laura Doyle shocked some of her feminist peers in 1999 when she released *The Surrendered Wife*. The title alone caused great controversy in New York publishing circles; when the book hit the top-ten list, people really started talking.

In her book, Laura admitted that she felt unhappy with her marriage, so she started asking other husbands what they wanted from their wives. After listening to their comments, Laura concluded that her husband probably wanted the same things, so she tried to put them into practice. Laura stopped nagging her husband; she cut out the complaints and criticisms, and then she started letting him lead in important decisions. She did what she could to help him, and she even — this really raised a controversy — started having sex whenever he wanted it. Treated this way, Laura's man suddenly became a "fabulous" husband.

I'm not endorsing the tactics found in Laura's book, because I believe our motivation has to come from reverence for Christ more than doing one thing in order to get something else. But at the very least, it shows that even feminists are discovering how a man "works." The typical man remains unmoved by power plays or criticism or by a wife who disrespects him. He's moved by a wife who lets him lead and then helps him get where he wants to go.

This isn't merely cultural. Neuroscience has shown this is how men's brains are wired. Men, for the most part, are physiologically inclined toward certain attitudes at work and home. If you really want to move your man, you must treat him the way God designed him to be treated.

You can't make your husband serve you or care for you — but you *can* focus on helping him, and more times than not, that action alone will prompt him to serve and to care. Even if it doesn't, it will, in the words of one wife (whom you'll read about later), unleash a great spiritual adventure in your own life.

Thankfully, you're not in this alone. If you can first accept God's plan for marriage, then you can receive God's help to make the marriage work. God wants to help you and your husband build a family that honors him; his help is more than sufficient for your needs: "[Christ] is not weak in dealing with you, but is powerful among you" (2 Corinthians 13:3).

My wife and I have the same goal for our home that Paul has for the church: "And in him you too are being built together to become a dwelling in which God lives by his Spirit" (Ephesians 2:22). How do we become such a dwelling? I need to faithfully discharge the duties of a husband, while my wife needs to faithfully fulfill the duties of a wife. We intend to witness to the beauty of God's life and God's church in our own house and neighborhood.

This doesn't always come naturally for us. I'm not a type A personality; I'm not always the strong leader I need to be. I tend to frustrate Lisa more by letting things slide than by acting in an overbearing way. And Lisa, I'm sure, hasn't always had the easiest time fulfilling God's call to submit to an imperfect and sometimes weak husband. But we both remain committed to God's design. Because God's plan seems to go against my nature doesn't mean I question God's plan; it means I submit to his will and ask him to help me overcome my natural and sinful weaknesses.

The issue isn't what makes me or Lisa happy; the issue is what makes *God* happy. We don't direct our lives by what makes us comfortable; we try to order our lives by what brings the maximum glory to God and by what will fulfill our call to proclaim the message of God's reconciliation. This has given us a joy that far surpasses any temporary happiness.

Both of us have to regularly throw ourselves before God to fulfill his calling in our lives. In the twenty-plus years we have been living this out as husband and wife, we have found that God is more than able. And we have discovered the truth of Ephesians 3:20–21: "Now to him who is able to do immeasurably more than all we ask or imagine, according to his power that is at work within us, to him be glory in the church and in Christ Jesus throughout all generations, for ever and ever! Amen."

I challenge you: if you really want to move your man, begin by praying this prayer: "Lord, how can I help my husband today?"

Tired Helpers

"Hannah" works full-time while raising a preschooler and feels guilty about the waning romance in her marriage: "I wake up at six o'clock, get my daughter ready, get myself to work, put in eight or nine hours, come home, spend time with my child, try to get us all something to eat, put the child to bed — and there's just not much energy left for physical intimacy."

Such weariness is legitimate. It's cruel to make wives feel guilty for not measuring up when their schedules literally overflow. The last thing I want to do when talking about helping husbands is to lecture working wives that they're not doing enough. I'm a realist, and real life involves compromises. A husband whose wife works outside the home has to realize that other elements within the home will give way. If you're raising small children and working full-time (or even thirty hours a week), this is, in fact, essentially how you're helping your husband in this season of your life.

If the situation exists because of the husband's inability or unwillingness to earn enough for the woman to stay home, he has to bear some responsibility for this and cut his wife some slack. In many cases, the issue isn't the reasons the wife feels too tired to have sex; it's the priorities and lifestyle choices that have led to the wife's weariness.

But occasional sacrifices can still speak volumes. Since I work full-time, let me use myself as an example. I face the same struggles you do — trying to faithfully love my spouse while working well over forty hours a week. One morning, I awoke and uttered a prayer that in "Sacred Marriage" seminars I encourage other couples to use: "Lord, how do I love my wife today like she's never been loved and never will be loved?"

It didn't take long to become convinced that I needed to take my daughter to a physical therapy session that afternoon. Normally, my wife carried out this four-hour task; but the more I sat and listened to God, the more I became persuaded he wanted me to do this — even though it would blow a hole in my work schedule.

When I mentioned my plans to Lisa, she responded with a tepid "OK, whatever."

Frankly, I expected something a little heartier, such as, "You know, I could search the world over and not find such a generous, loving man as you, one who is willing to give up his own work time so that I can have an afternoon off!" No such luck. But since I had already made the commitment, I was stuck.

As the morning wore on, Lisa began feeling ill; she actually took a nap right after lunch, something she almost never does. Then her sister called, informing us that she intended to visit. We had just moved into our house, and none of Lisa's siblings had seen it — so Lisa went on a tear to get the house ready for the next day.

When I prayed about loving Lisa, and God answered with a very practical suggestion, neither Lisa nor I knew she was going to feel ill — but God did. Neither Lisa nor I knew her sister would call to ask if she could pay an unexpected, last-minute visit — but God did. And he wanted to love my wife through me by removing a major time commitment from her day — at my expense.

On another occasion, I prayed that same prayer and sensed strongly that I needed to let Lisa sleep in while I got the kids up and made sure they ate breakfast and left for school, lunch bags in hand. At this direction, panic rose in my heart — I was due to give a keynote address the next day and still had to pull my notes together. Plus, I had to organize two workshops, and I enjoy my most productive time during the early-morning hours. But God made it clear I was to put my wife's needs over the nine hundred people scheduled to hear me the next day. Lisa would essentially become a "single mother" the rest of the week in the absence of her husband, and her heavenly Father wanted her to get a little rest before that task overtook her.

Of course, I can't do this every day. I don't even do it most days. But I still think that, at times, God will ask us to let work suffer so that we can care for our spouse. I didn't arrive at that conference as prepared as I wanted to be, but my first and best commitment must be to Lisa, not to any employer.

In the same way, you too should expect God to call you from time to time to make some vocational sacrifices so that you can help your husband. My friend Melody Rhode has often impressed me in this regard. I'm convinced she has a groundbreaking book in her, but she has chosen to refrain from actively pursuing it right now because of family responsibilities. She works three days a week as a marriage and family therapist and believes that any more vocational effort would interfere with her ability to love and care for her family.

She does, however, fully intend to pursue the writing of her book when her family commitments allow it.

As Melody and I discussed vocational and family responsibilities, I found her advice very refreshing. "Life is about compromises," she observed. We shoot for the ideal, but we have to live in the real. Family, of course, always comes before personal ambition. Some couples may decide to drastically change their style of living so that the wife doesn't have to work full-time or perhaps at all. Some of our friends made that choice and have achieved thrilling results. Of course, they had to learn how to do without certain things, but the intimacy that followed, combined with the sense of family togetherness that resulted, has convinced them that the trade-off has been more than worth it.

Whatever choices you and your husband make, I pray that your decisions will draw the two of you together. Working two jobs to provide a home and food for your children can become a cooperative effort when you support each other, show interest in each other, and make those occasional sacrifices that show you care.

If, in the midst of all this, you can convince your husband that you're on his side, committed to his welfare and well-being, then you'll likely discover an intimacy and a loyalty that know no bounds. *How* you help your husband depends on your family's situation, but the call to help your husband remains.

How can you help your husband today?

Chapter 7

A Claim, a Call, and a Commitment

Focusing on Personal Responsibilities

I had my seminary students laughing one day as we compared Mother's Day sermons with Father's Day sermons. The former are almost always odes to the glory, strength, wonder, and beauty of a woman's love; the latter invariably chastise men for not stepping up to their responsibilities and calling.

When we discuss the word *responsibility*, for some reason the church community usually thinks primarily of men. Sermons directed at men almost always talk about responsibility; I don't think I can recall a single time I've heard the word used with women — except when I read the Bible.

In Titus 2:4, Paul uses a curious word when talking about older women training younger women to love their husbands. According to Dr. Gordon Fee, "The verb translated 'train' ... is highly unusual, literally meaning to 'bring someone to his or her senses.'" Dr. Fee suggests that in its context the verb may mean "something like 'wise them up' as to their responsibilities as wives."[1]

Paul had a keen interest in the issue of women's responsibilities. In his first letter to the Corinthians, he makes clear that marriage gives a very specific responsibility to a very specific person. He assures women that they may live freely as singles and that they have no obligation to marry, *but once they do marry*, they *must* fulfill their marital obligations.

First Corinthians 7:3–5 deals specifically with sexual obligations, but the principle applies much more widely. Paul makes it clear that the only way out of a marital obligation is through another person's consent. The day I got married — and the day you got married — we signed over exclusive rights to our bodies to another person. *We became responsible to them.* This relationship constitutes a *claim.* Because I'm a husband, I am not allowed to do certain things, while certain other things I must do. I can never again act as a single individual, because I renounced my individuality the day I got married. I freely chose to renounce a future "freedom," and in a sense I enslaved myself with obligation.

For example, when my wife had our first child, I passed up the opportunity to pursue a PhD in England (*somebody* had to earn some money). Later on, as a father with three children, it took me many years to build up the resources to be able to work full-time as a writer; I couldn't just "pursue my dream" without working two jobs for almost a decade. Because I'm a husband and father, when I was in my forties I turned down a very attractive offer to become a writer-in-residence at a seminary; accepting the position would have required my family to move to a place where they didn't want to live. About the same time, I also turned down an incredible opportunity to work with what many are saying is the most influential church in the nation because, once again, it would have disrupted my kids' lives. I say this not in any way to pat myself on the back but to put my comments in context: I'm *not* saying that *only* women must sacrifice. I'm saying that *both* men and women, husbands and wives, obligate themselves to certain sacrifices on behalf of their spouses and children.

Yet we live in a culture that glorifies selfishness more than responsibility. Books and movies urge us to "follow our hearts," regardless of our commitments. We need to recapture the beauty of responsibility and the glory of faithfulness. A supermodel peaks in her early twenties, while the beauty of a godly, responsible woman grows with each decade. Some women try in vain to preserve a fading past, while others experience the joy of forging a new future. It all depends on what they value the most.

Families crumble because we've lost our respect for responsibility. Instead, we allow romantic intensity to enthrall us. Since God created our feelings, they must be good; there must be a divine purpose behind infatuation. Unfortunately, however, we've become romantic gluttons. Instead of giving thanks for romance when it comes, we crave it, demand it, and even build our lives around it. We rarely give ourselves the opportunity to experience the more steadfast satisfaction of loyalty, commitment, and responsibility.

This makes us ill-prepared for what God intends through the lifelong commitment of marriage. Marriage is difficult, so much so that we must never force anyone to assume its responsibilities apart from their own free choice. Once we choose that relationship, however, we must fulfill the roles that the relationship demands of us. Our prior decision to take on the responsibilities of a wife or a husband will ultimately determine our ability to pursue other responsibilities — and if we have kids, it takes the situation to an entirely new level.

I have seen firsthand how the strength of a woman can make a major difference in a family and even in a nation. Sometimes, it takes a woman's strength to virtually shame men into taking responsibility. I think of Deborah assuming the reins in Israel; Esther moving the heart of a king; and the former British prime minister, Margaret Thatcher, telling her male contemporaries essentially that it was no time to go warm and fuzzy — her male colleagues needed to grow backbones in order to effectively confront Communism.

Responsible wives may not mean much to our culture, but the spiritual implications are as precious as they are profound. Ironically, if more women would concern themselves with being responsible instead of obsessing about whether they feel happy, fulfilled, and "important," we would have a lot more women who are happy and fulfilled — and a much stronger church and world. Jesus says to seek *first* the kingdom of God *and* his righteousness; when we pursue them, "all these [other] things" will be added as well (Matthew 6:33).

Responsible in the Face of Irresponsibility

My children must grow weary of hearing me say, "Your greatest temptation to sin is when someone first sins against you. But *their* sin never justifies *your* sin."

This is as true for spouses as it is for siblings. Fighting your husband's irresponsibility with irresponsibility of your own is like pouring gasoline on a fire; it just makes things that much more explosive, that much worse. The Bible recommends a more subversive approach: let love conquer evil; let responsibility shame irresponsibility.

It's a spiritual fact that kindness kills wickedness far more effectively than nagging, complaining, or disrespect. Remember, God won us with grace when we were his rebellious enemies. He doesn't ask anything of you that he hasn't already done himself. And this God says that we are responsible to love, even in the face of another's irresponsibility.

Peter wrote, "Do not repay evil with evil or insult with insult, but with blessing, because to this you were called so that you may inherit a blessing" (1 Peter 3:9). Did you catch that? We are called to respond to evil with *blessing*. It's not human nature to be sinned against and think, "How can I bless this person who just hurt me?" But such a spiritually powerful practice yields very effective results. Regardless of how anybody else acts, we are still accountable before God for our response.

Paul elaborates on this in his letter to the believers in Rome: "Bless those who persecute you; bless and do not curse" (Romans 12:14). He then quotes from Proverbs: "If your enemy is hungry, feed him; if he is thirsty, give him something to drink. In doing this, you will heap burning coals on his head" (Romans 12:20; see Proverbs 25:21–22). Jesus said essentially the same thing: "Love your enemies and pray for those who persecute you, that you may be sons of your Father in heaven" (Matthew 5:44–45).

The Bible is amazingly relevant and practical for married people! It's not a "pie in the sky" kind of book that pretends no one will ever hurt us or sin against us. On the contrary, it promises us that we will be hurt and wronged and then gives very specific and practical advice to help us respond appropriately. We bless those who hurt us.* We feed those who make themselves our enemies. And over time, such a practice usually succeeds far more in prompting redemptive change than does arguing, complaining, gossiping, or threatening divorce.

In the ugliness of trying situations, the beauty of responsibility shines brighter than ever.

Even if this approach proves ineffective, however, it's what God calls us to as Christians, and that's of paramount importance. I love Linda Dillow's take on this:

> I cannot promise you that if you respond with a blessing when you're hurt or wounded, your husband will change. I cannot promise you a life of happiness and personal fulfillment, but I can promise you that you are living according to your purpose and calling as a Christian; you are obeying the will of God and there is peace in obedience. The first reason you are to respond this way is not so that you can secure a hoped-for change in your mate, but because it is God's desire that you make this kind of response.[2]

When I respond according to God's plan, even if the person who sinned against me doesn't change, *I'll* change. It's a victory either way. When I respond out of spite, repaying evil for evil, two of two things usually happen, both negative: the situation gets worse; and I become more bitter, more resentful, and less like Christ. The brilliance of Christianity is that God can grow you in an unhealthy marriage as well as in a healthy marriage. He can shape you in prosperity or need, in comfort or stress, in intimacy or loneliness. And intimacy with him is the most precious reward any of us can ever know or experience.

*But please see chapter 11 on male temper for how this is qualified. I don't believe any wife should tolerate physical abuse.

Just as we build our muscles little by little, lifting a bit more weight every other day, so the beauty of responsibility evolves gradually, built up by the tiny, seemingly insignificant decisions we make week by week.

"Would You Change Your Husband?"

This idea of "improving" your husband by patiently serving an imperfect man and living up to your own responsibilities and commitments is actually ancient advice. The famed theologian and moralist Erasmus (1466–1536) lived during the Middle Ages. In *The Colloquies*, he has a section titled "Marriage," in which he recounts the conversation of two women discussing their husbands. One woman paints a terrible picture of her spouse: he doesn't provide very nice clothing for her; he's lazy; he even comes home drunk and vomits in the bed. "I would rather sleep with a brood sow than with such a husband!" she declares.

In response to his earthy behavior and appearance, she attacks him verbally and even, on occasion, physically. She screams at him, berates him, belittles him. "If he won't treat me as a wife," she explains, "I won't treat him as a husband."[3] In essence, she's saying, "If he's going to be irresponsible as a husband, then I'm going to be irresponsible as a wife."

This is a common and often relationally fatal attitude.

This woman's friend concedes that marriage with such a man must indeed be a trial, but she wonders if perhaps the woman isn't making a bad situation even worse. "In the first place," the friend says, "remember you must put up with your husband, whatever he's like. Better, therefore, to put up with one who behaves himself or is made a little more accommodating by our politeness than with one who's made worse from day to day by our harshness."[4]

This very practical advice, though ancient, has many contemporary applications. You may indeed be married to a difficult man — but is your response making the situation even more difficult? Would you rather respond in a way that makes the situation slightly more tolerable, or would you prefer to give in to your anger and keep making the situation worse? The beauty of *your* responsibility is likely to rub off onto your husband; but even if it doesn't, it'll still make your home a more pleasant place and at least testify to your children about what a God-honoring life looks like. If you can't give your children two godly parents, at least give them one.

Remember, Jesus' advice is radical. We're responsible to love even the unlovely (see Luke 6:32–36). Such a love can work transforming wonders.

"Would you change [your husband] from drunk to sober, spendthrift to thrifty, idler to worker?" Erasmus's wise woman asks her friend.

"Indeed I would, but where can I find those arts?"

"But you've those very arts in yourself, if only you're willing to make use of them. He's yours whether you like it or not; that's settled. The better you make him, the better off you'll be. You have eyes only for his failings. These intensify your disgust, and with this handle you're simply catching him where he can't be held. Mark the good in him, rather, and by this means take him where he can be held. The time to weigh his faults was before you married him, since a husband should be chosen not only with eyes, but with ears too. Now's the time for improving him, not blaming him."[5]

I love that phrase: "Now's the time for improving him, not blaming him"! It's a stark admission — since you're stuck with him, and since God is still going to call you to live up to your responsibilities and commitments, what are you going to do? Wallow in your misery, or decide to make the marriage more pleasant by your own actions? It may never become as pleasant as you once dreamed; but can you make it more pleasant than it is? Will you rise up and assume this responsibility, or will you shrink back and let things grow even worse?

The frustrated wife goes on to complain about how long this process of change might take, and her friend gently chides her: "Would you shrink from working hard to reform your husband, with whom you might spend your life pleasantly? How much labor men put into training a horse! And shall we be hesitant about laboring to make our husband more tractable?"

"What should I do?"

"I've already told you. See that everything at home is neat and clean and there's no trouble that will drive him out of doors. Show yourself affable to him, always mindful of the respect owed by wife to husband. Avoid gloominess and irritability. Don't be disgusting or wanton. Keep the house spick-and-span. You know your husband's taste; cook what he likes best. Be cordial and courteous to his favorite friends too.... See that everything is cheerful and gay at home. If he strums his guitar when he's a bit tipsy, accompany him with your singing. Thus you'll get your husband used to staying at home and you'll reduce expenses. At long last he'll think, 'I'm a fool to waste my money and reputation away from home on a drab when I have at home a wife much nicer and much fonder of me, from whom I can get a more elegant and more sumptuous welcome.'"

If you're a working woman, you need to modify this advice; but the spirit behind it remains relevant. Maintain a positive attitude; don't resent your husband. You might even use some of your hard-earned income to occasionally buy him tickets to a favorite sporting event. Decide to bless him and make his life more pleasant. Be responsible with regard to God's calling to be a practical helper to your husband.

As the wife finally becomes persuaded to give this a shot, she tells her friend, "May Christ favor our effort!"

She replies, "He will — if only you do your part."[6]

Yes, the conversation seems dated, given today's views on marriage, but much truth remains buried in this account. Moving your husband toward better character and godliness may indeed involve a lot of work and take many years, but I've talked to many people who have gone through divorce — and the work, heartache, and pain involved in *that* choice is far greater than you could imagine. Just about every divorced individual I've talked to has encouraged me to urge others to spend at least the same amount of time and effort trying to save the marriage as they'll have to spend coping with the pain, heartache, and financial cost of a split.

Helping *Your* Husband

This is the place, in books such as this, where you usually find the "statistics": 98 percent of men say such and such is their most important need; 88 percent of men say they wish their wives would do so and so. You won't find those kinds of statistics here, because I believe true helping is a personal, individualized work. What "most" husbands want doesn't mean anything if it's not what *your* husband wants. Instead of evaluating statistics, you need to find out what your husband would most like to see in his wife.

Here's an example. Unless I'm buying running gear, I hate shopping. On one occasion, I had been looking for a new watch. Lisa tore out an ad from a newspaper and asked me, "What do you think of this one?" I loved it, took it to the store, and bought that watch in about 120 seconds of shopping time. I handed the jewelry store clerk the picture; he ordered the watch, and a week later I picked it up. I didn't have to do a bit of looking around.

I *really* loved my wife that day.

Other men might actually like to shop — but maybe they want you to do something else. The key is to make this personal.

Does any bond go deeper than simply helping your husband? I don't know of any. Beauty inevitably fades, but responsibility grows in power, ability, judgment, and wisdom. Faithfully fulfilling your calling as a true life-partner forges bonds stronger than any physical attraction.

Just yesterday, my wife called me while I was at the library. She knew I was making notes for a book with the working title *The Ministry of Sitting Around*.

"Hey, Gary," she said, "you need to check out this book — *The Five Silent Years of Corrie ten Boom*. I just read about it, and I think you might find something in it for your book." That type of thing really makes a man feel like he's being supported.

Have you come across something on eBay that your husband has been looking for? Can you pass on some information about one of his favorite sports players? Maybe you could surprise him with a drink from Starbucks or simply take on a chore (getting the oil changed, ironing some shirts) that has felt like an anvil around his neck. Are you being responsible toward your calling as your husband's helper?

Ask him this question tonight: "What frustrates you most about your job?" If you can find a way to help him work through that, you'll create the climate for a profound positive influence. I think this is especially true of working wives. Your lack of time limits your ability to help, but if you can find one or two really strategic ways to make your husband's life run more smoothly, you'll cement his affections. If you do that just once or twice a year, by the end of your third decade of marriage, you'll have laid down a lifetime of practical care, removing maybe fifty or sixty things that have frustrated him. In the process, you will have built up an enormous amount of gratitude and corresponding intimacy.

Today's conversations about the emerging roles of men and women invariably garble the thinking about roles in marriage. That's why I urge young women to sort out God's call on their lives. Nowhere does the Bible insist that young women marry; in fact, Paul even seems to suggest that, in certain circumstances, they should seriously consider singleness. But once you do marry, you assume, spiritually, all the duties and responsibilities of marriage: "Brothers, each man, as responsible to God, should remain in the situation God called him to" (1 Corinthians 7:24). For wives, that means being a helper.

It's not spiritually healthy to get married and then to resent the state of being married. History overflows with single women who did amazing things on behalf of God's world and God's kingdom. And God has used many married women as well. But if you intend to run for president or become a CEO, that should have an effect on the decision you make about the kind of man you marry and the kind of family you build.

Marriage constitutes a claim, a call, and a commitment. I firmly believe you will have the richest, most fulfilling life when you take seriously your responsibility to fulfill each of these.

Do you *truly* want to influence your husband? Then work hard to become a responsible wife. The world may not applaud your efforts, but your God will reward you, and your husband will praise you. Granted, "responsible wife" may not sound very sexy — I guarantee you they won't ever film a prime-time television drama using that phrase — but the concept is biblically important and powerful and life-giving. Responsibility really will bring the joy and excitement of spiritual beauty into your home and heart.

Chapter 8

Understanding the Male Mind

Learning to Make Allowances for Your Husband's Masculinity

Every winter, grown men spend thousands of dollars and hundreds of hours trying to lure high school seniors to their campus with one goal in mind: building the best college football team in the nation. In essence, these coaches are masters at moving men. They have to know how to attract them and how to motivate them.

Former Oklahoma coach Barry Switzer had a reputation as an excellent recruiter. One time, on a trip to Texas, he walked up to a boy's house and noticed a trash can filled with Pearl beer cans. When the boy's dad walked into the living room to greet Coach Switzer, he asked him if he'd like a beer.

"Only if you've got Pearl," Switzer responded.

Coach Switzer landed the recruit.

A classic case of a woman misunderstanding a male coach occurred when Rice football coach Ken Hatfield visited the home of a high school punter. During a lengthy conversation with the parents, Hatfield said something that most guys would readily understand.

Keep in mind that Hatfield was trying to recruit a *punter*, and punting means that your offense has failed and you're going to give up the ball to the other team. So the coach casually said, "You know, we hope he doesn't play much next year."

"What do you mean?" the mother asked, alarm evident in her tone.

"Ma'am, we're trying to score touchdowns, and we hope the punter doesn't play a lot."

The boy's mom took offense at this remark and said, "We're not coming here. We're going somewhere where he can play a lot."

Hatfield felt as sorry for the boy as he did for his own team's loss of a recruit. "The boy really wanted to come [here]."[1]

To influence a man, you have to learn to talk his language. Many marital problems arise not because of an issue between Rob and Jill or Robyn and Kevin but because of a breakdown in understanding between a male and a female. In this chapter, I hope to give you an insider's view of the male mind so that you'll learn how to better understand and communicate with your husband.

The Male Brain

Modern science has obliterated the "nature versus nurture" debate. Not long ago, some groups argued that no innate difference exists between boys and girls. They insisted that girls tend to choose dolls, communication, and romance, while boys fixate on war, funny noises, and competition, solely because that's the way each are raised.

The last ten years of neuroscience have disproved this. Well before the baby comes into this world, while it remains safely tucked within the mother's womb, the brain of a male baby gets bombarded with testosterone, while a female baby receives greater quantities of female hormones. Between the third and sixth month of that unborn baby's life, hormones begin to shape the tiny brain, influencing how that individual will interact with the world. Yes, males receive some female hormones, and females receive some testosterone, but the quantities of these hormones (males have up to *twenty times* more testosterone than females) will stamp that child's brain by the sixth month of pregnancy — three months before any mother or father has a chance to "socialize" it.

(Admittedly, there exist what neuroscientists call "bridge brain" males and "bridge brain" females. Our tendency toward masculine or feminine brains occurs on a continuum, resulting in various degrees of stamping. But even here, a "bridge brain" male will have more testosterone than a "bridge brain" female.)

The male brain therefore functions much differently than the female brain. PET scans (positronic emission tomography), MRI scans (magnetic resonance imaging), and SPECT scans (single photon emission tomography) have exploded the quaint and false notion that gender difference is determined mostly by nurture rather than by nature.[2] Since brains develop by degrees, stereotyping can lead us astray; but certain things tend to be true. For example, male brains usually have less serotonin than female brains. Since serotonin calms people down, men are more likely to act explosively and compulsively. Surprised? Probably not.

Here's another example. Men also have less oxytocin in their brains. Michael Gurian makes this observation:

> Oxytocin is part of what biologists call the "tend-and-befriend" instinct, often contrasted with the "fight-or-flight" instinct. The higher the oxytocin levels, the less aggressive the person is likely to be. Furthermore, the person with higher oxytocin levels will tend to be more immediately and directly empathic, and more likely to link bonding and empathy with verbal centers of the brain, asking, "How are you feeling?" or "Is everything okay?"[3]

Why is your husband less likely to tune in to your emotional pain and verbalize his concern than, say, your sister, your mother, your daughter, or your best friend? His brain doesn't work the same way a female brain does; it just doesn't occur to him to connect his affection with verbal inquiry. Why does your husband take longer to bond with an adopted child, or maybe even his own child? His brain possesses less of the "bonding" chemical; he'll get there — it just may take more time.

Men's brains also need to "rest" more than women's brains, with the result that men are more inclined to seek "mental naps."[4] Why do men gravitate toward the television screen and then launch through the channels instead of focusing on one program? Our brains get tired. At the end of the day, we don't want plot, story, or character development; we just want escape (think buildings blowing up, cars crashing, tires squealing). All the while, *your* brain — which has 15 percent more blood flow — is still running late in the day and therefore better able to process complex entertainment.

Remember, this is true not only of your husband in particular; it's true of men in general. Be careful that you don't fault or resent your husband for being a man! Gurian notes, "As most of us have learned intuitively in our relationships with the other sex, the maleness or femaleness of the brain is not as changeable as many people might wish."[5]

If you want a more technical discussion, pick up Gurian's *What Could He Be Thinking? How a Man's Mind Really Works*. For our purposes, it's enough to say that if you really want to motivate your man and communicate with him, as well as enjoy a fulfilling marriage with him and raise healthy kids with him, *stop expecting him to act or think like a woman*. He can't do that.

Nor should he.

Rid yourself of every tactic and skill you use in talking to your sisters, best friends, and mother, and realize that a man's mind functions very differently. Some similarities exist, of course, so a few things will interrelate. But if you expect him to talk to you like your lifelong best friend does, or your sister does, or your mother does, you're being unfair. And you're going to be disappointed — and probably unhappy.

I've received a lot of positive feedback from my assertion in *Sacred Marriage* that many, if not most, problems in marriage crop up, not between two individuals, but between two genders. That's why divorce and remarriage never solve much. A man still marries a woman, and until both partners accept this reality, tremendous tension will continue to exist. In fact, if a second marriage is more successful than a first marriage, it's usually because one or both partners finally "get it" and accept that this is just the way men (or women) are. It's much healthier for all concerned (and far more economical) to learn this lesson in the first marriage.

If you accept and apply every other strategy in this book and *still* approach your husband like you would a close friend or a daughter, expect to fail. So many books written about men by women fail to address some of the key issues. In my survey of these books, getting a grip on the differences between genders seemed to be "the great divide." Laura Schlessinger's book *The Proper Care and Feeding of Your Husband* (New York: HarperCollins, 2004) succeeds so well because Dr. Laura "gets" what men are like. Many other books give advice that makes most men laugh. Many times I said to myself while reading one of these books, "Only a woman could believe a man would respond *that* way to *that* advice."

Give Him Time

Here's another big difference in the male brain that lies at the root of many marital confrontations: neurological studies show that men may take up to seven hours longer than women to process complex emotional data.[6] Think of that: *seven hours!* Why this delay? Many physiological facts help to explain it: men have a smaller hippocampus in the limbic system (which processes emotional experiences); females have more neural pathways to and from the emotive centers of the brain; and the bundle of nerves that connects the left and right portions of the brain — allowing the processing of thoughts and talk with emotions — is about 25 percent smaller in men than in women.[7]

Consider the implications. Suppose you have an argument or disagreement just after breakfast, and you take about fifteen minutes to get a grip on why you feel so angry. Your husband may not get to that place until *dinnertime.* But women often find it hard to wait that long; they want to discuss their feelings right away, and they want their husband to discuss his feelings — yet all the while his brain lags behind, stuck in the earliest stages of processing what just happened.

Let me paint a word picture. Let's say your husband invites you to an evening meeting at church. Just as you pull into your parking place, he says, "Oh yeah, I forgot. The pastor called last week and asked if you'd be willing to give a ten-minute devotional this evening right after worship. I told him I was sure you wouldn't mind."

You'd probably be furious with your husband, even if you enjoy giving devotionals. Why? You'd still want time to prepare. You'd feel your husband unfairly put you on the spot. You know what? That's *exactly* how your husband feels when you quickly click through your emotional processing and expect him to be ready just because you are. He needs time, *much* more time, to get to this point.

I can't tell you how many times I've heard speakers on marriage tell husbands they need to focus more on foreplay when it comes to sex. Well, fair enough. But just as most women need time to warm up sexually, so most men need time to warm up emotionally. Jumping into a complex discussion with your husband is tantamount to his taking you by the hand and wanting to immediately start having sexual intercourse. Remember, men may take up to *seven hours* longer to process complex emotional data.

I read of one late-night argument in which the wife insisted on talking things out before she and her husband went to sleep. Her husband wanted time to think about the issue, but she refused, insisting that they work it out, get through the emotions, and settle it before sleeping. The husband then infuriated her even more by falling asleep in the middle of the conversation.

Understanding brain differences would have helped this couple see that the husband had a legitimate desire to process his emotional response. Certainly, no marriage counselor worth his or her paycheck would recommend falling asleep on your spouse; but in this instance, the wife unfairly insisted on talking through the emotional travail without first giving her husband a chance to work through it on his own. Remember, your husband isn't as efficient as you are in processing emotional data. It's simply unfair to push through a resolution just because you feel the need for one.

Leslie Vernick told me that she often hears women protest this advice, saying something like, "Well, the Bible says we shouldn't let the sun do down on our anger, so that's why we need to settle it before going to bed." Leslie provides a helpful corrective: "The Bible never says we have to resolve all differences or problems with our spouse before going to bed. If you're still dealing with your anger, you can let that go *by yourself*, before going to bed, even if your spouse won't or isn't able to discuss the issue until later."

If a woman responds, "But he *won't* discuss it later," Leslie works on helping wives "learn how to bring up something without attacking their husbands and while working on their own heart and approach. Most men are willing to discuss something if they're not feeling like they're being pushed into a corner or blamed for something they did wrong."

Here's a suggestion: if you have an emotional issue that needs to be addressed, why not give your husband a heads-up several hours before you actually have a chance to talk? "Honey, something's really been bugging me [or hurting me, or frustrating me, or worrying me]. Here it is in a nutshell. Can you think it over so that we can talk about it later tonight?" By using this tactic, you'll give him plenty of time to process complex emotional data.

Why Do Men Stonewall?

When a woman doesn't understand the way a male brain works, she risks fostering an extremely destructive male response, something that researchers call *stonewalling*. Stonewalling describes how men may shut down emotionally and verbally, ignoring you and essentially withdrawing from the conversation. Understandably, few things irritate women more than being tuned out — and yet it is a stereotypically male action.

A biological reason helps to explain what's going on: "The male cardiovascular system remains more reactive than the female and slower to recover from stress.... Since marital confrontation that activates vigilance takes a greater physical toll on the male, it's no surprise that men are more likely than women to attempt to avoid it."[8]

Michael Gurian warns that most men don't immediately like to talk through distressing emotional events (frustrations at work or in relationships, disappointments in life) because talking about such issues usually brings them great cognitive discomfort. In other words, it *hurts* men to talk through hurtful experiences! Because of the way the female brain works (with the release of oxytocin), talking through emotional issues has a calming effect, while the opposite is true for most men; such discussions can create anxiety and distress. Since it's more difficult for males to process the data, they feel distress instead of comfort. You probably feel soothed by talking through problems; for men, it can feel like torture. That's why men sometimes tune out; it's a desperate (though admittedly unhealthy) act of self-defense.

When you understand that a verbal barrage takes more out of your husband than it does out of you, and that it takes him longer to recover from such an episode, you may begin to realize that criticizing, complaining, and displaying contempt will not allow you to effectively communicate with your man. Proverbs 15:1 tells us, "A gentle answer turns away wrath."

Dr. John Gottman, one of the nation's foremost experts on predicting divorce, helps wives understand what often lies behind the stonewalling. When a wife constantly criticizes her husband, acts harshly toward him, and displays open contempt for him, her behavior commonly leads to an explosive situation. This almost invariably causes the husband to shut down. Gottman writes, "Think of the husband who comes home from work, gets met with a barrage of criticism from his wife, and hides behind the newspaper. The less responsive he is, the more she yells. Eventually he gets up and leaves the room. Rather than confronting his wife, he disengages. By turning away from her, he is avoiding a fight, but he is also avoiding his marriage."[9]

This last thought is key: you may well be addressing a legitimate issue, but if you address a legitimate issue in an illegitimate way, you'll turn your husband away from your marriage. He'll shut you out. You'll get more frustrated because you realize he's not listening, which makes you criticize him even more and throw in even more contempt — and his stone wall rises higher and higher and higher.

How can you tell if your husband is falling into this pattern? Dr. Gottman notes, "A stonewaller doesn't give you ... casual feedback.

He tends to look away or down without uttering a sound. He sits like an impassive stone wall. The stonewaller acts as though he couldn't care less about what you're saying, if he even hears it."[10]

In Dr. Gottman's experience, stonewalling usually happens in more mature marriages; it is much less common among newlyweds. It takes time for the negativity to build up to sufficient levels for the husband to choose to tune out his wife altogether. Gottman gives more insight into this issue:

> Usually people stonewall as a protection against feeling *flooded*. Flooding means your spouse's negativity — whether in the guise of criticism or contempt or even defensiveness — is so overwhelming, and so sudden, that it leaves you shell-shocked. You feel so defenseless against this sniper attack that you learn to do anything to avoid a replay. The more often you feel flooded by your spouse's criticism or contempt, the more hypervigilant you are for cues that your spouse is about to "blow" again. All you can think about is protecting yourself from the turbulence your spouse's onslaught causes. And the way to do that is to disengage emotionally from the relationship.[11]

Instead of reacting with fury, take a breather and ask yourself, "Why is my husband tuning me out?" The answer may have something to do with the way you're treating him. If you respond to the stonewalling with the same behavior that created it, you'll only reinforce it. Be gentle, be patient, and give him time.

Emotional Rest

Just as a verbal barrage can overwhelm the male brain, so can an emotional barrage. When a woman "crowds" a man, he starts to panic. The biology of a man's brain requires that he get occasional vacations from emotional involvement.

Here's a practical example that may help you understand what I'm trying to say. Many guys have a love relationship with their cars. Women often puzzle over this. Why do guys argue about which piece of metal is more reliable, or which company builds the best engine? Why does a guy buy Chevy stickers or Ford stickers, or name his truck or car? Why will he walk out of a bedroom stuffed with laundry, pass through a cluttered kitchen with dishes piled high on the counter, go through a dining room that needs dusting and vacuuming, and then go outside and wash a vehicle that already looks clean?

I remember, as a young man, bonding with a work truck. I read electric meters for a public utility, and I drove this little yellow truck all summer long. When summer ended and I had to return to school, I felt a need to say a formal good-bye to that truck. It might sound sappy, but we had faced a lot of battles together; we drove through fields, we shared daily lunches, we outran dogs.

Even today, one of my favorite possessions is my Honda CRV. It's not a fancy vehicle; it's not a classic vehicle or even a luxury vehicle — but I just love the thing. It's been so dependable and comfortable. I feel at home inside it.

What's going on? Why are we males this way? Here's how Michael Gurian describes the brain biology behind this love affair with metal: "There is a biological tendency for men to seek a set of care objects that allow for brain rest and the pleasure of independent relationship without the stimulation of emotional conversation. A car is, not surprisingly, an object of choice for many men."[12]

A car takes me where I want to go without asking me how I'm feeling. A car lets me yell at other drivers without saying, "Why are you so upset?" A car lets me listen to the sports radio program without asking me what color I want to paint the kitchen. My car has never — not even once — asked me if something was wrong or uttered those four famous words, "We need to talk." And my car is absolutely clear about its needs. I know if the gas tank is full, half empty, or almost completely empty. My car would never respond to my inquiry about how much gas remained in its tank with the words, "Guess," or "You should know without me having to tell you."

In short, my car lets my brain rest. I have 15 percent less blood flow to my brain than you do, so my brain needs more rest than yours does. My car understands this. My car respects this.

That's why I love my car.

It is the rare man who grows in intimacy by being chased. A good, healthy marriage happens *by degrees*. So give your husband space; if he doesn't feel like talking, every now and then let it go. Don't even ask him to justify it.

This is especially true after work. Most men need to decompress. Our brains have been working hard all day long. We've been solving problems, putting forth our best efforts, and mentally we need some time to crash before we pick up and assert ourselves again. It's not personal; it's not a statement about you. Rather, it's a statement about our brains and their weariness.

One husband told Shaunti Feldhahn, author of *For Women Only*, "I wish I could make my wife understand that sometimes when I don't talk to her or act like a loving husband, it has nothing to do with how I feel about her. I just sometimes need to be left alone with my own thoughts."[13]

You have to wait for your husband to give more of himself to you. If you don't panic and if you resist the urge to try to force him into intimacy, things will go much better for you in the long run. Let him have some times of silence. If you can just give up a little, you can get so much more.

In fact, it's the wise wife who encourages her husband to occasionally go off on his own. My friend Dave Deur, the pastor I mentioned in chapter 4 who asked his class members to list five ways they love to be loved, said that the third most common response (after affirmation and sex) was this: many men mentioned that they simply wanted the freedom to occasionally do something "fun" without being made to feel guilty, without a sigh of disappointment or a guilt-inducing, "So, you'd really rather go scream at some football players than spend an evening with your children?"

If a guy asks for two nights out a week, I'd say he has priority issues. But a hardworking man does occasionally need some time away to do something he truly enjoys. Some men will feel guilty asking even for this, but a wife can build tremendous gratitude by taking the lead. In fact, my wife did this for me recently.

Because of an approaching book deadline, several speaking trips, and a seminary class to prepare for, I canceled a planned golf outing with three friends. Lisa phoned me and said, "Gary, the weather is beautiful; you really need to go." I started to protest, but she said, "I don't mind making the extra trips to get the kids; you deserve an afternoon off." I went — and enjoyed the break immensely. It meant a lot to me that Lisa willingly did the afterschool pickups so that I could spend a late afternoon with some close friends.

In this, Lisa showed me Jesus' love. Consider a telling episode of Jesus with his disciples; what I'm talking about is exactly how Jesus cared for his men: "Then, because so many people were coming and going that they did not even have a chance to eat, [Jesus] said to them, 'Come with me by yourselves to a quiet place and get some rest'" (Mark 6:31). Notice that when Jesus said this, many pressing needs remained, and much work needed to be completed. People were still "coming and going." But Jesus, concerned for his disciples, told them to leave the work and get some rest.

Lisa loves me like Jesus loved his disciples.

Author Linda Weber tells of the time she let her husband go on a trip. She initially wanted to be part of it, but she knew that "he needed a little time away to enjoy reflecting on a lot of things that are important to him." She goes on to make this observation:

Because I was happy for him to have this time away, he knew that I cared about what was important to him. In his frequent calls home, he was bubbling to share with me the fun of seeing this or doing that or just remembering good times. I loved getting excited with him, and I was glad that he wanted to share his feelings with me. It was my privilege to enter his world by being interested and showing my pleasure for him. It was good for us.[14]

That last phrase, "it was good for us," can be difficult to understand. Keep in mind, what's good for your husband is good for the two of you. Repeat after me: *If it's good for him, it's good for us.* A healthy husband is a happier husband, a more caring husband, and a more attentive husband.

There's a positive corollary to this, of course. Few women today get the refreshment time they need. Just as your husband needs an occasional break from work and family life, *so do you.* You're more likely to get this time if you remain sensitive to your husband's need for it. I'm much more eager to go out of my way to make sure Lisa gets time for herself when she's encouraging me to take that same time. Guys may not be terribly altruistic, but usually we're sensitive to fair play.

Don't Expect to Understand Him

Because of the different ways in which our brains function, you will serve your marriage well by accepting the fact that there are some things about your husband you will *never* understand. Some of the following comments may sound all too familiar:

- "I don't get it. You wouldn't hang up the Christmas lights last year because every weekend day was rainy, yet you just played eighteen holes of golf in a monsoon?"
- "You won't wait for me for five minutes in a store at the mall, but you'll get up at four thirty in the morning to go sit in a deer blind in the woods and do what? Wait! For ten hours!"
- "How can you forget our anniversary and every social engagement we've ever committed to, yet know to the mile when you're supposed to change the oil in your truck?"

You'll be trying to live a science-fiction novel if you ever expect to fully understand your husband. He probably can't even understand himself! Men seem better able to accept this, while wives often feel as though they *have* to understand their husbands. They can't accept that some things about their men don't make sense and may never make sense. Sometimes, you simply have to accept that *this is the way a guy is* — and love him accordingly.

I learned with my kids that when something annoys me, sometimes the real problem is my annoyance. I used to think I needed to change what annoyed me; then I realized that sometimes the problem is simply that I allow myself to be bugged by something that is morally neutral or merely inconvenient. Solomon once wrote, "A man who lacks judgment derides his neighbor, but a man of under-standing holds his tongue" (Proverbs 11:12).

Be a woman of understanding — learn *how* to communicate and *when* to communicate in such a way that your husband can fully participate. Part of living with someone is learning to accommodate them, and that includes all their nonsensical habits and rituals. Don't let petty annoyances poison your relationships. Live with — and even celebrate — the mystery: "It doesn't make sense, but that's the way he likes it, and that's good enough for me."

Chapter 9

Jeanne-Antoinette

The Power of a Persistent Pursuit

Louis XV inherited the French throne at the ripe old age of two, after both his parents and his elder brother had died from the scarlet fever. Almost immediately, adult nobles and dukes quarreled over who got to help dress him, serve his meals, hold his hand, and even carry his candlestick. Imagine a political campaign geared to secure the vote of a two-year-old, and you'll have a pretty accurate picture of what was going on. It's not hard to imagine the narcissistic personality that might result from being treated as someone so special from the time you started crawling.

Many males today grow up with a similar sense of entitlement. In all honesty, a part of us wants to be worshiped. Advertising executives understand this. The next time you leaf through a magazine, pick out the ads targeted toward men, and consider how many pictures show a beautiful woman looking adoringly, almost worshipfully, at a man wearing a specific cologne, consuming a particular drink, or wearing a certain designer's shirt or slacks. That adoring look in the woman's eye? That's what we want to see from you.

Should we men be seeking this? Of course not. Theologically, it's repugnant. I should live to worship God and bring *him* glory, not seek glory for myself. But a sinful core in all men seeks this adoration nonetheless. So it shouldn't surprise us that the narcissistic tendencies of an eighteenth-century French king appear in men today.

How can a woman handle such a man — not so that she reinforces the narcissism but so that she earns the right to offer positive influence?

I believe the story of Jeanne-Antoinette contains some clues — but I have to confess, I'm really going out on a limb here. In fact, this may be the first Christian book to use an official *mistress* as an example for godly Christian wives.

I have a high view of marriage, a strong stance against unbiblical divorce, and a firm belief that extramarital affairs offend God and destroy couples. In no way am I justifying the immoral conventions of eighteenth-century France. But I believe a little bit of Louis XV lives in most men's souls, and I know that Jeanne-Antoinette learned how to motivate such a man. So I think she may have some helpful lessons to impart to women today. So bear with me, and see if you don't agree.

Courting the Court

Jeanne-Antoinette's life got off to a rocky start. When her father was forced to flee France for political purposes, she ended up in a convent. After three long years, Jeanne returned to her mother, who had a quite different theological persuasion. She took Jeanne to a medium, who predicted that Jeanne would one day become the mistress of the king.

In an age of arranged marriages and political alliances, adultery had become practically a way of life (though the church still considered it scandalous). Many kings — including Louis XIV and Louis XV — had multiple mistresses, to the extent that "the favorite" became a semiofficial title carrying prestige.

On the face of it, however, any prediction that Jeanne-Antoinette would one day become a royal mistress must have sounded absurd. In pre-Revolutionary France, your birth determined your place; society considered it unseemly even to *attempt* to rise above your station in life. Kings simply did not take on a member of the bourgeoisie for a mistress: "Sharing the royal bed was an aristocratic privilege," observes French historian Evelyne Lever.[1] Even though Jeanne-Antoinette had many qualities in her favor — great beauty, poise, musical talent — at that time, beauty was seldom enough to leap the high walls of social prejudice.

It *was* enough to get Louis' attention, however.

Somewhere around 1745, the debonair king (frequently called the most handsome man in France) couldn't help but notice this young woman in her early twenties whose property lay close to where he often hunted. Somehow (nobody knows the specifics), Jeanne-Antoinette did the unthinkable, attracting the king so resoundingly that he determined to bring a commoner to Versailles as his declared mistress. It simply wouldn't do to *completely* buck convention, so the king needed to invent a title for her. Fortunately for the king's aims, the last of the aristocratic Pompadours had recently died without leaving an heir. Virtually overnight, Jeanne-Antoinette became the Madame la Marquise de Pompadour. The famous writer and philosopher Voltaire schooled her in her new surroundings.

Almost immediately, the young woman developed many enemies. One noble-born woman scoffed that Madame de Pompadour was "excessively common, a bourgeoisie out of her place who will displace all the world if one cannot manage to displace her."[2]

Madame de Pompadour's only hope of success lay in maintaining her favor with the king. She did not have the security of marriage, so her acts undoubtedly took on a more desperate character. Yet her success shows how such a woman can move a man.

Serving the King

The beautiful Madame de Pompadour knew that beauty fades and that she couldn't possibly hope to compete with the best of France — indeed, the best of the world — for very long on beauty alone. Looks may have gotten her into the palace, but with so many enemies, they certainly couldn't keep her there.

So she studied her man. She figured out what a busy king who bears the weight of his country on his shoulders most wants and needs, and then she worked hard to make it happen.

First, she realized that the king needed an escape from his responsibilities and duties — little pockets of enjoyment that would make his burden less heavy to bear. Accordingly, Madame de Pompadour set up small and intimate social gatherings that the king could enjoy two or three times a week. Biographer Christine Pevitt Algrant describes the dinners this way:

> The marquise realized very early the importance of the *petits cabinets* for her own ends. She understood that the king liked this intimate, comfortable, pleasant, and cheerful setting — very bourgeoisie; she came to comprehend that, by establishing an ambience at once cozy and royal, relaxed and refined, she would become essential to his life. After becoming accustomed to such congenial society, after a tedious council or exhausting ceremony, Louis would not be able to do without it. And if it were she, and she alone, who was responsible for the good cheer, the discreet friends, the voluptuousness of it all, then without her, he would enjoy none of this.[3]

Few could match the way Jeanne-Antoinette put herself almost entirely at the king's disposal. When the king lapsed into a semi-depressed funk, the marquise "never left him alone; she tried to liven him up, stir him and divert him from his gloomy thoughts; she reassured him and surrounded him with a giddy gaiety.... She invited more and more people to the suppers in the private apartments and increased the number of escapades to the smaller chateaux."[4]

Madame de Pompadour *had* to entertain the king to maintain her place; but I wonder if wives can't find something to apply here. After all, why do so many marriages break down? Many times, one or both partners simply stop trying to please their spouse. While dating, they may have put great effort and gone to great expense to make a good impression. They deliberated over thoughtful gifts. They demonstrated great concern. They felt eager to serve with a back rub, a plate of cookies, a special meal, a kind and thoughtful gesture.

If you think back, you may recall a time when gaining your man's favor made you happier than almost anything else. You went about it very intentionally, didn't you? But somewhere into the second or third year of marriage, instead of trying to please your spouse, perhaps you found that you wanted to be pleased *by* him. Resentment may have frozen your motivation, and you may have stopped even trying to please. Perhaps you began to take your spouse for granted and started coasting in your affection, care, support, and service.

This happens in the bedroom as much as anywhere. I was eating an airline dinner, flying somewhere over the Midwest, when I put on some headphones and caught this piece of dialogue from the Sandra Bullock/Hugh Grant movie called *Two Weeks Notice*: "Don't let this lawyerly facade fool you," Sandra warned Hugh. "I'm actually really good in bed."

In a Christian worldview, a single person shouldn't *know* whether he or she is "good in bed." But since I was stuck in an aluminum tube thirty thousand feet above ground, I had plenty of time to think — and the question challenged me in another context. When did I, a married person, last ask that question: "Am I really good in bed?" I'm not trying to reduce sexual intimacy to mere mechanics; but why should I care less about pleasing a spouse who has committed her life to me than some drunken girlfriend cares about pleasing a guy she just met? Sadly, many people in marriage simply stop caring about whether they're "good in bed." They abuse the security and commitment of the relationship, allowing their physical intimacy to fall into a predictable routine. They stop trying and do just enough to "fulfill their duty" and keep their consciences at bay.

While it's justifiable to question Madame de Pompadour's low character, how much sadder that this mistress from the eighteenth century tried much harder to build an illicit relationship than many contemporary (even Christian) wives try to build healthy marriages! How deplorable that an adulterous woman put more thought into her relationship with a lover than many spouses do in their lifelong unions!

Why do we care less about a spouse than a mistress might about a king? Because we've forgotten the power of a *persistent* pursuit. Jesus warned us, "Because of the increase of wickedness, the love of most will grow cold" (Matthew 24:12). Is your love for your husband growing cold?

For some women, marriage is the ultimate life goal — once attained, what's to try for? When you stop trying to please your man, eventually, by degrees, you lose him; or at the least, you lose the intimacy that leads to influence. You become someone other than the person he married, and the two of you begin to drift apart.

Please don't misunderstand me. I am not exonerating Jeanne-Antoinette's morals. But I am applauding her effort!

The book of Proverbs contains a sober warning:

> *I went past the field of the sluggard,*
> > *past the vineyard of the man who lacks judgment;*
> *thorns had come up everywhere,*
> > *the ground was covered with weeds,*
> > *and the stone wall was in ruins.*
> *I applied my heart to what I observed*
> > *and learned a lesson from what I saw:*
> *A little sleep, a little slumber,*
> > *a little folding of the hands to rest—*
> *and poverty will come on you like a bandit*
> > *and scarcity like an armed man.*
>
> Proverbs 24:30–34

Does your marriage look like the sluggard's vineyard? Have you stopped planting healthy plants, with the result that weeds — unhealthy habits — have replaced them? Are your stone walls — the boundaries that protect your marriage — lying in ruins? Is your marriage vulnerable because of neglect? If you start slumbering in your marriage and let the relationship slowly drift, year by year, the riches of your marriage will collapse into emotional and spiritual poverty.

It takes great effort to love a man well. Marriage is work! Even the highest, most intense passion can cool if not maintained.

Just because your husband once felt head over heels in love with you doesn't mean he'll die that way. If you take your husband for granted, if you let yourself grow lazy in the arts of love and relationship — then you run the very real risk of losing his heart.

Think about your past week. How much effort have you put into really *pleasing* your husband, into bringing joy and happiness into his life? Have you given it a single thought? If not, go back a month. How many times in the past four weeks have you made this a matter of prayerful concern? If you can't remember the last time you actively strove to please your husband, if you've stopped caring whether you're "good in bed," then you're giving less effort to your marriage than many a mistress would give to her adultery. Does that attitude honor God?

On a practical level, if you aren't putting forth the effort, then you're far less likely to influence your man. As we'll see shortly, Madame de Pompadour ultimately became King Louis' most influential adviser. Why? For one thing, she remained *persistent* in her pursuit.

The Most Delicious Woman in France

By 1748, the marquise's position looked solid. Her work at distracting the king with intimate dinners and plays created a growing bond that seemed permanent. Madame Pompadour's longtime enemy, the Marquis d'Argenson, grudgingly referred to her as the "oracle of the Court."[5] After one play in February, the king showed his affection publicly, openly kissing the marquise and referring to her as "the most delicious woman in France."[6]

The title of "most delicious woman in France" did not come unearned. Madame de Pompadour spent considerable time and effort on the elaborate costumes that she wore to the plays. Algrant writes, "The marquise excelled on stage, dazzling her audience with her acting, singing, and dancing, not to mention her spectacularly glamorous costumes. For her dancing role in *Almasis*, she wore a low-cut bodice of rose taffeta decorated with a pattern of silver, embroidered in flowers of pastel colors."[7]

The lesson here should be quite clear: Jeanne-Antoinette never stopped trying to captivate Louis XV. She knew the king would take other mistresses — Louis XV was no more "faithful" to his favorite than he was to the queen — but she never ceased working to keep herself looking her best.

Appearance does matter to men. I realize such a statement can make many women wince, and let me assure you that, even as a man, I can at least empathize with a contemporary woman's situation. In previous ages, a woman competed with perhaps dozens of other women in her village or small town.[8] Today, with television and magazines, you're likely to be compared to hundreds of thousands of women! Modeling agencies scour the earth to find the next gorgeous supermodel, who will promptly retire by the age of twenty-five, with a new crop soon replacing her. But in those few short years, she'll have clothes made just for her, makeup artists who spend hours getting her ready, and photographers who take hundreds of pictures and then display the ones that best showcase her beauty (after digitally enhancing them).

You can't compete with that — and even if you could, your victory would be short-lived. Yet it might surprise you to learn that when dozens of men filled out a recent survey, listing how they wish their wives would love them, *not a single one* mentioned a desire for their wife to lose weight. About half of them, however, expressed a desire for their wives to cultivate a different attitude toward sexual intimacy — a comfortableness with sex and their bodies, the willingness to be emotionally engaged, initiating, enthusiastic. In a sense, this should be good news. You can't lose ten pounds in an afternoon, but you can change your attitude anytime.

In this regard, I think men generally get shortchanged. Their sexual desires get dismissed as animalistic — "they just want a perfect body," the saying goes, and frequent sexual activity. But none of the men responding (and none I've talked to) are like that. No mature Christian men I know expect their wives to look like a twenty-two-year-old supermodel.

In fact, if you feel uptight about your appearance and thus act more reserved in bed, your attitude, far more than your body, takes away from your husband's enjoyment. I talked to one man whose wife is in her forties. Because of the wife's commitment, they have sex more often now than they did in their twenties. And guess what he told me? "I'm more attracted to her today than I've ever been."

I think it's safe to assume that this man's wife probably weighs a little more today than she did twenty years ago. I'm sure there are a few more wrinkles, very likely some stretch marks that didn't exist when they were on the honeymoon, and a few body parts that don't look as "tight" as they once did. But her husband loves her body more than ever. Why? It's her *attitude* — she generously gives what she has, and her husband has bonded with that familiar but oh-so-glorious body in a very big way.

I guarantee that if you polled a hundred husbands, asking them if they'd prefer a supermodel look-alike who is cold emotionally and who never initiates sexual intimacy, or a woman carrying a few extra pounds who is eager, enthusiastic, and sometimes takes the lead, ninety-nine husbands out of a hundred would choose the latter.

But here's the catch. While your husband probably doesn't expect you to look like a supermodel, he does want you to look *feminine*. One time, Lisa and I were talking about how unmarried teens were becoming Victoria's Secret's biggest customers. A dad once told me that when he and his wife folded the laundry, he couldn't help but notice that his unmarried daughter had far more attractive undergarments than did his wife.

All this *does* seem backward.

Men like to be captivated by their wives. They understand that advancing years and the experiences of childbirth and nursing take their toll on a woman's body and appearance; but they still want their wives to look like women. The feminine enthralls us. It is so different, so beautiful, to us. And it is God's good desire that this be so.

Solomon says to husbands about their wives, "May you ever be captivated by her love" (Proverbs 5:19). This rather weak translation would sound a bit more erotic had I included the previous lines, which describe the actual body parts the husband should be captivated by. Keil and Delitzsch paint the picture here of a husband in a "morally permissible love ecstasy" as he gazes at his wife's naked body.[9] That's how strong the idea "captivated" is here. And, according to Scripture, this is a *blessing*, God's good gift to your husband. Let me try to re-state this biblical prayer in a contemporary context: "May you receive God's good gift of being captivated and enthralled by the beauty of your wife's body."

When guys talk in private, without fear of sounding politically incorrect, they often lament how so many wives have stopped look-ing feminine. That doesn't mean you can't dress down — a ponytail sticking out of a baseball cap can be a beautiful thing! But guys want their women to look like women. If you can master this, your influence in your husband's life will become that much stronger.

You could seriously misconstrue what I'm about to say, but please give me the benefit of the doubt. Within the holy security of Chris-tian marriage, can you still maintain the motivation of a mistress? Will you be just as zealous and eager to keep your man enthralled out of the goal of reverence for Christ as some other women are to draw attention to themselves for more selfish aims?

The Chains of Habit

As the marquise became concerned about her age, she received the advice, "Make your company more and more valuable to the king through your gentleness; don't turn him away at other times, and let things take their course; the chains of habit will bind him to you forever."[10]

Later in life, she received similar advice: "Princes are above all creatures of habit. The king's friendship for you includes your apartment and your surroundings. You are used to his ways and his stories; with you he is not embarrassed, he's not afraid of boring you. Where would he find the courage to uproot himself from all this?"[11]

Perhaps because it doesn't sound romantic, many women may never fully appreciate these "chains of habit" — being familiar with and accommodating the personal likes, patterns, and rhythms of your husband's life. But they can grow strong. Maybe I'm tempted to overstate this (as I'm almost neurotically a person of habit), but with most men, these "chains" can be a real force.

It's interesting and noteworthy that when Paul tells older women to "train" younger women in how "to love their husbands" (Titus 2:4), the word he chooses for "love" is *phileō*, one of several Greek words for "love." *Phileō* is a practical kind of love that in other contexts can mean "to be in the habit of." John Stott describes it this way: "Thus love [*phileō*] is the first and foremost basis of marriage, not so much the love of emotion and romance, still less of eroticism, but rather of sacrifice and service. The young wives are to be 'trained' in this, which implies that it can be brought under their control."[12]

I talked earlier about keeping your man "enthralled," but realistically, that doesn't speak to the twenty-four-hour reality of married life. The *phileō* type of service-love cements the relationship. It respects the "chains of habit" by which a woman can bind a man to her for life. Since you know your man like no one else, you can anticipate his needs and create a great sense of loyalty when you accommodate and meet those needs. It can be as simple as keeping his favorite beverage and snack food stocked, taping his favorite television show when he's away on business, buying a book by one of his favorite authors when you're shopping at your local bookstore, or remaining sensitive to his daily rhythm when you schedule appointments or entertain others.

It's really about kindness and thoughtfulness. Just as Madame de Pompadour studied King Louis' preferences and sought to ride those "chains of habit" right into his heart, so you can build great affection in your own marriage by doing the same.

I like to advise newlywed women to *be patient*. So many young wives seek an intense relationship, unrealistic in the case of most young men, once the initial romantic intensity wears off. Loyalty, oneness, and deep intimacy all take time to develop and mature. When a man feels consistently pleased, when he feels enthralled over time, when his wife has learned to use his "chains of habit" to bind his heart to hers — *then* the relationship reaches that level of intimacy, trust, and oneness that most young wives seek. But this process happens by degrees. Too many young wives want to immediately reap a long-term investment from an initial deposit called "marriage."

Though this won't sound very romantic, consider loving your husband the relational equivalent of making an investment in your IRA. You don't deposit a check in 2006 and expect it to double by 2007, or even by 2012. You know that value accrues over time. Mature love is just like that. A Christian man should be absolutely committed to you as soon as he speaks the marriage vows. He should die for you without fear or regret. But his soul doesn't immediately knit to yours in a relational way. That takes time. It's not automatic, and a man can't force it to happen any more than he can plant a sapling and expect to see a fruit-producing tree by the next morning.

Sadly, too many women grow impatient with men. If the man doesn't respond in the first decade of marriage just as they want him to, they trade him in for someone else. They don't realize that they've just thrown away a decade of relationship building that they can never get back — and they have to start all over at square one. Their second husband will also take time to fully bond, once the initial romance has faded. If they ever want to move past romance to true love, they have to stick it out long enough for mature love to grow.

Jeanne-Antoinette's relationship with the king changed over time. Eventually she became more of a friend than a lover. Whether out of sincerity or intrigue, Madame de Pompadour underwent something of a religious conversion around that time. Now that she no longer committed public adultery, the church welcomed her return, and many hoped that her newfound devotion might somehow influence the still-philandering king. Jeanne-Antoinette banked her future on becoming an invaluable adviser and confidante.

By 1751, she let it be known that she was no longer "intimately involved" with the king, though she became even more involved in matters of state and diplomacy. Where once she had used seduction, now she built a relationship based on trust. Louis XV was not a particularly confident or decisive king; he didn't wear his authority as comfortably as did others. Confidence was never a problem for Madame de Pompadour, however, and she recognized that such a king could use her services. In time, as Evelyne Lever explains, "nothing could be done without her. The king was inaccessible and left most of the military, diplomatic and administrative appointments up to his mistress."[13]

In short, Jeanne-Antoinette became indispensable in King Louis' life. She had studied his patterns and knew his needs, and she persistently pursued him until he realized he couldn't function without her. Based on this foundation, she had enormous influence, and she was able to motivate and move the king in many ways.

Let me stress that this reliance, this dependence, this cooperation, came about through *years* of service and relationship. You have to win a man with a persistent, passionate pursuit before you can move him — and men aren't won easily. Yet their loyalty can be fierce when carefully encouraged, patiently earned, and proven over time.

Unimaginable Honors

Madame de Pompadour's chronic ill health finally caught up with her in 1764. As her death became imminent, King Louis XV insisted that she be allowed to die in the king's palace in Versailles, despite a very strict rule that only those of royal birth should receive such an honor. Just as Madame de Pompadour had broken boundaries all her life, so she broke them in her death. A despondent Louis XV told his doctor, "Only I know the extent of my loss."[14]

Contemporary women may be disgusted at the way Madame de Pompadour tried so hard to please a man, but the king rewarded her efforts prodigiously — in death as in life. Though Jeanne-Antoinette had started out as a commoner, she became a member of the nobility, a leap that almost never happened in French society. From humble financial beginnings, she acquired enormous wealth, with numerous mansions and gardens built solely for her pleasure. And then, in her death, she received royal treatment.

Even so, the rise of a mistress can never compare with the passion of holy marriage and absolute commitment. The author of Ecclesiastes wrote, "I saw that wisdom is better than folly, just as light is better than darkness" (2:13). Imagine putting the positive side of Jeanne-Antoinette's actions into the healthy situation of a

God-ordained marriage. No longer having to please out of fear but out of love, yet not trying any less! Consider what a rich relationship could result from such a passionate and persistent pursuit.

This isn't about coddling a narcissistic man; it's about fulfilling biblical commands. Jesus tells us to love each other as he has loved us (John 15:12). Jesus' love is no less persistent, no less passionate, and no less extravagant with each passing day. To love biblically, we must not let our love grow cold. Paul describes persistent love as a "continuing debt" that we owe to one another (Romans 13:8); and if that is true of people in general, how much more so with regard to our spouse! In the great love chapter, Paul reminds us that love "always perseveres" (1 Corinthians 13:7). It does not give up; in fact, it never fails (verse 8).

Do you love your husband with this kind of love? Are you faithfully building your marriage with the power of a persistent and passionate pursuit? When you give your marriage adequate time, when you work diligently to keep your man enthralled, when you seek to serve and to love and to become familiar with your husband's rhythms of life — then he'll honor you with all he has, just as Louis XV honored Madame de Pompadour.

When Lisa and I got married in 1984, my entire net worth wouldn't buy a season ticket to the Seattle Mariners. For years, while I was working in ministry, we qualified for the earned income tax credit. We had our first parental argument over an eight-dollar toy that I impulsively bought for Allison. Lisa didn't think we had the money to spare.

So much has changed. While we don't live extravagantly, for the first time in our lives, money isn't a big concern. When one of us needs an expensive crown at the dentist's office, we don't have to go without groceries for a week or go into debt; we just write the check. If one of the kids wants to take dancing lessons or guitar lessons or even requires a program that doubles the tuition at a private school, by God's grace we can cover it without having to give up too much. We try hard to be good stewards of what we have, and God has provided a nice home, occasional vacations, and a comfortable living. And Lisa hasn't had to work outside the home for more than fifteen years.

I want to say to young wives: this didn't happen overnight! Lisa supported me emotionally during some rocky, barren times. During one stretch in my life, my writing *cost* us money (postage, paper, computer supplies, and so on) without earning anything. For years, Lisa had to put up with a husband who went to bed ridiculously early and who arose very early so that he could pursue a new occupation. She put up with my working on weekend mornings and throughout many a vacation. She juggled a budget that often ran in the red. I shudder when I think of the debt load we once carried.

But together — and that's the key, *together* — we walked through it into some fertile fields. Should it all be taken away tomorrow, we'd still have each other and the loyalty of a firm partnership forged over two decades. Lisa has become irreplaceable in my life. She accepted the marriage proposal of a man who had no job, a ten-year-old Ford Maverick, and an offer to live for free in a mobile home park. Amazingly, she accepted. She tried to decorate the mobile home as best she could. Months later, she put up with a basement apartment that flooded every time it rained two days in a row (and we live in the Northwest, where two consecutive days of rain is the norm nine months of the year). She endured years of additional schooling that would take me away many evenings as I completed seminary. And then she watched me go into a ministry that snatched away many weekends.

She has proven her love for me over time — not just months, not even just years, but *decades*. And everything I now have is hers. I would spend my last penny to take care of her, and I would give my life to protect her.

Though I believe in spiritual headship, I'm very malleable in Lisa's hands. From little things, like no longer drinking Pepsi every day, to bigger things, like major vocational choices, she has influenced me, moved me, and shaped me. She is no mistress; she's much, much more. She is my *wife*, my sister in Christ, and the single most influential person in my life.

The Climate for Change

By now, I'm sure you see that motivating a man isn't nearly as linear a process as programming a computer or fixing a car. People are shaped by degrees. You can't force someone to change, but you can create a climate conducive to change.

I know almost nothing about gardening, but I do know that all the attention in the world won't help a plant if it sits in poisoned soil. Think of the section that's wrapping up here as pointing you to the proper soil mix in which your man can grow. I didn't offer simplistic, 1–2–3 steps that will result in instant change; instead, I suggested basic ingredients that, over time, will foster maximum growth. Do you want to influence your man? Then put these suggestions to work to create a climate in your marriage in which positive change will most likely occur.

In part 3, we're going to address some of the most common issues that women confront today: men who have fiery tempers; men who are so involved in their work or hobbies that they fail to be fully present in the home; men who struggle with pornography or Internet affairs; and men who are unbelievers.

I suspect this next section may be the biggest draw for many of you, but I also think it would be a big mistake to try to address specific issues apart from the context of the overall relationship — and providing that context is what I've tried to do in the first two parts of this book.

Part 3

Confronting the Most
Common Concerns

Chapter 10

Ray and Jo: Taming the Temper, Part 1

Self-Respect as a First Defense
against Your Husband's Anger

D id you marry an angry man?
Maybe you even married a violent man.

Perhaps you saw signs of this rage or violence before you married, but in your eagerness to become a bride, you chose to look past it or excuse it as a onetime occurrence. Maybe you thought you could control him. Maybe you thought marriage would make everything better. But now you're stuck in a frightening situation. You want to do the right thing, for yourself and for your children, but fear and guilt and confusion so fill you that you don't know what the right thing even *is*.

This may not be your situation, but I can assure you it's the situation of someone who attends your church, lives in your neighborhood, or works in your office. So even if this chapter doesn't describe your husband, you may want to read it anyway in your quest to become a woman God can use to reach out to others.

Escalating Anger

Like so many women who have walked down the marriage aisle, Jo Franz[1] knew that her prospective bridegroom had bouts of "intensity and anger," but she reasoned that, because Ray loved God, the two of them as a couple could overcome them. Not until they became married did Jo realize just *how* intense Ray could be.

"His voice intensified so dramatically that it felt like he could physically hurt me, even though I didn't think he would," Jo remembers. Ray sometimes unleashed his anger over seemingly small things, like when Jo would forget to buy something at the store.

"You can't even run a house well enough so that we don't run out of soap," Ray yelled at her one time.

Jo was shocked. "I had no idea he would nitpick like that or be so attacking."

In case I'm talking to an unmarried woman, let me pause to say I have never heard of a situation where marriage made a man *less* angry. You should assume you are seeing, at most, about 75 percent of your future husband's temper while dating him; it's virtually guaranteed that more temper will erupt after the wedding. If the man you are dating already seems too angry for your taste, he'll be *much* too angry after the honeymoon.

Unfortunately, single women often make excuses for their angry boyfriends. If these women were abused by their fathers, they may even blame themselves for causing the anger. As long as a woman blames herself for causing her husband's temper, she ignores the real problem: she's the *target*, not the cause. As long as a woman thinks she causes the anger, she accepts blame for her husband's problem. This allows her husband to keep hurting her, and the situation will never change. Of course, you could be making a bad situation worse; a little later I'll talk about strategies to avoid this. But for now you need to know that it's impossible to live with an angry man without making him angry. Make sure you catch that: *it's impossible to live with an angry man without making him angry.*

But you *can* remove yourself as the target.

"I Have Value"

Ray grew up with a very critical alcoholic father who taught him that relationships are built on extremely high expectations. Ray admits, "Sometimes I have little patience, and yes, I can be intolerant of other people's patterns — like forgetting to buy more soap."

At first, Jo responded to Ray's angry tone with defensiveness and guilt, thinking she was most likely in the wrong. But after Jo analyzed several confrontations, she eventually decided Ray wasn't always right, which led her to react with anger of her own — and that only made things worse. Ray would yell at her, and then Jo would yell back, "Don't you *dare* speak to me like that!" and the anger soon spiraled out of control.

Proverbs 15:1 is key here: "A gentle answer turns away wrath, but a harsh word stirs up anger." As I said before, you are most vulnerable to sin when you are sinned against. Your husband's inappropriate expression of anger doesn't excuse your inappropriate expression of anger: "He who loves a quarrel loves sin" (Proverbs 17:19). Become spiritually grounded so that you can respond out of reverence to Christ instead of "giving more of the same." If you give more of the same, all you'll get is more of the same.

That, at least, was Jo's experience. One day, she finally said to herself, "Enough is enough. I can't live like this."

Jo took her dilemma to the Lord.

"As I prayed, I thought, 'Do I deserve this?' And I realized, 'No, I don't!' As a Christian, I have value to God, and my husband should value me too, but I can't force him to value me. How can I cause him to respect me and to show that to me in his communication?"

Over the next several weeks, Jo became convinced that God wanted her to learn how to communicate to Ray in such a way that he could hear her concern. As Jo reflected on her previous actions — responding to Ray's temper by letting her own temper flare — she had to admit that she was making the situation worse. Then God led her to the wisdom of Ecclesiastes: "The quiet words of the wise are more to be heeded than the shouts of a ruler of fools" (9:17).

Jo sought to use "the quiet words of the wise." She explains, "What I sensed God saying to me was to use communication that was direct and nonattacking and that showed self-respect: 'This is what I need from you,' or, 'Would you please communicate in a way that isn't so frightening?'" Essentially, Jo heard God tell her to respond with a gentle and quiet spirit (see 1 Peter 3:4).

It would be an oversimplification to suggest that their disagreements changed immediately; however, over time, this quiet, gentle approach began to work. Note the spiritual foundation behind this transformation: Jo allowed God to change *her*, which resulted in her husband's spiritual growth.

Ray explains, "Before, if I was condescending to her or demeaning or critical, then she would respond very quickly and very angrily back: 'Don't talk to me that way! Don't use that tone of voice when you're talking to me!' Her face would get tight and tense, and I thought, 'Boy, she's really hurting. I've touched a deep nerve in there somewhere,' but I didn't understand why she was making such a big deal out of it."

In the midst of subsequent blowups, Jo concentrated on being firm but gentle. "I need for you to reword that so I don't feel so defensive." Recognizing that Ray was raised in an alcoholic family, Jo decided she needed to tutor him on how to talk to a woman.

Ray reflects, "It's so important for the woman to share that she's been hurt, but to first take the intensity out of the response. Otherwise, we men tend to think you're overreacting. Jo put it this way: 'I care about you very much, and I need you to know that what you said was very hurtful.' She dropped the sharp, 'Don't talk to me that way!'"

According to Ray, Jo's previous method of communicating "just made me feel guilty. I already knew that I had screwed up, and here she was, piling it on, making it more of an issue than it was. And when you already feel low about yourself, and then you're attacked, you're more likely to strike back and escalate the intensity."

Ray says that what made him the angriest was being misunderstood. He believes that Jo sometimes just looked at his behavior without giving him the benefit of the doubt. That perplexed and frustrated him, which would escalate into anger. In fact, Ray believes, on many occasions he had good intentions, but when Jo assumed the worst, he became frustrated, which in turn made him angry — and then he chose to lash out.

Looking back, Ray sees how God used this situation to challenge both him and Jo. "God may frustrate us at times, but we should give him the benefit of the doubt because we know his motivations and intentions are good."

This may seem like a small point, but I think it's a profound one: learning to love and communicate with a very imperfect man can teach valuable lessons about how to love and communicate with an absolutely perfect God. Sometimes we *do* tend to assume the worst — not just of our spouses but of God too: "He doesn't care; he doesn't see; he's playing with us." At the very least, when we know this is never true of God, perhaps it can teach us to show a little less arrogance in our assumptions and much more humility and grace in our attitude toward others.

Personally, I believe this will be one of the greatest challenges that wives married to angry men will face: it's going to be very difficult for you, if you're married to such a man, not to look at every new response of his as simply "more of the same." That's why forgiveness is so crucial; we need to let go of the past so we don't keep coloring the present with it. Otherwise, the future is going to look very bleak, indeed. In spite of your past hurt, can you choose to suspend your immediate judgment and try to give your husband the benefit of the doubt?

Spiritual Preparation

There's another principle we can learn from Jo's experience: in order to confront anger in your man, you're going to need to put your own spiritual house in order; otherwise, you'll likely lack the strength, courage, and perspective to help your husband.

Jo realizes that her marriage is about more than her and Ray; it is also very much about her and God. When you live with an angry man, you not only crave but literally *need* God's affirmation. Men can be very cruel with their cutting comments; if you aren't receiving affirmation and affection from your heavenly Father, you're going to feel emotionally empty and perhaps even worthless — and that will feed into your husband's response and tempt you to become even more of a doormat. Jo went to God, understood her value as his daughter, and approached Ray from a position of being spiritually loved instead of desperately empty. Had she been spiritually destitute, she probably wouldn't have had the motivation, the courage, or the will to risk confronting Ray.

So if you're living with an angry man, please accept my encouragement to spend all that much more time in worship, prayer, and Christian community so that you can soak up the love, affirmation, and affection you need for a healthy spiritual life. From such a strong spiritual core, you can face the hurt and frustration in your marriage, as Jo did.

Armed with her standing before God, Jo made it clear to Ray that, while she wanted to understand his frustration, she would not put up with verbal harassment. Because Ray desired a better relationship with his wife, Jo's tactic worked; he started to see that letting his temper get the best of him was hurting his relationship with Jo and was getting in the way of communicating his frustrations.

"I really wanted, more than anything, to be a good husband," Ray says. "I wanted to recognize her needs. When Jo stood up to me, it told me she valued herself. So I valued her. It made me understand that Jo is a person with a lot of character; she cares about herself, and I think every man wants that. I don't think men want a woman they can just run over. We want to value our wife's character. The way Jo stood up to me revealed a lot of character."

This goes back to the point made in the very first chapter: respect is vital in a marriage, and not just for a woman toward her man, but also for a man toward his wife. If your husband doesn't respect you, you're going to have a very difficult time influencing him in any significant way. And if you don't respect yourself, you'll make it that much more difficult for your husband to respect you.

It took time for Jo's gentle and self-respecting approach to bear fruit, but she kept at it. "The more that I persisted in asking him to lower his intensity, the more he began, gradually, to see what he was doing."

Remember Dr. Melody Rhode's concept of "functional fixedness"? Men usually don't change unless their wives give them a reason to change. This requires specific, direct, gentle, and self-respecting communication.

"My husband is so grateful that I stood up to him," Jo says today. "He actually said that in one of our conversations! When he learned to lower his intensity, he started to like himself better, and he realized he was loving me better. That made him feel so much more like the man God wanted him to be that he was *thankful* I stood up to him."

Angry men sometimes tell me something they rarely tell their wives: they feel ashamed of how they've acted; they hate what they've become. In most cases, when you help your husband tame his temper, you're helping him to become the kind of man he wants to be.

Helping Him Love You

In her role as an inspirational speaker, Jo has met many women whose husbands have cowed them into an "unhealthy doormat mode." Sadly, sometimes this posture gets couched in religious language and represents a complete misreading of biblical submission. Jo observes, "Women don't tell men what they need because we've been taught that it's selfish to even think of ourselves. In fact, some of us aren't in touch with our own feelings enough to even *know* what we need. Schools don't teach females how to do this — we're supposed to be strong enough on our own, without asking a man to help us; and many families today aren't healthy enough to model it, so these women go into marriage ill-equipped to relate to a man who is likewise ill-equipped to love them."

This "martyr method" of marriage, though common among well-meaning Christian women, shortchanges both husband and wife. Your husband will prosper spiritually and personally by excelling in loving you. God designed marriage, in part, to help both husband and wife grow in character. If you do all the sacrificing, if your husband runs over you, he's not growing; he's shrinking, spiritually speaking. He's becoming lower in character. You may well become a saint after living with such a man for twenty years, but he is going to become increasingly miserable, because, ultimately, any man who treats others poorly begins to despise himself. This might sound backward, but you need to love your husband by teaching him how to love you, because *it's spiritually healthy for him to grow in loving you.*

At one time, the thought of telling her husband what she needed would have sounded selfish to Jo, and she would have dismissed the thought. She has since learned that *respect matters* and that a husband won't truly love a woman for whom he has no respect. Jo realized that if she didn't respect herself, her husband would adopt that same attitude of disrespect.

Second, Jo realized that a marriage that never addresses the issue of needs ultimately provides little intimacy. Husbands can't read minds. She understood that if she didn't tutor Ray in how best to communicate his frustrations in a way in which she could hear them, their marriage would fail to fulfill either of them. Likewise, she needed Ray to understand that she also had certain needs; Ray could focus on changing certain things, even as he had asked Jo to change. Doing so would keep the marriage from becoming condescending and one-sided. An angry husband often acts as if only his wife needs to change. This is a false view based on a lack of respect.

Sharing Needs

Focusing on having our needs met can be selfish, of course, but there's a way to share needs that builds intimacy and respect. It can even become an act of humility: "I need your help. Will you help me?" Clothed in biblical humility, sharing needs can become an incredibly vulnerable and thereby courageous act that gives birth to increased intimacy. Clothed in demands, sharing needs can become a selfish accusation that builds walls: "How come you never talk to me when you get home? Why are you always ignoring me? Is that any way for a Christian man to treat his wife?"

The proper way to share needs involves having the right *motivation* and using the right *presentation.*

Motivation

Your first goal as a sister in Christ is to help your husband more fully express the image of Jesus. Of course, God calls all of us to do that; it just so happens that in this instance, such a change will make your life more pleasant. If you make gaining a more pleasant life your first aim, however, your husband will likely pick up on that and resist your selfish demand. "She's not perfect either," he'll think, "so why doesn't she just get off my back?"

Here's the purest motivation for change: God calls us to "purify ourselves from everything that contaminates body and spirit, perfecting holiness out of reverence for God" (2 Corinthians 7:1). You call your husband to change in the context of reverence for a perfect God, not in comparison with an imperfect wife.

Get painstakingly honest with yourself in prayer before you approach your husband. Dig deep into those buried motivations. Are you praying this way because your husband makes your life miserable, or because you're concerned about how he is grieving God and destroying himself spiritually? Are you motivated out of selfish ambition, or selfless love? I know it is truly difficult to be so altruistic in the face of understandable and legitimate hurt — but that's what prayer and the Holy Spirit's comfort, guidance, and empowerment are all about.

If selfishness motivates you, you're far more likely to give up if you don't get the immediate response you hoped for: "It's not worth the hassle; I guess I'll just have to learn to put up with it." But if you truly dedicate yourself to your husband's spiritual welfare, you'll stick with it and persevere.

Presentation

Ray urges wives who are married to angry men to "use a loving tone of voice and let them know that you really care about them and are committed to them. If you say something the wrong way, you can kill the content. It's not what you say; it's how you say it. Tell your husband that you care about his character because you see a good man in him. That tells him you're on his side. And once he knows you're on his side, you can use a word picture to show him how his angry response makes you feel."

Remember our earlier discussion about affirmation? We men feel desperate to preserve your good view of us. When you say things like, "You're a better man than that," we want to rise to the occasion. If you belittle us, we don't hear your words; we just taste the disrespect and want to spit it out. I think of Ephesians 4:15 in this regard: "Speaking the truth *in love*, we will in all things grow up into him who is the Head, that is, Christ" (emphasis added).

Expressing Needs

Jo learned that her reluctance to speak about her own needs in a direct and straightforward manner caused confusion in her marriage. "I realized that when I didn't communicate clearly, I sounded manipulative and controlling. I could be indirect: 'Why don't you do such and such,' instead of just coming out and asking, 'Please do this for me,' and explaining why it was important. The direct approach is so much better; it honors him more and it doesn't sound controlling or manipulative. It's just a simple request."

Expressing needs is certainly healthier — relationally, spiritually, and psychologically — than stewing in resentment and bitterness because the husband (out of willful lack of respect or perhaps out of ignorance) doesn't seem to get it.

Ray admits that many men have this problem: "I didn't understand Jo's needs until she shared them with me. I always used to say, 'What's your point?' or, 'Just give me the *Reader's Digest* version.' But Jo wanted to process everything with me, and I didn't understand that."

A case in point occurred when Jo asked Ray to go shopping. Ray became goal oriented. "I intended to go into the shirt department, find a style we liked, check the size, buy it, and leave." But Jo finally learned to express that when she suggested they go shopping, she often just wanted to spend time with him. Shopping wasn't about buying anything; it was about going out on a date.

Ray counsels women, "It would be so much more helpful if wives would just say, 'I want us to go shopping, but I want to use shopping as a way for us to spend more time together and to talk. I really don't care if we actually buy anything. We may just walk around and talk about what we're going to do with the patio or how the children are doing. So let's just relax and not rush out of the store, OK?'"

Jo admits that Ray's desire to change played a key role in their success. But she believes that a principle behind her approach remains true for many marriages: "The more we share with our husbands what we need, the more our husbands can meet those needs. Women often fail to realize that many times, our husbands don't know what we need; unless we tell them how we want them to communicate with us, they'll stick with whatever pattern they learned from their father. And if they didn't have a healthy father, watch out!"

Spiritual Lessons

In addition to changing her verbal presentation with Ray, Jo went through a threefold spiritual process to relate to Ray much differently in her heart.

First, Jo looked into Scripture to see who she was in Christ. The biblical way in which God honors women — and the affirming way in which Jesus treated women — contrasted starkly with the subservient description she often heard applied to women in many churches. "When I looked into Scripture and realized who I was in Christ, I started valuing that. God thinks of me as a person of value, and I needed to agree with him!" She had learned the truth highlighted earlier: *God, not your marital status, defines your life.*

Next, Jo applied this same "person of value" approach to Ray: "Not only does God value me as a woman and wife; he values Ray as a man and as a husband. When Ray spoke to me out of anger, I didn't value him as God does. I resented him. I feared him. But I didn't value him. It wasn't until I stood up to Ray that I could begin to value him."

Again, it's good to pause here, because Jo touches on something very insightful. It's far easier to *dismiss* an angry man than to *value* him. Anger attracts no one; a guy throwing a temper tantrum can look downright silly to an observer. When a woman truly values a man, she stands up to him and says, "You're better than that. Don't do this to yourself, or to us." A faithful sister in Christ challenges her man to grow in grace, mercy, and humility.

Finally, Jo realized what it means to be a sister in Christ. She wasn't merely Ray's wife; she was his co-laborer in the Lord, and that meant holding him accountable for God's best in his life. It was *not* God's best for Ray to let his temper direct his relationships. "Many Christian spouses do not hold each other accountable," Jo warns. "We let things slide." A biblical marriage provides a smaller picture of the church. We should use the position and gifts God has given us "so that the body of Christ may be built up until we all reach unity in the faith and in the knowledge of the Son of God and become mature, attaining to the whole measure of the fullness of Christ" (Ephesians 4:12 – 13).

By holding each other accountable as brothers and sisters in Christ, we not only address issues that have the potential to wreck our families; we also help each other learn how to better relate to people in general. Genuine believers will welcome this process of sanctification.

Today, Jo raves about the changed relationship she has with Ray. "Ray has seen so much change in himself since I patiently persevered. My insistence showed him I want the best relationship with him, that I value the person he's become. He wants to continue to be that person. I know he wants to be the best husband he can be. I know he wants to love me like Christ loves the church. When I hold him accountable, I give him more of a chance to become that person."

The Rest of the Story

Up to this point, I've purposely left out one final, but crucial, element of Jo and Ray's story. Jo's husband married her *after* doctors diagnosed her with multiple sclerosis. A woman facing a debilitating disease that has the potential to leave her in a wheelchair faces certain temptations that other women will never know.

I imagine it would be easy for a woman in Jo's situation to feel so afraid of losing her husband — and so fearful of losing his support as she faces an uncertain future — that she would just shut up and endure the angry outbursts. After all, where would she be if her husband left her?

Jo is a woman of tremendous courage. Though her body is gradually losing some of its functions, she still knows that in Christ she is highly valued. And out of that courage, she calls her husband to value and respect her as well.

So if Jo, facing all her challenges and her uncertain future, can do this, you can too. You may be timid. You may have a husband like Ray, and although you may have gained a certain measure of satisfaction from hearing of another wife standing up to her man, you think, "Of course, *I* could never do that."

Yes, you can! Please go back and read Jo's formula: she called out to her heavenly Father and then studied Scripture to find out how highly God values her. Next, she called her husband to do the same. These principles hold true whether you are disfigured, obese, disabled — you name it. You are a person of *great* value to God. Paul's word of encouragement is for you: "Finally, be strong in the Lord and in his mighty power" (Ephesians 6:10).

Chapter 11

Taming the Temper, Part 2

Learning to Navigate through Your Husband's Anger

ale violence creates havoc in homes all across the world. You
can hardly pick up a newspaper without reading at least one
account of the destructiveness of male anger and violence — in virtually all aspects of society. And because men tend to be stronger
physically than women, male temper can become a very frightening
issue in many marriages. So I'd like to spend a little more time on it
as a general topic, beyond what we learned from Ray and Jo.

Appropriate Anger

One caution is in order as we continue to address this issue:
anger is a perfectly natural and even, at times, spiritually healthy
emotion. The Bible says that even God becomes angry (Nahum
1:5–6 and many other passages). Anger in and of itself is not a sin;*

---

*My friend Leslie Vernick adds an important point: while anger in and of itself is not a sin, it
can be a sin: "For example, when anger results from not getting what we want (James 4:1), or
selfish desires ('I want my way, and I'm angry because you're not giving it to me'), then it is

responding with rage, however, or letting anger fuel a threatening, hurtful, or abusive outburst, *is* a sin. You can't fault your husband (or yourself) for getting angry, but you must focus on what you or your husband *does* with the anger.

At times, you must allow your husband to feel legitimately angry with you. You're not perfect — "There is not a righteous man on earth who does what is right and never sins" (Ecclesiastes 7:20) — and sometimes your husband would have to be in deep denial or less than human *not* to be angry with you. If you act as though anger is always illegitimate, you'll merely confuse him, because asking him not to feel angry is like his asking you to never feel hurt. We have to manage our anger in appropriate ways, however, and for you this begins with gaining a better understanding of the dynamics of male anger.

Male Anger

In this issue, as with many others, it's helpful to remind ourselves of the differences between a female brain and a male brain. A "female" approach to male rage often makes the situation worse. Many times, women wrongly assume that talking things out always makes things better — but many men simply need time to process their anger. It's a biological fact that emotional conversation can feel very stressful for a man and actually *increase* his anger, particularly if that conversation gets pushed on him.

If you married a man whose anger and rage seem to build the more you talk, *stop talking*! Let your husband's brain process the stress as you wait for him to come back to you. Just because conversation calms *you* down doesn't mean it will have the same effect on your husband. He may need to go for a run, hit some golf balls at the range, fiddle around in the garage, or do some yard work while he processes his anger. His need for this activity doesn't necessarily amount to stonewalling. It may simply be his very different — but very legitimate — way of processing anger.

sin. In such situations, we need to examine more than just how we handle our anger, but also the very reason we feel angry. Do we have the mind-set that we are always entitled to get our way? Or that people who love me should always give me what I want when I want it?"

148

Far too often women expect to argue with a man just as they would argue with a woman. Furthermore, they assume the way *they* handle conflict is the best way, or even the only appropriate way. In *For Women Only*, Shaunti Feldhahn asks a provocative question: "If you are in conflict with the man in your life, do you think that it is legitimate to break down and cry? Most of us would probably answer yes. Let me ask another question: In that same conflict, do you think it is legitimate for your man to get really angry? Many of us have a problem with that — we think he's not controlling himself or that he's behaving improperly."[1]

The question needs to be asked: why do women tend to respond with hurt, and men tend to respond with anger? It all has to do with the male need for respect. Shaunti goes on to quote Dr. Emerson Eggerichs, who explains, "In a relationship conflict, crying is often a woman's response to feeling unloved, and anger is often a man's response to feeling disrespected."[2]

Shaunti conducted her own survey that confirms this reality. Here's the statement:

> Even the best relationships sometimes have conflicts on day-to-day issues. In the middle of a conflict with my wife/significant other, I am more likely to be feeling:
>
> - that my wife/significant other doesn't respect me right now: 81 percent
> - that my wife/significant other doesn't love me right now: 19 percent[3]

Men get most frustrated — and angriest — when they feel disrespected. If your conversation takes on a demeaning tone, you have as much a chance of resolving something as you would baking a cake by throwing the ingredients down the garbage disposal. You *can't* control your husband's anger — but you *can* provoke it by being disrespectful. That doesn't excuse any inappropriate actions on his part, but if you truly want to be part of the solution, then learn how to disagree with your husband without showing a lack of respect — and that includes nonverbal routines such as folding your arms, turning away, rolling your eyes, or making mocking gestures.[4]

Also, carefully consider your words. Do they suggest inadequacy? When you continually question your husband's purchases, his ability to run the house or fix things, his choice of clothes, the way he handles the kids, and the like, you create a "frustration bomb." These things build up over time, and eventually, one blatant act of disrespect lights the fuse that results in a blinding explosion.

Every man is different, so with your man you must learn where you need to let go. You may not agree with how he's fixing something, or you may think it's long past the time for him to bring in an expert — but in most cases, let him make the call. Women, in general, simply don't understand how offensive and annoying it can feel to a man to be constantly challenged and corrected, especially in a disrespectful manner.

For years, men have been told to be more sensitive to women; perhaps it's time to help women understand how to become more sensitive to men. For example, when you blatantly question or ridicule the way in which your husband is doing something, it feels to his male mind exactly like it would feel for you to hear, "Honey, your face is really looking bloated and puffy; don't you think it's time to lose a few pounds?" Only an extraordinarily insensitive husband would ever talk like that — and only an extraordinarily insensitive woman would blatantly and callously question her husband's abilities.

It has often helped me to see objectively how this works out in the relationship between my wife and adolescent son. Now that our boy is becoming a man, I'm trying to help my wife see that her motherly concern and correction must never disrespect him, or she'll shut Graham out entirely. Nothing will make a man or a boy angrier than showing blatant disrespect or cultivating an attitude of disrespect. She still needs to correct him, but if that correction becomes demeaning, every male fiber in his testosterone-laced body is going to want to rise up in defiance. And so we enter the dilemma of either "swatting the mosquitoes" or "draining the swamp."

I suggest you do both.

Stop those little acts of disrespect — the tone that ridicules him; the teasing barbs that feel like little splashes to you and like tsunamis to him; the constant complaints to friends; the frequent questioning, "Are you *sure* you know what you're doing?" and the like. Instead, focus on the positive. Make sure he knows you believe he is adequate, competent, and capable. Talk up his strong points. Praise him in public. Show your unconditional support.

If you do all this, his "anger meter" will reach record lows in a surprisingly short span of time. From that platform, you can then begin to apply the principles we learned from Jo's experience.

The Queen of the Virtues

James 4:1–2 explains the genesis of every marital argument: "What causes fights and quarrels among you? Don't they come from your desires that battle within you? You want something but don't get it. You kill and covet, but you cannot have what you want. You quarrel and fight. You do not have, because you do not ask God."

According to James, we fight because we're selfish, because we're disappointed, because we're not getting our way, and because we're depending on someone other than God to meet our needs. There's one word that describes this hideous disposition: *pride.*

The ancients called humility "the queen of the virtues" because they rightly understood Scripture to teach that pride is the greatest of all sins. Humility will serve your home well, and it can also play a preeminent role in reducing angry outbursts.

Ray told me that one of the most helpful things his counselor suggested was to learn to ask for God's wisdom to compose himself so that he could focus on Jo's needs, making her the center of his attention. By nature, men can be self-centered; Ray needed to learn that Jo *matters.*

This cuts to the heart of the issue, because an angry man often acts as though he is the only one who matters. An angry man tries to assert control, seizing the situation by force and trying to use his anger to intimidate or scare the other person into doing what he wants. Humility — focusing on someone other than yourself — provides the best spiritual remedy for this.

But here's the catch for *you*. You must work to stay humble as you oppose pride. Maybe your side of the argument is that you don't want to put up with an angry man! Maybe what you want but don't get (referring to James) is a peaceful relationship, and so you are tempted to lash out with the same attitude of pride and expression of anger.

There's a very important spiritual principle behind this: just because someone I'm opposing is wrong doesn't make me right! There are a hundred ways to miss a target but only one way to hit it.[5] It's very possible that on any given day, and in the midst of any particular argument, both you and your husband are succumbing to pride, which in turn will blind you from the wisdom of God's humility. Your husband may be wrong, and he may be expressing himself in an improper way, but that alone doesn't make you right.

Pray for humility. Read books that deal with this topic more directly.[6] Pray with some friends, always keeping James 4:1–2 in mind. Pride is an ever-present foe, so make humility an ever-present friend.

Confronting Rage and Physical Abuse

I want to switch gears for just a moment here and address temper that burns out of control. There's a moment when anger becomes rage and when rage becomes physical. Such a situation calls for a more drastic response.

In *Sacred Marriage*, I talk extensively about how God can use a difficult marriage to shape us. He uses trials to transform us, and he teaches us to respond to evil with blessing. God has used many difficult marriages to help prepare people for ministry. Having said this, it is a misapplication of scriptural principles to believe you must stay in a situation where you are being physically abused.

Some women "spiritualize" domestic violence. They assume it's their "duty" to bear up under the assault and certainly not to report it to anyone, lest their husbands get in trouble.

I want to be as clear and as honest here as I can: If your husband hits you, both of you need help. You won't solve this problem alone. You *must* speak to someone — a trusted pastor, a wise counselor, maybe a dear friend. But you shouldn't ever have to face this problem alone.

You are not being unfaithful to your husband when you seek help. On the contrary, you are acting in love by helping him confront a behavior that offends God and could prove fatal. Paul writes, "Have nothing to do with the fruitless deeds of darkness, but rather expose them" (Ephesians 5:11).

Biblical submission *never* means you must serve as a punching bag. We are called to submit to one another "out of reverence for Christ" (Ephesians 5:21), which qualifies our response. If my wife asks me to do something or participate in something that offends Christ, I am not bound to join her. On the contrary, I have a duty to God to resist her. The same is true for you as a wife.

Depending on the situation, temporary separation may be necessary to end domestic violence.* You may not believe in divorce, but remember that not all separation ends in divorce; sometimes it's a move toward healing. It allows both spouses to regroup, get their bearings, receive counsel, and break destructive patterns before they come back together.

You *must* seek help in this situation, because you never know where the violence might lead. You need protection and wisdom, and your husband needs accountability. Once his problem no longer remains a secret between the two of you, he will be less likely to escalate the harm; he knows he's finally "on record" and could get into a lot of trouble if he continues acting out. If you try to solve this "just between the two of you," you put yourself at increased risk. Your husband may become afraid of being found out and do something desperate to silence you.

So please, please, please — get help!

While some women spiritualize domestic violence, others live in denial, dismissing it as a "joke" that got out of hand. Ximena Arriaga,

---

*But *please* seek advice from trained professionals before taking this approach. Sometimes, when a woman separates from an abusive man, she puts herself in even more danger of abuse. You need to work with someone who has enough experience to help you choose the wisest and safest course of action.

an associate professor of psychological sciences who studies relationship commitment and domestic violence, gives this explanation:

> We hear people say my partner was joking when he hit, kicked or burned me. They also may excuse degrading comments as simple jokes. When a partner is violent, the victim must wonder, "Why is this person who is supposed to love me also hurting me?" One way to make sense of this puzzle is to view the violence as benign. If the person can explain it as something else — something less negative, such as joking, and attribute it to their partner's sense of humor — then they can deny that they are abused and don't have to put up with the possible shame that goes with staying in a violent relationship.[7]

It pains a woman so much to know that her husband is hurting her that she might try to pass it off as "rough humor" or "an accident." An "occasional joke" is easier to face than the fact that you married a wife abuser. But physical harm is never funny. There is no humor in hurt.

If you're in this situation, don't be ashamed. You are not alone. Sadly, research shows that one out of every eight couples suffers from partner violence.[8] Think of it this way: in a church with two hundred couples, twenty-five couples may be struggling with this to varying degrees, which is why churches can do great good by posting in their women's restrooms notices of helpful programs. When you courageously step forward and talk to a pastor or counselor, you could become the lead person in helping your church to confront an issue that all too often is kept in the shadows. If no one talks to the pastor, he may not realize there's a problem and never address it from the pulpit.

Addressing the rage and violence doesn't necessarily mean the marriage has ended. Don't let the fear of your financial needs and parental responsibilities get in the way of confronting this problem. Other couples have worked through this. Ignoring it or putting it off will only make things worse. The habit will become more ingrained, and you and your husband may reach a point where the marriage cannot be salvaged. Furthermore, it devastates your children to re-main in a violent home. Allowing yourself to be abused "for their sake" is a contradiction in terms.

Many groups and organizations can help you face the immedi-ate financial implications. I always suggest you turn to your church first, but if that's not an option, consider calling the National Do-mestic Violence Hotline at 1-800-799-7233 (or visit www.ncadv.org for information on the National Coalition Against Domestic Vio-lence). You can also find a local YWCA by calling 1-800-992-2871 (or visit www.ywca.org).

Reporting your husband may, indeed, make him very angry. If as a result of this confrontation he chooses to repent and seek to grow, in the end he'll thank you. After he confronts his behavior and begins to make changes, he'll find it far more fulfilling to love, nurture, encourage, and support a woman than to abuse one. If he doesn't repent, you certainly do face some dark days ahead; but in the end, that will be better than remaining in a home where you fear for your life. Furthermore, you'll teach your children that their father's behavior simply isn't acceptable. Your daughters will learn not to put up with that kind of behavior, and your courageous action can help to stop a generational pattern of destruction.

From Strength to Strength

I've been part of a marathon training group for a couple of years now. I've seen women who had never run five miles slowly work their bodies into shape so that five or six months down the road they com-pleted a marathon. I'm not talking about women in excellent physical shape either! You'd look at some of them and think, "The last thing they'll ever do is run twenty-six miles in a day." But through months of small decisions and patient preparation, they do it.

If you live with an angry man, this is your "spiritual marathon." You're going to be challenged in ways that may terrify you. Women who marry abusive men often had abusive fathers, and they've de-veloped a lifelong portrait of themselves as victims. It will go against every learned response in your hurting soul to finally stand up and say you're not going to take it anymore — but doing so is the pathway to healing, hope, and a healthier marriage.

You may feel terrified, but think with me about a future in which you are supported instead of threatened, in which you feel adored instead of attacked and appreciated instead of insulted. Isn't it worth the risk, for you and your children, to work toward such a marriage?

Furthermore, God can use this situation to help you become much stronger. Sadly, often only when we feel like we're in over our heads do we fully throw ourselves on God's mercy and learn to walk with his empowerment and grace. For perhaps the first time in your life, decide to let faith and spiritual resolve win out over your fear. Remember, courage is not the absence of fear, but it entails putting your faith in God and moving forward even when you feel terrified and convinced that everything will go wrong.

Your situation may resemble Jo's — anger but no violence. You need the courage to accept God's view of yourself as a valuable person and then the wisdom to teach your husband how to respond to you appropriately. If your situation is beginning to become violent, you need to act now, find some help, and be part of creating a crisis that will lead to change.

Above all, remember that while you might feel frightened, uncertain, guilty, or confused, you are *never* alone. Your God is with you, and his people will surround you. Spend some time asking God to bring some helpers into your life before you act; this may be the wisest step you can take. And then move forward from there. If you keep stepping out in faith, you'll discover just how strong you can become in Christ — and that's a valuable life lesson. If you persevere in this, you won't even recognize yourself several years down the road. That timid, fearful, victimized personality will vanish in favor of a strong, wise, bold, and courageous woman of faith.

As the apostle Paul wrote, "To this end I labor, struggling with all his energy, which so powerfully works in me" (Colossians 1:29). This is your refuge and your hope.

Chapter 12

Rich and Pat:
The Magic Question

Helping Your Husband
to Become More Involved at Home

Although Rich and Pat have three children together, for some time they led mostly separate lives. According to Pat, "We did little together except argue about the kids."

Rich concurs: "Home life was pretty combative."

Pat once complainingly described Rich as an overinvolved worker during the week and an avid hunter and fisherman on the weekends. What little time remained he spent watching TV or using the computer, making him a relatively uninvolved husband and father. When Pat brought up Rich's frequent absences on weekends, Rich would say, "Don't worry, honey. Hunting season is almost over." He forgot to mention that fishing season was waiting just around the corner!

From Rich's perspective, life seemed much easier *outside* the home — a view shared by many men. "I probably was overinvolved in work, and when I wasn't working, I wanted to hunt and fish. Outside of home, there were all sorts of things to succeed at: birds to shoot or issues to solve at work. There's great satisfaction in getting my limit of trout or ducks, or resolving issues at work. Also, these were *solvable* problems that I could tackle with a certain degree of success; the problems at home didn't seem all that solvable."

We men have a tendency to avoid battles that we know we can't win or that make us feel incompetent. Unfortunately, this means that when we start to feel like we're in over our heads in our family life, home may become the last place we want to be. The sad result is that we may slowly increase our hours at work and then extend our involvement in recreational hobbies, perhaps not even realizing that we are virtually hiding from our families.

Pat realized what she was up against when she asked her husband to take care of their infant son, Ben, one evening a week so she could get some work done or have some relaxation time without being interrupted. Rich declined with the words, "I'm not really that interested in babies." By Rich's reckoning, since he worked all day, the evenings belonged to him, and he shouldn't have to bother with child-rearing. By the same token, since he worked all week, the weekends were his to relax and recharge. What's more, since he worked all year, vacations allowed him to pursue hunting and fishing or camping. In Rich's view, watching the kids and taking care of the house were solely Pat's responsibility.

Meanwhile, Pat saw her job as twenty-four hours a day, seven days a week, with no vacations and little or no help.

Pat blames herself for letting this go on for so long. "I didn't have negotiating skills or boundaries," she remembers. "I kept thinking that if I worked harder, it would get better somehow — but it didn't, and then I'd explode, and that just made things worse. I didn't know how to confront people in a good way or look for alternatives. For example, I could have hired a babysitter to take the kids to the park while I stayed home. And I should have set better limits on my children, like setting a timer and having a one-hour flat-on-bunk time every day, or having a list of chores to get done and then going to the park. Fortunately, I did start seeing my hours as flexible and Rich's as inflexible. I decided to start having some fun during the day so I'd feel more rested when Rich came home."

Shortly after their oldest child turned fifteen, "things began to fall apart. Our house was characterized by arguing, yelling, and business. Our children fell into the classic pattern of rebellious child, overpleasing child, and withdrawn child. Rich was usually gone and didn't really want to be home — and I had given him every reason not to! I greeted him with a list when he came home, was in a chronically bad mood, and was usually either depressed or angry."

Pat tried to talk to Rich about becoming interested in family activities (besides hunting and fishing), but Rich responded, "Look, I work hard, I don't drink, I don't gamble, and I don't chase other women. All in all, I'd say I'm a pretty good husband."

"He did provide well for us," Pat admits. "In his eyes, that made him a good husband and father. He also went to lots of the kids' games. He just couldn't see that he was very cold and distant and that he avoided problems."

Carving Out a New Path

Eventually Pat realized that, even after years of confrontation and arguing, Rich remained overinvolved at work and relatively absent at home. Now in her early forties, Pat didn't want to spend the rest of her life with a man who always had his mind somewhere else.

"To be honest," Pat admits, "I wanted a divorce, but I knew the only biblical grounds for one were if he died or committed adultery or left me. So I prayed that he would die or find someone else."

Instead, *Pat* found someone else — the Lord, whom she credits with saving her life. "Without God, I would have ended up in jail or the insane asylum." Pat thought she had always been a Christian because she went to church, but a frustrating experience with her pastor had led her to visit Bethel Church in Richland, Washington, where she encountered a rich, deep, and authentic faith.

At her old church, Christianity seemed more of a cultural thing; most of the congregation considered those who actually read the Bible as either strange or religious zealots. People just didn't use phrases like "God spoke to me" or "the Bible says." Pat started listening to Christian radio, reading the Bible, applying her new pastor's teaching, reading the works of Dr. James Dobson, and growing spiritually by the hour.

When she started reading about "biblical submission" of wives to husbands, Pat initially felt wary. "That was a radical, new thought for me," Pat says. "I wasn't raised that way, and I was more into the women's liberation philosophy of equality. Furthermore, I felt pretty nervous about submitting to someone who wasn't reading his Bible. Doing so will either break you or develop your faith in the love and power of God."

Pat's church also introduced her to basic Christian virtues, such as being thankful in all circumstances and pursuing love, joy, peace, patience, goodness, and kindness. "I thought I deserved to be cranky; anyone who had to put up with what I had to deal with would do likewise. It was hard to admit that, regardless of circumstances, people can choose their response."

The Magic Question

Pat began this journey of biblical submission by asking Rich the "magic question." "Rich," she said, "what things would you like me to do that I'm not doing?"

Rich's answer caught Pat completely off guard.

"Somehow I expected him to tell me he would like the house to be cleaner — I could have dealt with that. But he asked me to start preparing meals that the kids would like. I was in shock. I was raised with the notion that there is only one thing worse than a murderer, and that is a picky eater. 'You got two things to eat: take it or leave it!'"

When the kids didn't enjoy what Pat had made, she'd insist they eat it anyway, creating regular friction and confrontation around the dinner table. Rich just wanted peace. When Rich was a boy, if any of the kids in his family said, "I don't like this," they never saw it again. If Pat ever heard that response in her family, she would have been served the same meal, in double portions, for breakfast the next morning!

"I was appalled that Rich let the kids eat dessert if they didn't like the main course. But over time, he helped me see that there is some wisdom in the fact that people do feel loved when you give them the things they want; and he's come around to my view, too, that healthy eating and polite table manners also matter."

Previously, Pat made the kids' lunches, and that was that. Now, at Rich's request, she became more aware of what they liked and didn't like and started customizing their sack lunches. "Before, I had simply ignored what the kids liked. My attitude was, 'I made it; you eat it.'" One of Pat's daughters liked her sandwiches cut in a fancy way; the other kids didn't care about such niceties. For the first time, Pat began to regularly accommodate this daughter's preference, and years later, she felt very glad she had. On a high school retreat, someone asked this daughter to name something that someone had done to make an impact on her life, and she said, "My mom cut my sandwiches like I liked them. It made me feel special and loved."

"At the time, I thought it was so crazy," Pat remembers, "but listening to Rich helped me to demonstrate love to my daughter in a way that she could receive it. Also, I remembered as a child that I wanted my sandwiches cut a certain way. It seemed a small thing to ask because it requires no money and almost no time. But my mom refused. I felt stupid and insignificant. Unless I had submitted to my husband, I would have done what my mom had done. I never would have learned to balance practicality with graciousness."

Pat's question can transform a marriage. Perhaps you are reading this book because you want to see something change in your husband. It's always a good exercise in humility, however, to occasionally put the spotlight on yourself. Do you have the spiritual fortitude to put aside your own frustration and disappointment long enough to ask your husband, "What would you like me to do that I'm not doing?"

Notice, Pat didn't ask this of a perfect husband; she asked it of one with whom she felt very angry, one who seemed to ignore her and the kids. *But she also believed that if change was going to transform her home, it would have to begin with her.*

Let me challenge you to take some time in the next few days to offer that simple, yet potentially marriage-changing, question, "What would you like me to do that I'm not doing?"

"The Last Thing I Wanted Him to Ask"

After getting used to meal changes and seeing some good results, Pat decided to repeat the question. Once again, Rich's answer astounded her. He replied, "I don't care if the house is clean; I just want you to be in a good mood when I walk in the door."

"That was the last thing I wanted him to ask of me," Pat admits. "I could see how it was theoretically possible, because if all I had to do all day long was to be in a good mood when he walked through the door, I figured I should be able to do that. But complaining, criticizing, and arguing were old, faithful friends. Be in a good mood? That was not me!"

Rich also asked Pat to focus on having more fun with the kids instead of correcting them all the time. Pat's constant admonitions kept pouring tension into the home, and Rich craved peace.

Beyond these things, Rich felt reluctant to talk about what Pat could do for him, so she thought up a few things on her own. Instead of complaining about Rich's fishing trips, Pat started going with him. And not just the fishing trips — she'd accompany him to the sporting goods store and even to Rod and Gun Club meetings ("where they eat venison, moose, or bear, and some speaker shares slides of his latest hunt").

"This was real hard for me because I felt that fishing and hunting was something my husband should give up," Pat acknowledges. "At first it sort of felt like wanting an alcoholic to give up going to bars, and then going out drinking with him; to me, it felt the same anyway. This was a real idol in his life, and I didn't want to support it. I *still* think hunting and fishing have a bigger place in his life than they should have, but I finally had to admit, there *is* a difference between fishing and drinking. It wasn't sinful for me to go fishing with my husband. I had to learn to let God be God and let *him* work on things with Rich."

After adopting this very difficult transformation, Pat laughs about driving past places now and thinking, "That would be a great place to fish!" "I actually *enjoy* some fishing," she marvels. "We went to Sun Valley for our twenty-fifth wedding anniversary and had a great time fly-fishing."

For both of them, it's been a long transformation by degrees. "Basically, when I asked Rich what he wanted of me — regarding us — what he wanted sounded most difficult. He just wanted me to be in a good mood, to be more fun, and not to complain about things that don't get fixed." Some of those things, Pat now fixes herself. And as for her mood — well, Rich will tell you that she's a lot more pleasant to live with.

Overwhelming Benefits

Much to Pat's surprise, when she started focusing on helping Rich instead of fighting and resenting him, he became more involved at home. "Home became a lot more pleasant place to be, so I'm sure that had something to do with it."

Pat heard two guys on the radio joking about a 1950s home economics textbook that encouraged women to serve their husbands; but that comedic exchange affected Pat in a different way: "Most men, if they're honest, really would like that in their wives," she says. And she's trying to provide some of that service for Rich.

What initiated the first major change in Pat's marriage? Pat decided to focus on helping Rich. She started having dinner ready when he got home. She went fishing with him instead of complaining about him leaving. She cleared her calendar, cutting out a lot of her outside activities, so that "instead of trying to find fulfillment in other things, I could focus my energies on my home and my family."

Pat doesn't sugarcoat the difficulty of any of this. "It's impossibly hard to put so much energy into a home and marriage when you don't enjoy your home or family. At first, you literally feel like you're dying. We all crave recognition, power, and honor. Sacrificing and serving seem to move you away from those desires."

But Pat fought off the resentment. "I felt that, in one sense, what I was doing was contrary to everything I am. I felt like I was dying, but the paradox is that I am more me now than I ever was. I am kinder, gentler, and more submissive, but I am also more strong-willed and opinionated than I ever was. I used to think those were contradictions, but now I see how they work together. Although at the time, I thought I was giving things up, I can see now I was gaining. I wouldn't go back to the way I was for anything. I have more joy, forgiveness, and grace, and more friends — *a lot* more friends! My family has changed dramatically, and for the first time, I get along with my siblings, Mom and Dad, and my in-laws."

Pat went on. "The way I moved my husband was by changing myself. I honestly believe that when you do what your partner wants you to do, you heal yourself in the process. God gives you your spouse as the person who can fix those things in you that you really don't want to fix."

Rich agrees. "Pat softened a lot, and that made a big difference to me. It's a lot easier to feel empathy for someone who is soft than for someone who is coming on hard."

"You can't do this without faith in the Lord," Pat adds. "And though you probably will, like me, feel like you're dying, all I can say is that it's *so* worth it. By submitting to my husband and doing what he asked me to do — even though there was so much I wanted *him* to do differently — I became the person I wanted to be: a more loving wife, a better friend, a better mother. And then I found that those things bring me a lot of joy. The benefits to *myself* have been overwhelming. Even if my husband acted like the biggest jerk from now until the day he dies, submitting to him has brought an incredible change in me, and I wouldn't go back to the way I was for anything."

The Big Adventure

To wives whose husbands play darts on the weekend or who constantly haunt the golf course or who accompany their buddies to the local bar, Pat advises, "Consider how you might be driving your husband out of the house and into the basement, the golf course, or the computer."

Think very honestly about this past week. Put yourself in your husband's shoes. What did it feel like to be greeted by you? What kind of mood do you set in the home? Are you pleasant? Confrontational? Apathetic? Would you like to be welcomed home in the way you welcome home your husband?

Maybe you get home from work after your husband does. You can ask yourself some other questions. Do you regularly complain about your day instead of listening to him about his? Do you pour out your resentment that other women have it easier than you do? Do you make him feel as though he doesn't measure up? Are you preoccupied with the in-box on your desk at work? What are you doing to make your husband your "buddy"? Are you a pleasure to be around?

Since Pat has undergone these changes, she says that "Rich now *wants* to come home. He *wants* to be with me; he wants to support me if I'm going through a bad time. When he does go away on trips, he's careful to organize them in such a way that he can see the family as much as possible before and afterwards."

Pat adds, "If you want a big adventure, submit to your husband. That will be the greatest adventure of your life; it will be more exciting than being shot to the moon. It will open up a whole different way of looking at things — a way you perhaps can't envision right now. Few topics are more controversial than that of submitting to your husband, but it's absolute truth — and it's worked so well in my own life."

Rich's Perspective

Rich points to three factors that influenced his evolution from absentee father and husband to a man eager to come home at night:

- Pat's renewed commitment
- Pat's expression of her own hurt
- Rich's renewed faith

"To me, the big change occurred when I felt that Pat was really *committed* to the marriage. Before, I began to wonder just how committed she was. There were times she said that she didn't love me, that she even hated me, and suggested that I might want to leave — which I did not want to do. But I think what became important was when she realized we have a commitment. Marriage isn't just about *feelings* of love; there are times when only a commitment carries you through. When marriage is based on a Christian faith, it's much more solid. You can depend on it. That, to me, was the foundation that was most important — after we both realized that we were committed to this marriage, I wanted to change, and I always had hope after that point."

Rich brings up a good point: why would a husband change for a wife who shows no commitment to him — who might, in fact, even leave him or encourage him to leave? From a guy's perspective, that's like filling up the gas tank just before you sell your car. If your husband has no confidence that the marriage will continue, why go through the hassle of character transformation?* Most men need to know that their wives will be there before they feel motivated to make a change.

Second, Rich was genuinely surprised when Pat finally got through to him about how badly he was hurting her. Rich obviously enjoys being around his wife, and he really didn't want to lose her. "Pat is an extraordinary woman," he says. "She once asked me why I wouldn't leave, and I said, 'Because I like you.' There's just something about her that's different that I really like. This may not be true of every marriage, but I personally couldn't *ever* see myself being married to or dating another woman. I had no interest in other women."

When a man feels this deeply about a woman and then sees how his actions cause her such pain, he's going to feel motivated to change. Before then — as much as this may frustrate Pat — Rich says he really didn't understand just how much pain he was causing.

The third major stage of Rich's evolution came about when he saw Pat's renewed faith. Her renewed relationship with God became contagious. Like Pat, Rich exchanged a "cultural Christianity" for a real faith. If you ask him why he's more involved at home now, Rich says, "There's no treasure in the other activities, no inheritance; it all gets burned away! I still put in a good day at work, and I still love to hunt and fish, but I realize that, from the standpoint of eternity, they'll all pass away."

*I believe husbands should be motivated "out of reverence for God" (2 Corinthians 7:1), not out of our wives' reactions. I'm describing here what *usually* happens, not what *should* happen.

How interesting! The man who once threw himself into work and outdoor sports because of their solvable nature and tangible rewards now recognizes that their rewards pale in comparison to God's promised rewards in eternity.

In my view, that's why Pat's mission "worked." Instead of trying to change Rich for her own sake, she drew closer to the Lord, captivated Rich with her own example, and in a godly way encouraged Rich to reevaluate his priorities according to God's standards. Rich needed another measuring stick. Marriage, faith, and family life take more effort than work and fishing — but they offer much greater rewards: "Everyone who competes in the games goes into strict training. They do it to get a crown that will not last; but we do it to get a crown that will last forever" (1 Corinthians 9:25).

Rich has some simple counsel for wives married to overinvolved husbands: "First, they really need to let their husbands know how it feels to be left alone. Second, I would tell them that their man needs to get into an accountability group. Doing so helped me to see other role models at church. Our small group evolved into an accountability group, and those guys started challenging me about how much time I spent with my wife compared to time at work or hunting. Plus, it was very helpful for me to see what other successful couples were doing."

Rich and Pat's story emphasizes the importance of a healthy Christian community. It'll go much easier for you if other men can challenge your husband. Some men resent it when they think their wives want them to change for the wives' sake; it's a different matter entirely when some committed friends say, "Hey, buddy, you need to do this because *God* calls you to do this."

Rich also urges wives to follow Pat's example of entering into their husbands' world. Pat says to wives, "Find a way to be his buddy and do the things he wants to do," and Rich affirms this wholeheartedly: "It really helped to find common ground on things we like to do. I really appreciated it when Pat made the effort to start fly-fishing with me. After she did that, I thought I had an obligation to spend time with her shopping or doing the things she likes to do."

I believe marriage involves a commitment to, as I say in *Sacred Marriage*, "fall forward." Just as I started following figure skating (something I have zero natural interest in) when figure skating became important to my daughter; and just as I'll occasionally watch the HGTV (Home and Garden Television) channel with my wife, even though finding the "right" wallpaper ranks one millionth on the list of things that interest me — so you might think about doing something or becoming informed about a topic simply because your husband enjoys it. Doing so creates momentum for your husband to also fall toward you.

Rich freely confesses that conversation doesn't rank high on his list of favorite things: "The hardest thing for me is just sitting down and talking. Oh, that's hard!" But now he's at least willing to give it a try.

Rich stresses, "Wives need to understand the commitment part. Marriage is love *and* commitment; a husband won't stay or even want to stay in a marriage if the wife isn't committed." Commitment is about more than simply staying put; it also requires moving toward someone. If you want your husband to move toward you, ask yourself how you are moving toward your husband. This goes far beyond staying legally married to include the spiritual commitment of continuing to love, pursue, and serve.

Your first movement toward your husband should be, as it was for Pat, a movement toward God. Paul praises the Macedonians for this: "They gave themselves first to the Lord and then to us in keeping with God's will" (2 Corinthians 8:5). When you give yourself first to God, you open yourself up to his correction, affirmation, and redemption.

How might God be using the situations in your life to help you reevaluate yourself, your priorities, and your actions? For Pat, the answer came loud and clear that she needed to learn the meaning of biblical submission. I doubt she could have given herself to Rich if she hadn't first given herself — including her emotional desires, her relational frustration, and her personal despair — to God.

And then follow this up with the second question: "What would you like me to do for you that I'm not doing?" If you heed your husband's words instead of taking offense, you can slowly transform your home into a more pleasant place for him to be — and therefore make him *want* to come home.

Chapter 13

The Biology of
a Busy Man

How to Help Your Man Put Family First

"Rothschild" was to the financial world of Victorian England what "Kennedy" or "Bush" is to political power in the United States. Because of their acclaim, the Rothschilds usually married their English children to their German cousins. The fact that Lionel and Charlotte had an arranged marriage did not in any way lessen the couple's delight or happiness with their upcoming nuptials. Even arranged marriages could be refused, but both Charlotte and Lionel readily agreed to the match. Lionel wrote to his mother, "[I] have to thank you for my fair bride."

At first, the seventeen-year-old Charlotte had difficulty adjusting to her life as a young wife. Lionel's business kept him away for most of the day, and Charlotte lapsed into self-pity, thinking of herself as a neglected bride. It's not difficult to understand why. Lionel had been quite the romantic before the wedding. He wrote to Charlotte that, without her, "his life of interminable if unpredictable business would seem newly tedious." He confessed in another letter that he had "no amusement nor occupation, but that of preparing for and thinking of the happy times when I can call you Dearest Charlotte mine and mine for ever."[1]

But now that it had become entirely appropriate to call her "Dearest Charlotte," Lionel stayed away most of the day, building his business. As happens so often, the romantic husband soon became a preoccupied pragmatist. He had a business to run and vocational duties to attend to. Charlotte lapsed into self-pity and criticism and may even have begun to regret her decision to marry.

While we can understand her conflicting emotions, later in life, Charlotte faulted *herself*, not Lionel, for this "wasted" season: "Lionel was never with me between the hours of tea in the morning and six in the evening. Oh! Why did I waste those hours in warm regrets, in tears? Why did I not then, ardently and assiduously, apply [myself] to study? Possibly, that would have dried my tears and made my thoughts play into pleasant and profitable channels. I could have accomplished much in those days."[2]

Most modern wives certainly wouldn't judge their husbands for working nine-hour days — especially since many have jobs themselves that run just as long or even longer. But most can relate to Charlotte's surprise at how much a couple's emotional life changes after the wedding. Charlotte suffered from the common syndrome of being romanced and adored leading up to the wedding, and then watching in shock as her husband immediately turned his focus back to his business once the couple declared their vows. Romance, to the man, is all too often like a vacation; once the vacation ends, he's ready to get on with life. The wife, on the other hand, frequently hopes and assumes that the romance will continue as a way of life.

Love Abides

Charlotte's father eventually stepped in and urged her to stop feeling sorry for herself and instead find ways to offer immense practical help to Lionel and stop making a scene when he came home. "Tell your husband he should assiduously visit diplomats in order to hear the news.... You should try to find out what is happening in London."[3]

Charlotte took this advice to heart. Instead of wasting energy on complaining, she put that same energy to work on Lionel's behalf. "Soon it was Charlotte ... who was efficiently entertaining diplomats, Cabinet ministers, princes, and peers. Her guests evidenced her pragmatism; Charlotte knew she did not even have to like them."[4]

While it was fashionable for public men of prominence to have several mistresses, no hint of indiscretion ever tainted Lionel's life — perhaps, in part, because of how indispensable Charlotte soon became to him. The two lovers merged into an indissoluble team, a united force to make their mark in this world. They become arguably the most commercially successful couple of their day. Lionel even made political history by becoming the first person of Jewish descent to win a seat in the British House of Commons. By the time he achieved this lofty aim, Lionel was virtually an invalid. He managed only with Charlotte's invaluable aid and assistance. Charlotte spent many hours listening to speeches in the gallery so that she could discuss the issues with Lionel when he got home. Their biographer, Stanley Weintraub, writes, "Charlotte was seldom afflicted by boredom. Her responsibilities were too many, and her family seemingly always in motion."[5]

The biographer sums it up well:

Her husband had left a legend, and a formidable enterprise to confront the generations after him. Beyond her tireless benefactions and her role as Lionel's chatelaine, Charlotte's bounty was unique. Not just as the most memorable woman in three Disraeli novels, but in her sparkling letters and her family legacy, Charlotte still lives. With Lionel, she embodied one of Victorian England's most remarkable and unfading love stories. A marriage arranged by ambitious mothers between cousins who hardly knew each other and came from different countries, it endured and was even enriched by adversity and challenge. As Charlotte had said, wealth was not enough. Love abides.[6]

Love abides.

What a powerful description of a marriage! If only the young Charlotte could have looked ahead five decades and pulled herself out of her stupor with the thought that becoming a helper would knit a romance that the years would only intensify! That instead of fighting her husband's drive to succeed, she could become an integral part of it and thereby win his affections, while creating a marriage that one of the most prominent novelists of her day would celebrate in several books.

It's my hope that Charlotte's experience will encourage young wives in particular. It's quite normal for a man to romance his fiancée eagerly, only to turn his attention to his business after the wedding. I understand this must hurt and may even feel like fraud and deception; I also agree with you that husbands shouldn't be given a free pass: "That's just the way men are; what are you going to do about it?"

But I also want to help you begin to look at this from a slightly different perspective. One of the reasons most men focus intensely on their occupation is that God wired us this way. Yes, we can take it to sinful extremes, but the drive to succeed is innate in masculinity, by our Creator's design.

The Male Drive to Achieve

Here's a common scenario: the kids have grown, the husband has achieved relative success in life, and the wife finally feels ready to buy that vacation home on the beach or take more time off to visit the grandkids. Then, much to her shock, her husband announces his plans to build a brand-new business or to take on a completely new challenge (golf, triathlons, buying and repairing run-down homes).

To many women, such actions may seem like a denial of one's age; but it's a biological imperative that drives them. Male brains are bent toward a calling of some sort. According to Michael Gurian, "At the biological core of manhood is the drive and will to prove self-worth, not just as a person, but as a male.... There is a biological tendency in men to seek self-worth through personal, independent performance; in women, there is a greater tendency to experience worth through relationships and intimacy. This difference, while certainly socialized in all cultures, finds its origins in human biology.... In men, the biological foundation is laid for performance imperative."[7]

If you were to study the brains of a man and a woman while they gazed into the eyes of a child or grandchild, you would see that the typical female gets more out of such an encounter, physically, than does the male. Relationships simply reward *you* more than they tend to reward your husband.

Gurian states, "The hero is biologically wired into men's minds. Testosterone, vasopressin, greater spinal fluid in the brain, less serotonin, less oxytocin, and the way the male-brain system projects life onto an abstract and spatial universe lead men to see the world in terms of action, heroes, warriors, even lovers who must negotiate landscapes of challenge."[8]

What does this mean, practically? For some men, to stop accomplishing is to stop living. "Settling down" feels like a near-death experience. Why do you think coaches and athletes often hang on to sagging careers long after their prime, always promising that next year things will really come together?

Not all men reach this extreme, but if you're married to one who has, you won't help matters by taking this personally. He can't stop the chemical drive in his brain that pushes him to accomplish and succeed any more than you can stop caring about your kids or grandkids.

"But people are so much more important than building another business!" you protest. But do you see how such a statement unfairly simplifies the situation? Of course, we need people who put people first, and in a very true sense God calls *all* of us to adopt such a philosophy. But we also need people who feel driven to take care of the big picture — building better houses, fighting the wars that keep brutal enemies away, spending long hours in a lab to find a cure for a disease, building the businesses that support countless families. Such heroic aims do, at least indirectly, put people first. If not for the women and men who spent long, lonely hours in a laboratory, many more kids would live without a father or mother who has survived cancer because of modern medical treatments.

Through the differing brains of males and females, God has ensured that what needs to be taken care of *will* be taken care of. This world would be much different — and much poorer — if everyone spent just three hours a day at work so that they could enjoy long picnics and lengthy walks on the beach. There's a place for beach picnics and family barbecues, but there's also a place for getting things done.

So while it's a healthy thing to motivate your husband to spend more time with the family, you should never try to strip away the essence of what it means for him to be a man. Gurian observes, "[Males] just keep pushing themselves toward developing and showing potency, toward acquiring and utilizing social and hierarchical power, even as it kills them eight years younger than women and often takes them away from other human values."[9]

This male drive can be harnessed to serve evil (think 9/11) or good (think of the American soldiers on D-Day) — but channeling it is different from trying to cancel it. The sooner you understand this, the more realistic will become the demands you make or the desires you have of your husband. An old German proverb, written long before we could scan a human brain, understood this: "If you take the cause out of a man, there is no reason for the man."[10]

Celebrate His Drive

All of this is to say that you can help your husband become more involved at home, but you can't make him stop wanting to achieve. You must find a way to *respect* and *appreciate* his biological drive — you wanted a man, and you got one! Don't fault him for finding some meaning outside the home. Celebrate this as you also try to motivate him to spend more time with the family. More times than not, you'll find that Pat's method, built on "the magic question," works most effectively: work hard to make your home a place he can't wait to come back to. In fact, Martin Luther gave this advice five centuries ago: "Let the wife make the husband glad to come home, and let him make her sorry to see him leave."

As a Christian man, I want to submit my male tendencies to the lordship of Jesus Christ. But nowhere does the Bible say I'm supposed to act like a woman when God made me to be a man. Jesus talks about a willingness to leave homes and families for the sake of serving the kingdom of God: "Anyone who loves his father or mother more than me is not worthy of me; anyone who loves his son or daughter more than me is not worthy of me; and anyone who does not take his cross and follow me is not worthy of me" (Matthew 10:37–38). From a biological point of view, this is a very "male" statement that must seem abhorrent to many females — until they realize that Jesus himself spoke those words. Of course, the Bible elsewhere says that to ignore family is to deny the faith (see 1 Timothy 5:8). Obviously, we must find the happy medium.

This will call for humility on the part of wives who chide their husbands' God-given ambition, assuming that a man who is wholly and centrally focused on his family is somehow holier than a man with a mission. That's a female view of the world, though not necessarily a biblical one. And it will call for humility on the part of men who truly *are* ignoring their family responsibilities. What women need to realize is that, biblically speaking, a man can err on *either* side of that continuum. Do you really want to be married to a man who only wants to stay home and play with the kids, who has no desire or concern to provide a decent life for you and your children, and who has no motivation to bring glory to God by doing great things on behalf of his kingdom? Some of you may, but you're in the minority:

> Studies all over the world indicate that women between puberty and middle age select, for romantic relationships and marriage, the men who are on a quest toward achievement and status. Women want men who aspire to be kings (even if only at a local level), warriors (protectors who make them feel safe), magicians (men who have, even if in a love of gadgets, some magical power that leads to success), lovers (men who make women part of their quest).[11]

The problem is that once women *get* these quest-oriented men, they sometimes want them to become sedate shepherds who like to talk about their feelings.

My good friend Dr. Steve Wilke tells me that the very thing that draws most couples together actually drives them into marital counseling, and this principle certainly applies here. As singles, women tend to be drawn to high-achieving men, but as wives, women sometimes resent the schedules of accomplished men.

Be honest about what attracted you to your man, and about whether you now resent some of that. You have to carefully consider which impulses to challenge in your husband. He wants to succeed. If you impair his opportunity to succeed at work, he may throw himself into poker and gambling, risking your financial security; illicit relationships with women, risking your marriage; excessive sports participation (golfing or working out several hours a day, every day); or any number of activities that may, in the end, hurt your family. At the very least, you should feel thankful that your husband channels his focus in a way that complements your life rather than tears it apart.

Also, try to show some empathy. If your husband languishes in a boring or dead-end job but continues to hang in there because he knows it's the responsible thing to do, he needs some other outlet where he can succeed and excel. Many females (not all!) can work eight hours in a job with little fulfillment and then come home and spend relational time and consider the day to have been OK. But most men aren't like that. The psychological cost of a frustrating job debilitates them, and males tend to receive less from conversation or emotional relationships than do women.

I draw immense satisfaction from my work — and have for the past ten years. I get more positive feedback than I deserve and more sense of self-worth than warranted. But I remember those days when my job felt merely like a way to gain a meager paycheck — mundane work that didn't challenge my mind and gave me little sense of accomplishment. I actually got chastised for setting goals and getting my route done too soon, because doing so made the "regulars" look bad. "Go slower," they told me, "and take longer lunches; enjoy yourself more."

That type of environment can destroy certain men — and if you're married to someone who feels "chained" to his job, have some empathy. Reward his discipline and sacrifice by giving him space to pursue something satisfying. Many wives who see their husbands hurting over such a situation want to "talk it out," to try to get them to "share their feelings." With most males, this only makes the situation worse. The *last* thing they want to do is relive their day! They want to forget it ever happened.

So, having accepted your husband's God-given determination to succeed, what can you do to keep him from living out this determination in such a way that he ignores his family responsibilities? The first thing you can do is what Luther hinted at: "Let the wife make the husband glad to come home."

Becoming More Pleasant

Years ago, during a professional basketball game, Rudy Tomjanovich rushed toward a fight that had broken out on the court. Kermit Washington, then one of the NBA's strongest men, "welcomed" Rudy with a punch that caught him just under his nose and shattered his face. The force of the punch snapped Rudy's head back; his body hit the floor so hard it sounded like a hammer slamming into a tree trunk.

Rudy was out cold.[12]

Even the seasoned doctor who saw the X-rays felt nauseous. The entire posterior portion of Rudy's face had been moved way out of alignment. Rudy's eyes had swollen shut, and his brain had begun to leak spinal fluid. Three days later, Rudy's face remained swollen to twice its normal size. When Rudy's eyes finally opened up enough for him to get a peek in the mirror, he thought he looked like the Elephant Man.

On that day, Rudy's wife, Sophie, flew in to see him. Rudy was nervous about what Sophie might say, and he searched her expression for clues about how hideous he looked.

After a very gentle hug, Sophie stepped back, took a good, hard look, and said, "You know something, Rudy? I think this is an improvement."

Here's a reliable truth about men: we love to laugh, and we love women who have a great, spontaneous sense of humor. Even more, we love to see our wives happy. My saying this might surprise some of you, since I wrote a book subtitled *What if God Designed Marriage to Make Us Holy More Than to Make Us Happy?* but valuing holiness over happiness doesn't mean we must discount happiness. A well-placed smile and a pleasant demeanor can work spiritual wonders. We men love to hang around a woman who's in a good mood.

One of the least quoted attributes of the Proverbs 31 woman is her sense of humor: "She can laugh at the days to come" (Proverbs 31:25). When the Bible says that the Lord "was gracious to Sarah [Abraham's wife]" (Genesis 21:1) by giving her a son in her old age, Sarah responded with the wonderful line, "God has brought me laughter, and everyone who hears about this will laugh with me" (verse 6).

If you're eager for your husband to be more involved at home, ponder these questions: Have you ever considered what you might do to make your husband's life a little more enjoyable? Have you ever thought about what kind of climate you're creating with your personality?

In their fine book *The Walk Out Woman*, Dr. Steve Stephens and Alice Gray offer two helpful questions for women who feel frustrated with their marriage. In such a situation, a woman's eyes usually focus on her husband's faults. These authors turn this around and urge women to ponder two questions:

- What's it like being married to me?
- What's it like hearing the words I say?[13]

I'd suggest a third question: "What's it like living with my attitude?"

An overly serious attitude can really suck the joy out of life. One of the best gifts — and one of the best motivators — you can give your husband is the gift of laughter. Can *your* husband find this at home?

I fear that too many women may look for a serious psychological diagnosis as to why their husband seems to be avoiding home. Others search for some deep spiritual reason, a biblical verse that will unlock their husband's mystery. Some may become obsessed with their husband's past, trying to uncover some personal hurt that they think needs to be identified, repented of, and healed so that things can change. Maybe the issue is simply that home has stopped being any fun, and the husband is reluctant to return to a place of stress, tension, and conflict!

There might be yet another reason: maybe your husband stays away from home because he's been embarrassed there too many times.

Cover for Him

At a large banquet held in London, Queen Victoria shocked her subjects when she lifted her finger bowl and drank all the water. Many marveled at Her Majesty's committing such a gross breach of etiquette. Later, the guests learned that the queen's guest of honor — the Shah of Persia — had done it first, and the queen didn't want him to feel embarrassed.

President Grover Cleveland's wife was cut from the same cloth. A guest visiting the White House felt visibly nervous about the grandeur that surrounded him. Mrs. Cleveland did her best to make the man feel comfortable, initiating small talk about an antique cup made of very thin china.

"We're very pleased to have these," the president's wife said. "They're quite rare, and we're using them for the first time today."

The guest picked one up, said, "Really?" and crushed it in his hand.

The man, clearly mortified at his clumsiness, didn't know what to do. Mrs. Cleveland immediately rushed to his rescue. "Oh, don't worry about it," she said. "They're terribly fragile. See?" And then she proceeded to break her own cup.[14]

At times, your husband will embarrass himself — and you. These moments create wonderful opportunities for you to develop a lot of "capital." If you support your husband, if you step in to cover for him, he'll feel nurtured and cared for and will walk across the desert to get you an iced tea. But if you ridicule him to cover your own embarrassment — if you point out his faux pas and laugh with everyone else about it — you'll crush him.

Every husband has his flaws. Maybe he mispronounces words. Maybe he has limited knowledge of world geography and says something really stupid, like asking an acquaintance if they visited the Eiffel Tower when they went to New York. Maybe he's clumsy or socially insecure. It could be any number of things. These embarrassing moments are your time to shine. Solomon tells us that it is a person's "glory to overlook an offense" (Proverbs 19:11).

Ridicule, jokes at his expense, looks of disgust — these all create emotional distance in a man. Some men even give up and start hiding.

If your man feels incompetent and senses he's being ridiculed or humiliated by you and your family, eventually he's going to find ways to avoid being with you. You may not realize it, but there's often an astonishingly high level of insecurity buried underneath your husband's seeming air of confidence.

The Secret Insecurity

Because success and achievement play such a vital role in a man's sense of well-being, we men tend to have a greater fear of failure, and even insecurity, than most women would ever guess. We may cover up our feelings with an attitude of certainty or even bravado, but many of us live with the sense that we are about to be "found out," that our limitations will be exposed — and this can create a secret insecurity.

If your husband works eighty hours a week, he may feel terrified at the thought of losing his job; and if he were to lose that job, he's terrified that he won't be able to find another one, or at least a respectful one; and if he can't find another respectable job, he's terrified that you won't love him as much. You may look at his schedule and accuse him of "neglecting the family," while all the time he's fighting for psychological survival because he fears you'll leave him.

Think of it from his perspective: Your husband may be doing his best to get a job done, even while feeling he's in over his head. He probably doesn't share this feeling with you because he doesn't want you to think of him as incompetent. Yet all the while you're indirectly telling him he's not good enough because he's not home enough — which, in the end, only reinforces his determination to succeed at work (since you keep telling him he's failing at home).

The answer? Become more sensitive to your husband's insecurity. If his job seems truly on the line, the best thing you can do is say, "I understand you have to put more time in at work; I'll take up as much slack as I can at home and even explain it to the kids. I know you're doing this because you love us."

This line of approach won't fly when the overinvolvement becomes a lifestyle instead of a season, but if it's truly a season, you can make some tremendous deposits in your husband's "gratitude bank" by supporting him verbally and emotionally instead of attacking him. As Solomon writes, "A word aptly spoken is like apples of gold in settings of silver" (Proverbs 25:11). Think of it this way: if your husband truly fears losing his job, and he comes home and hears that he's also failing at home, you've just about buried this man with disappointment. Adding to his insecurity will never cure the problem; it'll just tear apart your marriage at the same time he's losing his way at work.

In addition to his insecurity, your husband feels a compelling need to provide. You may inadvertently contribute to your husband's overinvolvement at work. Are you making it more difficult for him to provide by making unnecessary purchases while at the same time complaining about how long he works? He may think he *has* to work extra hard to pay for those purchases! Or are you indirectly telling him he's not earning enough by comparing his paycheck to yours, as you speak enviously of the vacations your friends get to enjoy or the new house or car they bought or the restaurants they visit? If your husband hears this, he may think, "I need to work longer and harder so my wife can have that too."

All of this comes back to *affirmation*. When you consistently, persistently, and creatively affirm your husband, you remove one of the most compelling reasons for him to get overinvolved at work or to find an escapist hobby that robs his passion for home.

If your husband stops off at the bar on the way home from work, try approaching the problem from this perspective: how can you make home sound more inviting than the tavern? Keep in mind, the people at the bar will act like they're glad to see him. They'll serve him his favorite drink — with a smile. They won't mention the calories or talk about his bulging waistline. On the contrary, when he's done, they'll ask him if he wants another drink. They won't talk to him about what needs to be cleaned or fixed. They'll let him have all the time he wants so that he can unwind.

Yes, there's a time and a place for you to address the behaviors and attitudes that need to change — but if your goal is to get your husband more involved at home, then make home a place he can't wait to return to.

Chapter 14

Pure Passion

Cementing Your Husband's Affections
and Protecting His Spiritual Integrity

The fact that you've read this far tells me something: you *truly* care about your husband. It's extraordinary, really, that you would take the time and effort to study ways in which you can help your husband become the man God wants him to be. At the risk of sounding presumptuous, I believe God is proud of you for taking your marriage so seriously and for being so conscientious about loving his son.

In this chapter, I'll discuss how you can use the sexual relationship within marriage to cement your husband's affections and help protect his spiritual integrity, which I believe is vital for a healthy marriage. Your husband's spiritual standing before God will have a major influence on his care for you, his participation in your family, and his growth in character.

I'm not qualified, nor do I have the space, to go into a complete discussion of sexual intimacy within marriage. Since Christian publishers seem to be releasing new books on the topic virtually every week, there's really no need for me to cover that ground anyway. Instead, I want to help you understand the role that a fulfilling sexual relationship plays in your husband's spiritual, emotional, and relational health. Sex represents one of the most effective ways by which you can care for — and motivate — your husband.

Threshold to Intimacy

The good news is that the majority of married Christians feel "satisfied" or "very satisfied" with their sexual relationship.[1] According to one *Christianity Today* research report, 53 percent of respondents fit those two categories; only 20 percent felt "dissatisfied" and 9 percent "very dissatisfied." These aren't bad numbers, especially when you consider that we ought to expect many of the stated causes of dissatisfaction in the course of a normal married life: busy schedules, children in the home, occasional sexual dysfunction, or a current illness.

This is doubly good news in that a satisfying sexual intimacy is such a key component in your husband's emotional availability. Dr. Melody Rhode has seen more than her share of couples in the course of two decades of family counseling, and from her perspective "most women want more emotional involvement from their husbands, but most husbands can't connect with a woman emotionally if their sexual needs aren't being met. So if women want a deeper emotional connection, they *must* provide the sexual one."

For many women, participating in a fulfilling sexual relationship is a joy, not a burden. There will always be times when the weariness of raising a family can dampen anyone's enthusiasm for particular sexual episodes, but most women value the intimate connection formed through years of generous physical affection. It may surprise you, however, to learn how closely connected your husband's emotional availability is to expressions of physical intimacy.

We've already talked about oxytocin, the "relational bonding" chemical more predominant in women than in men. While women normally have oxytocin levels ten times higher than those of men, a man's oxytocin levels match those of his wife in one particular instance — following a sexual encounter. Neurologically, reports Michael Gurian, "one of the primary reasons that men want sex more than women (on average) is because it feels so good to them to have the high oxytocin — it feels great to feel so bonded with some-one.... In male biochemistry, sex is the quickest way for a man to bond with a woman."[2]

After the honeymoon and the first year or two of marriage, it is so easy for couples to begin to coast in this area. Sometimes they coast because a baby comes along, and they're both too tired to think about another physical activity. On occasion, couples may coast because one or both partners simply lose the desire they had at the beginning. Yet sexual coasting, no matter what the reason, endangers the relationship. Studies reveal that coasting physically usually leads to drifting apart relationally.

I stress this because if your husband feels frustrated in this re-gard, if he feels his sexual relationship with you has waned to such a degree that his sexual advances will more likely receive a "You've got to be kidding" than an "Oooh baby, let's go!" — then he's going to have a difficult time maintaining the emotional bond so crucial to a fulfilling marriage.

To illustrate how this works, let's turn the tables. Say a man gave his wife the silent treatment for a week and then expected her to have sex with him. We would naturally assume that such a man knows little about either women or relationships, that in fact his request is cruel, selfish, and absurd. But when a woman consistently turns down a man's physical advances and then expects her husband to open up to her emotionally and engage in long conversations, es-sentially the same dynamic is taking place: "We haven't had sex for a week, and you want to *talk*? Why would I *want* to talk to you?"

Though single men often get caricatured as seeing sex only as a physical act divorced from any emotional involvement, and single women often get hurt because they likely see sex as a commitment rather than a simple activity (though this is changing), in marriage, for some reason, this reality often gets reversed. I think husbands get more emotional when it comes to sex; the husband experiences it far more personally than does his wife. Gurian believes that, neuro-logically speaking, a man's "self-worth is linked, to a great extent, to how often and how well he engages in the sex act."[3]

One husband told Shaunti Feldhahn, "When [my wife] says no, I feel that I am rejected. 'No' is not no to sex — as she might feel. It is no to me as I am."[4] The wife thinks she is rejecting an activity, but her husband feels she is rejecting *him*. This not only cuts off the opportunity for the oxytocin chemicals to create a refreshingly new bonding experience, but it will tempt him to shut down emotionally.

Another man told Feldhahn, "[My wife] doesn't understand how even her occasional dismissals make me feel less desirable. I can't resist her. I wish that I, too, were irresistible. She says I am. But her ability to say no so easily makes it hard to believe."[5]

I know you probably don't feel as though you are rejecting your husband when you say no to sex or if you seldom initiate physical intimacy — but that's exactly what it feels like to him. You're unintentionally telling your husband that your pillow is more irresistible than he is — and that carries a tremendous emotional impact, whether you intend it to or not. Feldhahn makes a good point:

> I believe that most of us aren't manipulatively withholding something we know is critical to our husband's sense of well-being. Much more likely is that after a long day at the office or with the kids, we just don't feel an overwhelming desire to rip off our husband's clothes and go at it. I suspect we simply don't realize the emotional consequences of our response (or lack of one) and view his desire for sex more as a physical desire or even an insensitive demand. Once we truly comprehend the truth behind our husband's advances, we're more likely to *want* to respond.[6]

A man who feels sexually fulfilled is much more motivated to become emotionally and spiritually intimate with his wife, as well as to want to please her. He is far more likely to be more heavily involved and invested in the home if his wife pursues him sexually. By being considerate, thoughtful, creative, generous, and energetic in this area, you can create a more stable foundation on which to make over your marriage — and you can open the door to the emotional intimacy you so rightly desire.

The Spiritual Good of a Physical Act

For your sake, for your children's sake, and for your husband's sake, the best way to influence your husband is to encourage his growing *intimacy with God*. A man who is deeply in love with God, who regularly listens to God's voice, and who seeks God's kingdom above all else will feel more motivated to love you, keep his focus at home, and to purify himself out of reverence for Christ. Probably 90 percent of the changes I've made in my marriage have come out of prayer and Bible study, not out of conversation with my wife.

An experience of compromised sexual purity is one of the great threats to your husband's spiritual intimacy with God, and therefore to the welfare of your marriage. The older I get, the more pastoral I feel toward many husbands for whom this area produces great struggle. In fact, responses to Promise Keepers surveys reveal this issue as the single most common temptation men face, and therefore the single most common threat to a man's continued relationship with God and his family.

Though sexual temptation plagues women just as much as it does men, the dynamics of your temptation differ significantly from those of your husband's temptations. Your brain is wired differently, which makes it difficult, if not impossible, for you to truly understand the internal sexual temptations your husband faces, including the violent struggle in your husband's heart when he passes a pornographic billboard or sees a woman "dressed to kill." Many wives simply don't understand how much effort it takes for some men to remain sexually faithful to one wife.

Let me be clear: there is no excuse, and no reason, for a man to use pornography. I don't care if his wife has doubled her weight or if she refuses to have sex for six months in a row. I'm not blaming any woman for a man's failure in this regard. But having said this, it is also true that a wife's seeming indifference to her husband's sexual needs *does* make a man's struggle more intense. Where these wives see sexual relations as a burden or a chore, I see God's sons wanting to be faithful, trying to be pure, working harder than you can imagine to keep lust at bay.

Satan will try to use your husband's sexual temptations to drive a wedge between your husband and you *and* between your husband and God. Illicit sexual activity, once chosen, tends to escalate in all the wrong directions. The husband soon finds himself spending far less time thinking about pleasing his wife and far more time trying to figure out how to hide, and indulge in, his fantasy life. Furthermore, a man whose mind brims over with inappropriate sexual fantasies will have a difficult time praying, studying the Bible, and meditating on God's truth. Temptation will bombard him every time he closes his eyes or tries to quiet his mind. Thus his sexual sin will bleed out into other areas of your marriage. When he stops spending intimate time with God, he will probably become, in general, more impatient, more critical, and more selfish.

I know you don't want that for your husband! God doesn't want it either. He broods over your husband's welfare with a passionate concern. He has called your husband to a holy lifestyle, and he zealously desires the growth of your husband's integrity. That's why he has anticipated your husband's sexual drive. He created marriage, after all, and while marriage is about much more than a holy sexual outlet, such an expression is part of it — and even provides one reason for considering marriage, as the apostle Paul observes: "But if they cannot control themselves, they should marry, for it is better to marry than to burn with passion" (1 Corinthians 7:9).

God knows exactly what it's like for your husband, because every day he sees every thought, every temptation. In the midst of your many responsibilities, you can easily forget about your husband's struggles — but God sees every one. Even more than that, God became a man in human form and lived within a man's body. Though Jesus never sinned and never entertained a single inappropriate thought, he certainly realizes what it means to live with a man's body and face a man's temptations.

Knowing what it's like for a man, God created marriage as a holy and healthy outlet for a man's sexual desires. In the ideal world, a man would marry a woman who understands her husband's situation, who cares about his spiritual integrity, and who accordingly lavishes her affection on him (while the husband remains thoughtful, unselfish, caring, and romantically inclined). She realizes that her husband will, at times, feel in desperate straits spiritually as he tries to remain faithful to his God, his family, his marriage, and his own integrity. She also will realize that she, by God's design, is the only appropriate outlet for her husband's desires. Anything she denies her husband becomes, by definition, an *absolute* denial, because he has no other place to which he can go to find satisfaction in a healthy or holy manner.

This believing woman may, at times, resent the fact that God gave her husband such frequent desire. At various stages in her life, she may even resent the fact that only she can meet that desire. At times, she may even contemplate the benefits of the Old Testament concept of a concubine! But if she's a mature Christian, she'll understand that God called her into marriage to help her husband — and in this area, he may need special help. She might wish this weren't so, but she reminds herself that God's design, God's will, and God's explicit instructions from the Bible are foundational here.

Lest I lose you, let me state that I know some of you may have an entirely opposite situation. Maybe you've made yourself more than available, even regularly initiating sexual relations — but your husband's lack of sensitivity and awareness of your needs keeps your sex life from becoming even remotely close to satisfying. The situation in your marriage may not be the wife's lack of interest but the husband's laziness or selfishness regarding how to please a woman. As my friend Leslie Vernick points out, some women have made themselves more than available to their husband sexually, only to have their hearts broken when they discover his lack of interest for them hasn't dampened his interest in pornography. In many cases, this abuse of pornography is a lifelong habit, indulged in long before the man even met his wife. Any man who tries to blame his wife for his sin is in serious denial.

Regardless of the situation in your marriage — whether it means there's a need for you to become more generous with your affection or to woo your disinterested husband into more significant intimacy — let me stress the spiritual health benefits of your working to maintain this threshold to marital intimacy, and the gift you present to your husband when you work with him to see this area of the marriage excel.

Take a moment to ponder God's passionate love for the man you married. If only you could see how God and the angels celebrated on the day your husband became a believer, a redeemed servant of God's kingdom! If you could have glimpsed just three minutes of the rejoicing that erupted in heaven over this seemingly normal man whom not one person out of a hundred would describe as anything other than ordinary! You might just begin to realize how your attitude toward your husband's sexual needs and desires is, in fact, a matter of cosmic concern. On the day your husband became a believer, he accepted God's plan, not just for his eternity, but also for his sexuality. The world mocks that plan — one woman for life. No mental undressing of a celebrity or coworker. Not even an occasional leer at a barely dressed woman. No pornography. God calls him to an exclusive integrity that much of his society calls puritanical, fanatical, and flat-out unrealistic.

Then God watches. Will this man have to live out God's call to purity without any real help from his wife? Will she participate reluctantly, grudgingly — motivated only by guilt — or with generosity, enthusiasm, and creativity? In today's world, a less-than-satisfying sexual relationship puts both husband and wife at risk. Your entire family could be at stake.

How well does God think you're helping his son walk in sexual holiness? The sexual life you foster, create, and maintain in your marriage isn't merely about you and your husband; it's about your husband's relationship with God, as well as his ability to provide a godly example for your children.

Please don't misunderstand: it is *not* your fault if your husband sins sexually. If my wife had a terrible accident and became disabled for life, never again being able to engage in sexual relations, God would still call me to absolute purity and sexual fidelity. Your husband is solely responsible to God about where he sets his eyes and on what he lets his mind meditate. But having said that, let me also say that you can make his job easier or more difficult by the spirit, energy, and affection that you express toward him.

Allow me to get personal. For me, sexual temptation takes on a much different form in the period after Lisa and I experience our own moments of physical intimacy. During the next few days, I feel much less vulnerable to sexual temptations of all kinds, and, to be quite honest, I'm more attuned to God in a prayerful attitude.

But here's the catch: most of us husbands are too proud, too embarrassed, or too ashamed to admit when we feel weak in this regard. We don't want you to think we find you unattractive, or that we're spiritually feeble. It is the rare husband indeed who regularly and intimately gets honest with his struggles against lust. In fact, out of desperation, your husband may make a clumsy approach or bring up the topic of sex in a manner or at a time that seems wildly inconvenient or inappropriate. Why? It's just possible that he feels beside himself with temptation and needs to experience authentic, legitimate, and holy intimacy with his wife. To get turned down at such a time, or to be made to feel guilty or unwanted or a bother, can put him at real spiritual risk.

That's why being proactive — working with your husband to build a fulfilling physical relationship — is so healthy for your husband's spiritual standing. At times, this will be a joy for you; at other times, it may feel like work, or even a dreaded chore. But on every occasion, I hope you see it as an expression of concern for your husband's spiritual well-being.

If you'll persistently pursue this side of your marriage, you'll reap tangible, practical, and long-lasting rewards. Your husband will feel emotionally closer to you than at any other time, while finding the spiritual reinforcement to go out into a world of constant sexual temptation and be an overcomer.

The Limits of Desire

My wife has a painful nerve condition that requires my amateur therapy. I need to help her do certain stretches and hit certain pressure points that alleviate her frequent pain. I certainly don't enjoy these stretches, nor do I look forward to using my elbow on pressure points until she cries out in pain. To complicate matters even further, Lisa typically wants me to do them either early in the day, when

I want to get to my desk, or right before bedtime, when I often feel tired and want only to lie down and read a book. What I enjoy or desire at that point, however, doesn't really matter. Lisa needs these exercises; I'm her husband, and I'm glad to do them.

What would you think if you heard me respond to her legitimate physical need this way: "Honey, get that look out of your eye. I'm *tired*. I just don't feel like doing those exercises tonight."

"Gary, I'm really hurting. Please! It'll really help me sleep better."

"We did them two nights ago! What's the matter with you? What kind of body did God give you, anyway? Are you some kind of a freak?"

"Fine. I guess I can make it another day."

"No," I say like a martyr, sighing deeply so there's no chance she'll miss my altruism, "I'll do them. Just give me half an hour to get ready."

I've just made my wife feel like dirt, all because I didn't "desire" to help her do those stretches.

If you heard this exchange, would you think of me as a loving husband?

Desire certainly has its place, and the wise couple will do everything possible to build a fulfilling and mutually enjoyable love life. But in some stages of life and on certain occasions, it's entirely appropriate to view sex as a loving ministry and a tangible expression of love. I've read that about 50 percent of women will never desire sex until they get physically stimulated. Until these women allow themselves to engage in foreplay, the thought of physical intimacy simply won't seem inviting. That's not their fault; it's just the way their bodies are wired. The apostle Paul doesn't say you must *desire* your husband; he just says you are not allowed to *deprive* your husband (see 1 Corinthians 7:5). We do many things in marriage that we don't particularly *want* to do.

I'm sure you don't "desire" to change your eighteen-month-old's diaper. Many times, I don't "desire" to help my daughter with her homework. But my duties as a parent call me to get involved in my kids' lives. I want to eagerly pursue the things that interest them.

So does desire not matter at all? Of course it does. But when sex is *only* about desire, we lose the bigger picture. Sex can be a ministry that feeds the marriage, with the added benefit of providing stability for your children. I honestly think most men in their thirties and older would feel more than pleased if their wives willingly participated in two high-quality times of sexual intimacy a week — we're talking about two to three hours total.

If God came to me with a proposition — "Gary, I have a chore for you that will take just two hours a week. It'll secure your wife's affections, thereby providing great security for your children; it'll make your wife feel loved; and it will be a crucial part of building a stable home" — I can't imagine turning him down. I really wouldn't care *what* the chore was; if it meant shoveling manure, I'd say, "Where's the shovel?" I'd do it gladly, knowing that my wife and children would receive such tremendous benefits.

Women who ignore this aspect of marriage because they're too busy with their children have it backward. They risk opening up their children to the devastating wound of divorce by not tending to the stability of their marriage. A wise woman understands her husband's desires and uses them to strengthen the relationship. She anticipates his needs and gives him something to look forward to when he comes home, reinforcing his need for her, his desire for her, and his focus on her.

Sexual desire can knit a man to a woman, or Satan can use it to build an ever-growing reliance outside the home. Satan has one goal in sexual temptation: to take that man's heart away from his wife and away from his family and to get him to desire something, or someone, else. The Devil doesn't care what or who it is, as long as that desire weakens the Christian family's foundation.

God calls you to entice your husband and make his desires, thoughts, and fantasies center on you. That way, his physical longings build up the family (and your children's well-being) rather than putting it at risk.

Yet some wives read something like this and say, "You know, he's right. I need to do better." And for a couple weeks, they'll try. Then they'll forget, or they'll get frustrated with their husband's lackluster response, and things will return to the subpar level at which they used to be.

As a husband, if I knew that a vicious enemy lurked outside the door, waiting until I fell asleep to strike his blow against my family, I'd stay awake all night. I'd do everything I could to keep that threat away — particularly if I knew that this enemy had but one aim, namely, to tear apart my family. I'd keep focused. I'd do everything in my power to build up the defenses, to keep watch.

Wives, such an enemy really *does* lie in wait at your family's door. It's called "sexual temptation."

The Proverbs 31 woman "watches over the affairs of her household" (31:27). She is diligent and alert. You may grow weary of meeting your husband's needs, but know this: neither natural temptation nor the spiritual tempter of our souls ever sleeps. In fact, the apostle Peter describes Satan as a "roaring lion looking for someone to devour" (1 Peter 5:8). Today, Satan even has the Internet on his side.

The Problem of Porn

Pornography has crept into many of our homes, crippling countless marriages. Over time, porn stunts a man's desire for his wife. The same God-ordained sexual desire that can knit a man's soul to his wife can get diverted to create a lust for women in general, thus creating distance and frustration instead of personal intimacy and satisfaction.

We can cultivate sexual appetite every bit as much as we cultivate taste for certain foods. Porn trains a man away from real sexual experience and makes him desire what in the abstract should seem creepy (think about it: what's even remotely appealing, to a healthy man, about having sex with a magazine or a computer monitor?).

If your husband is deeply into pornography, nothing I say can fully address the issue. You need much more than "three easy steps." I recommend that you purchase a copy of *False Intimacy: Understanding the Struggle of Sexual Addiction* (Colorado Springs: NavPress, 1997) by Dr. Harry Schaumburg. It features an excellent chapter written especially for women whose husbands struggle with porn. For your husband, *Don't Call It Love: Recovery from Sexual Addiction* (New York: Bantam, 1992) by Patrick Carnes provides a step-by-step approach to walking out of this sin. Dr. Mitch Whitman, who specializes in addressing men's sexual problems, especially likes Russell Willingham's *Breaking Free: Understanding Sexual Addiction and the Healing Power of Jesus* (Downers Grove, Ill.: InterVarsity, 1999).

This next sentence might surprise you. If your own marriage suffers from this problem, make sure you don't overreact. Your husband needs to see how much pain this causes you, but please don't begin treating him like a freakish sex pervert. I'll be honest with you: most men have viewed pornography at least once or twice. Now, that's no excuse for men to make this a regular habit. But you won't help matters by making your husband feel unusually weird, weak, or unchristian about seeking out porn. It's a common temptation, and many men have fallen. As Dr. Mitch Whitman has counseled so many wives, "Be glad it's finally out in the open. Secrecy feeds the power of giving in to the temptation."

Let me put it this way: 51 percent of pastors cite cyberporn as a possible temptation, and 37 percent confess it as a current struggle. In fact, four out of every ten pastors have visited a porn site. *Sixty-three percent* of the men attending a church seminar admitted to struggling with porn in the past year; two-thirds of these men serve in church leadership.[7] It may shock you, but according to this study, if you greet four men on a Sunday morning, odds are that at least two have looked at porn within the last twelve months.

Therapists claim that the Internet has changed everything; the shame associated with visiting a sleazy "adult store" in the bad part of town has vanished, and many men have a very difficult time fighting the temptation when their computer makes it appear to be everywhere. According to Dr. Whitman, the Internet has made the viewing of porn anonymous ("in a chat room, you can be whoever you want"), accessible ("you can get it from almost any computer"), and affordable ("lots of it is free, which also makes it untraceable through the family budget"), thus removing many of the roadblocks previous generations faced.

Now, *of course* you'll want to take your husband's interest in viewing other naked women "personally." Yes, your anger is appropriate. Certainly, your hurt is more than understandable. Absolutely, this is an offense against you and a breaking of the marital vows of faithfulness. Over time, and in certain situations, I believe persistent, unrepentant use of Internet pornography can even constitute an affair. But I also believe the viewing of pornography has at its root a spiritual cause. If the wife takes it only on a personal level, she can actually impede the man's healing process. Your husband needs redemption, spiritual intimacy, practical help, and forgiveness with accountability. You might be his last hope in the battle Satan is waging to pull him away from God. "Making a scene" merely feeds the spiritual dynamics that feed a hunger for pornography.

I believe God created sexual intimacy, in part, as a spiritual glue between a husband and a wife. If we live according to God's design, a wife can make her husband feel things no other woman has ever made him feel. She can touch him in places and in ways no one else has the right to. Together, a married couple can build pleasurable memories and years of mutual gratitude based on God's gift of marital sexuality.

But what can unite two hearts can also divide two hearts when sexual expression takes place outside of the marriage context — which is what porn does, on a regular basis. This is nothing short of a spiritual war.

You gain little by seeing your husband as an enemy in this conflict — but can you try to view him as a casualty? I'm *not* saying he's only a victim; I'm just saying he has willfully given himself over to a serious weakness, and he needs your support, forgiveness, and strength to walk out of it. You're probably going to need to vent, so find a close, discreet friend you can talk to, if this will help you act in a redemptive way in your husband's presence. Normally, I would never suggest talking about your husband like this with another person. But in this case, I'm trying to be realistic. You're going to be hurt, and you're going to need someone to listen to you talk things out as you support your husband. I may be wrong, but I wouldn't fault my wife for talking with someone if I knew she was motivated out of a desire to love me and stand by me through this terrible struggle.

Second, I've usually found that this issue — once it comes out in the open — is best addressed in a men's accountability group or, in the case of a serious problem or addiction, a therapy group. For some men, a support group won't work; they need a trained therapist to deal honestly and seriously with their sin. You want your relationship with your husband to focus on sexual fulfillment and enjoyment; always asking him if he's been "good" has a debilitating effect after a while. If Internet porn is the main problem, let a brother in Christ ask your husband if he has viewed anything inappropriate in the past week. Urge your husband to visit www.covenanteyes.org, and download some software that will capture the name of every website he visits. It will then forward that information each month to designated accountability partners.

One of the reasons I think it's helpful to have other men hold your husband accountable is the sad fact that the process of recovery and repentance is rarely error free. I was shocked when reading Dr. Carnes's book to discover that he considers most recovery programs a *five-year* cycle (with the second six months being the most likely time for a relapse). That motivated me to teach my son about prevention, urging him not to open a door that's so difficult to close. Some wives expect their husbands to drop a lifelong habit without any relapses, and in most instances, this is probably unrealistic. That's why having another man hold your husband accountable can spare you from the ugly realities involved in walking out of a pernicious sin.

Dr. Whitman gives women a clear explanation of what's really going on: "It's about the man's *fantasy*. In the porn-enhanced fantasy, everything is excitingly perfect and uniquely custom-made. Yet by definition, fantasy is not real. You, the wife, *are* real — for better or worse. You are competing with a fantasy that you can't possibly measure up to. Fortunately, you are really not *personally* in a competition. In a very real sense, it's not about you; it's about your husband's problem."[8]

There's a major difference, of course, between a repentant, struggling husband and one who's in denial. If your husband refuses to enter an accountability group or to take steps to address his behavior, then I think you have every right to set some clear boundaries. You shouldn't have to put up with a husband who regularly is unfaithful to you, even if only mentally. There may come a time when you need to say, "Look, for our marriage to continue, this behavior must stop, and that stopping point is *now*. If you refuse to address it, I have no choice but to take it before our church and begin seeking their counsel as to my next step." Ephesians 5:11 tells us, "Have nothing to do with the fruitless deeds of darkness, but rather expose them."

Unfortunately, as Mitch Whitman reminded me, "many pastors or churches really don't know what to do with a serious pornography problem. This is one area where many times a woman should insist that her husband seek professional Christian counseling."

Impure Desires

Pornography abuse can lead to incessant demands and ungodly requests in the marital bed. The Bible anticipated this. Hebrews 13:4 reads, "The marriage bed [should be] kept pure." This means you have no obligation to meet a man's sexual desire when that desire conflicts with God's design for marital sexuality.

Numerous emails have convinced me that ugly things are happening in married couples' bedrooms across the country. Some Christian women believe they have to accommodate their husband's every request. I don't believe the Bible teaches this, nor do I think you help your husband when you engage in any activity that feels offensive, demeaning, soul-destroying, or physically harmful.

I'm not being a prude. At times, a married couple may indeed "push the envelope" and on occasion look at each other with a sly grin when they consider what they've done, laughing about it and maybe even turning red-faced — "if only so-and-so knew!" But that's very different from looking back on an act that elicits feelings of shame, regret, and degradation. Holy sex builds up intimacy, strengthens the relationship, and creates mutual enjoyment and respect. Any act that involves coercion and builds regret, shame, and anger works against what God designed sex to do. Like anything else, you can usually judge an act of sex by its fruit: how do you feel the morning after? Of course, not all guilt-free sex is holy (one's conscience may be seared), nor is all guilt legitimate (one's conscience may be overly sensitive). But if the Bible doesn't prohibit the experience, if both of you enjoyed it, and if it brought the two of you together, it pretty much passes the test. One couple's view of fun, of course, may differ wildly from another couple's view.

It's sobering but true: a man's character can be corrupted even in the marital bed. If he regularly degrades or debases his wife, he destroys his own soul — and no wife should feel compelled out of guilt or obligation to willingly participate in her husband's soul destruction, even if he wants (or begs) her to. Saying no could be the most loving thing you do, but make sure you accompany each no with another yes that offers true intimacy, pure pleasure, and *holy* satisfaction.

Sadly, some men have so given themselves over to lust that "normal" pleasures offer little satisfaction; they think they need something immoral. Why? Because they have cultivated and given themselves over to an ungodly view of sexuality. Dr. Whitman warns wives that this is often a symptom of pornography abuse and/or addiction. He says, "The philosophical message of porn is that women are sex objects intended for the male's pleasure. The greater the sex addict's progression, the greater his need becomes for ever more exciting sexual thrills. As his demands grow, a wife will experience a notable change in the type of demand. If a wife feels like her husband's demands are degrading, there is a likelihood of his being influenced by pornography."

In this case, too, you would do well to bring in a trained Christian therapist. Only the rare husband, maybe one out of a thousand, will listen to you rather than resent you when you stand up to his sexual demands. He will need to hear it from someone else — and in the spirit of humility, counseling will be a good check to make sure you are truly operating out of godliness rather than out of a hypersensitive conscience or your own lack of love.

Also consider the indirect approach. If your husband attends a men's group, all members would benefit tremendously by studying C. J. Mahaney's *Sex, Romance, and the Glory of God: What Every Christian Husband Needs to Know* (Wheaton, Ill.: Crossway, 2004). Consider buying a copy and slipping it to a guy in the group (but be very careful about this, or else it could explode in your face; you might want to give it to a friend, who would give it to her husband, who just happens to be in your husband's group).

Finally, you may need the encouragement of the following comment from Dr. Whitman: "It's possible that a woman may do everything right in this area but still meet with no success. Something is wrong, but she can't fix it. When this is the case, seek help! That is why licensed counselors exist.* We can usually figure out what is going on with the guy."

Yes, it will humble you to pursue help with regard to such a sensitive matter; but if you can look ahead and envision the possibility of a fulfilling sex life for the rest of your marriage, wouldn't you consider the momentary discomfort a small price to pay for decades of healthier living?

A Blessing or a Burden

In some ways, sex seems like a very heavy burden. At other times, it may seem like one of the top two or three blessings — but if so, then why does it cause so much hurt and pain and confusion?

It is not for us to question our Creator's design. If he has called you into marriage, he has called you into regular sexual relations with your husband. Biblical marriage isn't a cafeteria in which we can pick and choose the dishes we enjoy. It's more like a soup — a lot of ingredients mixed together, and we must take the dish as a whole. God's design calls you and your husband to sexual fidelity and loyalty, as well as to sexual generosity and service, regardless of whether either of you feels like it. Anything less betrays marriage

---

*Please do not contact me via email to discuss theses issues. I am not a trained therapist, and email "counseling" is as ineffective as it is unwise. Approach someone who can sit down with you face-to-face, who can spend the necessary time with you — perhaps over the course of several months.

as God laid it out for us. To withhold one element of marriage is to rebel against God himself.

Be careful: your first argument may be not with your husband but with the God who created marriage! He knew, going in, that men and woman would be built differently. He knew, going in, that our levels of desire would often conflict. Yet he still created marriage, he designed the sexual relationship, he created you, he created your spouse, and he blessed your union.

Will you live in his design for you? Will you allow him to equip you to fulfill the tasks marriage asks you to perform?

Sexual relations are worth the effort to get it right. A frustrating sex life produces as much pain as anything. On the other hand, a mutually satisfying sex life does wonderful things for a marriage. It knits a man's heart to his wife. It helps to protect his sexual integrity and keeps him from sinning against his God. It motivates him to please his wife, and it cements his loyalty to his home. And, as an added benefit, it helps a wife learn how to love in a godly and selfless way.

Chapter 15

Ken and Diana: Affair on the Internet

Winning Back the Husband Who Strays

The crisis in Diana's house finally erupted on May 24, 2002, when "Ken" told "Diana"* that he "cared about her but didn't love her."

Three months earlier, Ken and Diana had discovered that their daughter, Hillary, was cutting herself; doctors later diagnosed her as clinically depressed. In the wake of Ken's shocking declaration, Diana decided to keep first things first: "It doesn't matter what you feel about me," she told Ken. "If you leave now, Hillary might not make it. *You will not leave this house*, for Hillary's sake, if nothing else."

Ken agreed, but the couple's long ordeal had just begun. They shared the same house and even the same bed, but emotionally, they lived miles apart.

Early on, Diana sought solace in her faith. She read Psalm 55, about how a companion, a close friend "with whom I once enjoyed

*To protect their daughter, Ken and Diana have used assumed names; other identifying details have been changed as well.

sweet fellowship" (verse 14), betrayed the writer, and her copious tears permanently stained her Bible. "The next seventeen days were horrible," Diana admits, "but God was so faithful."

As Diana looks back, she can predict the drift, including the part she played in Ken's dwindling affections. Earlier in the year, Diana's company suffered a major computer meltdown. It took a full month for Diana to get things back up and running. She stayed late at the office and brought work home.

The first night after Diana finally solved the work crisis, Hillary overdosed on prescription drugs. A boy Hillary really liked had said some cruel things to her. Heartbroken, Hillary turned to drugs to tune out the pain. To make matters worse, shortly after the overdose, another young man eagerly pursued Hillary, and in the wake of her hurt and recent abandonment, Hillary gave up her virginity.

Diana felt devastated when she discovered all that had happened. Every maternal nerve fired Diana's indignation, and she all but swore off sex in her marriage. Every time Ken proposed physical intimacy, Diana thought about Hillary losing her virginity, and she just couldn't respond.

It doesn't take a PhD to predict this one — overwork, serious problems with a child, no sex at home, and little communication. *Of course* one partner began to feel as though he were no longer in love. "If you don't water your plants," Diana admits, "eventually they're going to die; you *have* to nourish your relationship."

"Do You Realize What Your Husband Is Doing with My Daughter?"

For years, Diana and Ken had separate interests that they rarely shared. Diana loves going to the movies; Ken tolerates them. Ken enthusiastically follows NASCAR; Diana has never quite understood the fascination of watching cars drive in circles for hours on end. Diana sensed that Ken was pulling away, but a friend assured her that it was probably just pressure at work and that she shouldn't get paranoid.

But Diana *knew* something was wrong. When she pressed Ken for details, he finally came clean and told her he cared about her but didn't love her.

"Is there anyone else?" Diana asked.

"No," Ken said, to Diana's relief.

Unfortunately, Ken was lying.

On June 11, just a few weeks after Ken had declared his lack of feelings, Diana found herself praying to God to use whomever and whatever to save her marriage. She never expected it to come from "the other woman's" mother.

That very day, a woman phoned Diana and asked her, "Is your husband Ken Franklin, who works at Grizzly Industries?"

"Yes."

"Do you realize what your husband is doing with my daughter?"

Diana felt her heart beat its way out of her chest. "What are you talking about?"

"Your husband and my daughter met in a NASCAR chat room. They started out sending emails to each other, and now they've exchanged pictures. They're even planning to meet on the Fourth of July weekend."

Diana couldn't believe what she heard, but sadly, it all added up. Ken had already arranged for Diana to spend time at her parents' house while he went on a "business" trip over the holiday.

And then came the kicker: "And my daughter is married and has two kids!"

Diana could hardly believe that her husband had planned an affair with a married woman. Would Ken really blow apart two families, just when Hillary needed him the most?

That's when Diana took the action that both she and Ken believe saved their marriage.

A Friend in Need

Diana drove to a friend's house, her mind racing with questions and prayers about the future. "What will happen to me?"

"O God, what will happen to Hillary? Will she make it all right?"

"OK, God, technically, this is adultery; I can leave this marriage, right?"

And yet Diana had a strong sense that divorce played no part in God's plans.

Diana's mind launched into such a whirlwind of speculation that when she got to her friend's house, she blurted out the entire story on the front porch, venting her rage and anger, yelling at Ken, asking how much more she was supposed to take, and calling Ken some nasty names she hopes he never hears about.

Diana's friend had survived a similar situation; her husband had had an emotional affair several years prior, so she could understand Diana's feelings of betrayal.

Today, Diana believes that "venting my anger, disgust, and disappointment on Darla instead of on Ken saved my marriage." Darla patiently listened as Diana worked through her emotions. Once Diana gained control of herself, she risked returning home to her husband.

She arrived at about ten o'clock; Ken's car sat in the driveway. Diana immediately went up to him and said, "We need to talk."

"Why?"

"Cheryl's mother called."

Ken's face went white. The jig was up.

Diana and Ken went out onto the porch — and here the story becomes remarkable. With incredible detachment, devoid of accusation and fiery emotions, Diana talked through everything with Ken. Because she already had vented her emotions with Darla, she could be more objective and dispassionate in this conversation that had the potential to either save or wreck her marriage.

"OK, tell me about Cheryl," she began.

Ken slowly described how he had met Cheryl on the Internet. The two shared a love of NASCAR. They had never met, but Ken admitted they planned to do so. They had even talked about a possible future together.

"You mean to tell me you've actually contemplated a life with this woman?" Diana asked.

"Haven't you ever wondered what it would be like to be with someone else?" Ken said.

"Let me get this straight: you're prepared to tell Hillary you won't be her daddy every day, but you'll be daddy to these two other kids whom you've never met?"

Finally, Ken began to see the ridiculous nature of the situation. Diana's eyebrows lifted, almost comically. "You can't be serious about ending nineteen years of marriage for someone you met on the *Internet*," she said with a laugh, and Ken laughed with her. The entire evening went like that. Diana spoke forcefully but maintained a light enough air to raise her eyebrows and elicit some comic relief at just the right moments.

Not once did Diana swear or call Ken any of the names she had uttered on Darla's porch — even though Ken expected exactly that. Later, Ken told Diana that if she *had* reacted to him in the way she had talked to Darla, he would have bolted. Instead, he saw a picture of God's grace and mercy through Diana — and it made all the difference.

Diana remembers, "When I first walked out on the porch with Ken, the disappointment and sadness were still there, but the anger was gone, replaced by God's peace and the confidence that if Ken chose to stay in our marriage, it would eventually be better than it was before. It was so totally God, because I did not expect to act that way. I was very hurt and disillusioned."

The evening concluded with Diana giving Ken a challenge: "My challenge to you is to be obedient to God's Word, contact Cheryl, and say it's over — and work on our marriage. If you do that, I believe God can give you astounding feelings for me again."

The next day, Ken told Diana he was through with Cheryl. He closed the email account he had used with Cheryl and gave Diana the password to the new account so that she could keep tabs on what happened from then on.

Despite Ken's attempt to put the situation behind him, Cheryl continued to pursue him. Diana even received a couple of calls from Cheryl. But in the end, Ken ended the relationship, and Diana's words proved true. Ken's feelings for her came back.

What Went Wrong?

In the aftermath, Diana spent a good bit of time trying to dissect what went wrong. She asked Ken, "When things got tense, why weren't you talking to *me* instead of to a stranger on the Internet?"

Ken doesn't have an answer, but Diana does. She believes Satan saw a foothold and used it. Because of Diana's work schedule and their problems with Hillary, Satan took advantage of this natural lull in their relationship and tried to force a permanent break.

Diana wisely understood that Ken's breakup with Cheryl was just the first step. She needed to follow through and do her part to patch up an obviously shaky relationship. I asked her how she would counsel wives in a similar situation. When you sense that your marriage is drifting apart because of events you can't control (a work crisis, a child-rearing crisis, or both), how can you keep the intimacy going?

"First," said Diana, "you have to keep working on your marriage, because ultimately everything else is going to be irrelevant if your marriage falls apart. I don't mean to diminish the importance of child-rearing, but if you put the children first to the neglect of your marriage, what will happen to them if the marriage falls apart? It was for Hillary's sake that I realized I needed to take better care of my marriage. An intact marriage gives you better support and resources with which to face everything else.

"Second, I'd say don't forget the small things that keep a relationship going: keep your finger on the pulse of your marriage. If you haven't gone for a walk in a couple of days, do it! Just be up-front about it and say, 'Honey, we need to get connected again. Let's go have a cup of coffee.' Make sure you really are communicating; it sounds like such a cliché to say that communication is important, but it is! Regularly ask each other, 'Are we OK?' Do a periodic checkpoint — use a scale of 1 to 10, or empty to full, whatever works. But don't forget to watch out for relational drift."

While Diana admits that she really couldn't have put her job crisis on the shelf, in hindsight she does believe that she probably didn't need to bring home as much work as she did. "I thought I was the only person who could fix what needed fixing; it was egocentric of me, and it almost cost me my marriage."

Hillary presented a tougher challenge. With a child's life in peril, it's hard to keep the pulse on your marriage. "I wasn't asking how Ken was, because I was singularly focused on how Hillary was," Diana admits. It had been almost a year since the two of them had gotten away. Then add to that Diana's and Ken's wildly different reactions to Hillary's problems, which only seemed to push them further apart. Ken simply couldn't understand the emotion that would lead Hillary to hurt herself "over a boy."

Even so, Diana stresses that you cannot let your children's main base of support — their parents' marriage — crumble just when they need it most. It might sound crazy, when your child is in crisis, to contemplate breaking away for a walk or a cup of coffee or even a weekend, but to keep the family going, that's exactly what you have to do.

The book of Proverbs talks about setting priorities: "Finish your outdoor work and get your fields ready; after that, build your house" (24:27). First, you take care of the life-sustaining needs (like food), and then you worry about things like comfort (shelter, for example). Relationally, you must maintain the life-giving relationship of the home — the marriage — out of which you can provide emotional and spiritual sustenance for the children. If you starve the marriage, you risk creating a spiritual hunger that will end up injuring everyone else in your home.

Almost inevitably you will endure stresses at work, concern for the health of your parents, and anxiety over the choices your children make. Virtually everyone faces these kinds of issues at one time or another. But in no case should they distract us from that duty of prime importance — *feeding our marriages.*

Shared Interests

The third part of Diana's recipe involved making a bigger effort to enter Ken's world — a theme that keeps surfacing in the many talks I've had with couples who have renewed their marriages.

When we let common interests fade, over time we slowly drift apart. Diana went to her movies and Ken watched NASCAR, and both of them, for a while, felt fine with that. But when Ken met another woman who was enthusiastic about NASCAR, he realized that shared intimacy is far more fulfilling than solitary fun. That's why Diana now counsels other wives to "find a way to be interested in the things that your husband is interested in, because it shows him you care about things he cares about."

Will doing so be easy? Hardly. Diana admits that when she went to her first race, she was bored silly. "I was asking myself, 'Why am I here?' And then I remembered: 'I'm doing this to please him.' And it got better."

During that fateful conversation on the porch, Diana had asked Ken, "So what would you do if you left?"

"I'd go to more NASCAR races," Ken answered.

Keeping the conversation light, Diana half laughed, half inquired, "So you'd leave me to do NASCAR?"

"It's not just going to NASCAR," Ken said. "It's about being interested in the standings, the driver, who's won the last pole, who's in line to win the championship."

So Diana has chosen her favorite driver — Michael Waltrip — and on most weeks, she can tell you who leads the points race. She even enjoys the races — just as Pat learned to enjoy fishing and Catherine (whom you'll meet in the final chapter) learned to enjoy biking.

I can readily imagine many readers thinking, "That's all well and good, but when is he going to start doing the things *I* like to do?"

Give it time. Diana freely admits, "In the beginning, some of my needs were in the backseat, and I asked God to love me so I could focus entirely on loving Ken." Remember that Rich (from chapter 12) said he felt more inclined to engage in Pat's favorite activities once Pat started going fishing with him. Sometimes the person who is more invested in the relationship must accommodate the other: "We who are strong ought to bear with the failings of the weak and not to please ourselves. Each of us should please his neighbor for his good, to build him up" (Romans 15:1–2). By pleasing your husband, you're winning the intimacy that you can use to influence him in a positive way, including his building an interest in *your* life.

Problematic Priorities

There's another underlying issue we need to address here: what if a husband is so consumed by recreation that he loses his heart for eternal priorities? I can imagine some wives asking me, "We're called to seek first the kingdom of God — and I have to go to a NAS-CAR race?" Or, "I'm praying for the salvation of my city — but I'm supposed to put that on the sideline because my husband is obsessed with whether the Red Sox can beat the Yankees again?"

God tends to be far more patient than we are. He waited centuries for just the right time to send his Son to earth. And then Jesus spent thirty years doing menial tasks before he launched his public ministry. By engaging in common interests with your husband, you're winning his heart so that you can influence his soul.

I have found that authentic spiritual passion is contagious. A close friend of mine serves as a missionary to Japan, and his worldwide concern for the lost inspires me. We'll go golfing together, and as we pray before we have our lunch afterward, I listen to him pour out his heart to God for the person we played with that day, even though we'll likely never see that man again. Being around him reminds me of God's passionate concern for unbelievers.

The same principle can work for you and your husband. The best way for you to stimulate his spiritual concern is by living out your own. Paul used this model in his own ministry. He told the Corinthians, "Therefore I urge you to imitate me" (1 Corinthians 4:16). In case they didn't get it, he repeated himself seven chapters later: "Follow my example, as I follow the example of Christ" (11:1). To the Galatians, Paul gives essentially the same advice: "I plead with you, brothers, become like me" (Galatians 4:12).

But before Paul could *say* this, he had to *live* this.

Take a deep breath, enter your husband's world, and trust God to use your example in a way that will challenge your husband's heart. The apostle Peter urges, "Wives, in the same way be submissive to your husbands so that, if any of them do not believe the word, they may be won over without words by the behavior of their wives, when they see the purity and reverence of your lives" (1 Peter 3:1–2).

Besides, where better to meet the people who most need God's love than by occasionally going to a NASCAR race or a professional baseball game? Also remember that you're going to compromise your message of reconciliation if your own marriage blows up. By staying fully engaged in your marriage, you're creating a more solid base for spreading God's kingdom — even though doing so may require some activities that seem frivolous to you.

Lessons Learned

Most divorces or affairs don't occur as the result of one big decision; far more often, they take place after a series of mini-separations that lead to the final, permanent destruction of the relationship.

Diana unwittingly began separating from Ken when she put work ahead of her husband. She then made another choice toward emotional distance when she allowed the hurt she felt over her daughter to entirely extinguish her marriage's sexual intimacy.

Ken made numerous mini-decisions himself. He chose to enter a chat room. He chose to keep writing to the same woman. He chose to exchange a photograph. And then he chose to make plans to get together.

Diana and Ken teach us that we endanger our marriage when we put it on the shelf — even if only for a season — and then expect our spouse to put up with our temporary separation. Few people in our culture willingly endure loneliness, and we no longer live in small villages. With the Internet, cell phones, and air travel, the world is literally at our fingertips. Whatever causes us to ignore our spouse — work, a sick mother or father, a troubled child, a busy church, a growing ministry — makes little difference to the neglected spouse. If they feel ignored, they become achingly vulnerable. One Internet chat, one long lunch at work, one phone call from an old high school girlfriend, one chance meeting at a sporting event or a business convention, and suddenly they see an "instant cure" for their loneliness — a cure that has the potential to destroy your marriage.

We grow together by degrees, and we grow apart by degrees.

Diana realized that if NASCAR was so important to her husband, it must become more important to her. And Ken must realize that as Diana attends some of his races, so he needs to take her to the movies now and then. Of course, our primary interests and efforts should center on the kingdom of God — but we're talking about recreational times. When a marriage loses its shared interests, it becomes utilitarian — and most people will not stay in a marriage that has lost its emotional core.

Finally, we need to understand that marriage provides the foundation for our relational lives. Work is important. Parenting is crucial. Hobbies are healthy. But when work or hobbies or even parenting causes us to neglect our marriage, the whole house may fall down — and often work, parenting, and everything else will come down with it.

Here's a helpful "Ken and Diana" exercise: Look at the little decisions you've made over the past six months. Are you consciously growing toward your husband or away from him? Are the two of you building areas of shared interest, or are you slowly and unintentionally cultivating separate lives?

We have to be realistic — my wife is *never* going to run a marathon with me — but we also have to be intentional. The two of us take walks together all the time. You may not be able to share every interest with your husband, but you must cultivate several others.

A New Start

Two months after the lid got blown off his Internet affair, Ken finally could tell Diana he loved her. In July 2003, the couple took a twentieth-anniversary trip to Vancouver and Victoria, British Columbia, to see the sights — and the whales. They toured Butchart Gardens, had high tea with "the *best* strawberry preserves," drove up the coast and saw the tide pools, and overall had a "wonderful, really good time."

Throughout the trip, Diana marveled that she still had an intact marriage. Twelve months before, the thought of her and Ken celebrating two decades of matrimony seemed far from a done deal.

"In fact, it was kind of weird," she admits. "We were having such a good time that our problems felt like they had taken place ages ago; but then at other times, I'd be reminded that everything happened months, not years, ago. But mostly, I kept saying, 'Wow,' because God really *has* made us even stronger than we were before."

God also has begun using their healing to reach out to others. "We've been able to share our testimony, and that's been a really neat thing. It really is a remarkable story when you think about it. If I had to produce the recipe for our healing, I'd say it all came down to God's grace and our obedience."

Hillary has never found out about the "incident." She recently took a college course in psychology and made Diana smile when she talked about how unusual it was that her two parents "never had the types of problems you usually see in middle age."

"Listen, the last thing Hillary needs right now is something else to feel insecure about," Diana explains. "I'm relieved she hasn't had to carry this burden."

But at times Ken and Diana have shared their story discreetly, in ways that have helped other couples face similar crises. One young couple recently disclosed their struggle with Internet pornography. Since Ken's struggle included the Internet, he could confess some of his own temptations and the things that God had shown him.

As Ken reached out to this hurting, repentant man, he could offer more than sympathy or prayer; he provided practical help that was gained from experience. He talked about how he keeps the words of 1 Corinthians 10:13 taped to his computer and about how he's reorganized his office so that visitors can readily view the computer screen the moment they walk into his office.

Diana ministered to the man's wife. Because this young wife had heard Diana's story, she knew that Diana could understand her pain and help her to confront the question most wives in such a situation fear the most: "How do you ever trust again?"

Though Ken seemed to put the affair out of his mind quite readily, Diana has struggled to do so. "It's hard; even though this incident happened three years ago, sometimes the old suspicions still creep up, and I find I have to put my trust in God anew. Maybe I won't ever completely trust Ken again, but I trust God, including firmly believing that if Ken makes some bad choices, God will take care of me. Even Ken recognizes that it may never be the same."

Diana is thankful that Ken patiently accepts her need to occasionally talk about the situation. "He understands that he made a huge mistake and that we will deal with it, at some level, for the rest of our lives."

But Romans 8:28–29 — "And we know that in all things God works for the good of those who love him, who have been called according to his purpose. For those God foreknew he also predestined to be conformed to the likeness of his Son" — has proven true in their lives. Diana and Ken are stronger and wiser today and more like Christ. Their family remains together, and they provide hope and healing for other couples who, in the midst of their process of reconciliation, wonder how they will ever make it.

"It was *so* totally God," Diana says today. "I was very hurt and very disillusioned, but we're still together, stronger than ever. God is soooo good."

Chapter 16

John and Catherine: Finding Faith

Influencing a Nonbelieving or
Spiritually Immature Husband

About four hundred years ago, when Elizabeth married John, she created a love story for the ages. John's full name was John Bunyan; he eventually wrote *Pilgrim's Progress*, one of the most influential books ever published on the topic of the Christian life. John (a widower) already had four children; Elizabeth became pregnant with their first child just months after exchanging vows.

John passionately preached the gospel during a time when the state church regulated the faith like a professional poker player counts cards. Since the church didn't license John, it was technically illegal for him to preach; but rather than accept such a prohibition, John freely and publicly proclaimed God's truth — and promptly went to jail.

He and Elizabeth had been married for less than six months.[1]

In the seventeenth century, if your husband got sent to jail, you didn't have the luxury of simply visiting him once a week and forgetting about him. Family members had the sole responsibility to supply prisoners with food, clothing, laundry services, and everything else. So get this: married less than six months, the *pregnant* Elizabeth had to care for four children from John's previous marriage, as well as regularly travel to the jail to keep her new husband alive.

Some ungodly husbands can't seem to stay sober. Some can't stay out of a casino or the bowling alley or off a golf course. But John Bunyan — man of God — proved unable to stay out of jail. As soon as he got out, he started illegally preaching again, only to receive another visit from the church authorities and another no-expenses-paid trip right back to prison.

In fact, John's zeal for preaching meant that during the first twenty years of his marriage to Elizabeth, the couple lived together for less than *three* years. During those seventeen years of incarceration, Elizabeth had to raise the children on her own, earn the family's income, and supply her husband with the necessities of life.

George and Karen Grant describe Elizabeth this way: "Tempered by suffering and privation, bolstered by persecution and stigmatization, and motivated by faith and devotion, she was a voice of encouragement, comfort, and inspiration to her husband. Their marriage was marked by the strong bonds of covenantal friendship as well as the emotional bonds of love."[2]

Love Hurts

I chose to begin this chapter — on loving a spiritually immature man — with the love story of Elizabeth and John to give you some perspective. I can imagine the hurt you must feel if you can't share your spiritual journey with your "lukewarm" or nonbelieving husband. Of course, you experience a sense of loss when you lack the intimacy inherent in pursuing God as part of a couple. But don't overestimate how "easy" two mature Christians might have it! Faith can be a risky business, with its own set of sacrifices.

Whether your husband is spiritually mature, immature, or in between, your heavenly Father likely will call you to love him and to sacrifice on his behalf. Whether you feel frustrated by his apathy or burdened by his zeal, in the end it all comes down to the same thing: marriage is about sacrifice.

We sometimes forget how radical Jesus' words are, but consider this passage in the context of marriage:

> If you love those who love you, what credit is that to you? Even "sinners" love those who love them. And if you do good to those who are good to you, what credit is that to you? Even "sinners" do that. And if you lend to those from whom you expect repayment, what credit is that to you? Even "sinners" lend to "sinners," expecting to be repaid in full. But love your enemies, do good to them, and lend to them without expecting to get anything back. Then your reward will be great, and you will be sons of the Most High, because he is kind to the ungrateful and wicked. Be merciful, just as your Father is merciful.
>
> Luke 6:32–36

Jesus couldn't have said it any clearer. If you manage to love only an easy-to-love husband, why do you need God? Even non-Christian women can love a thoughtful, caring, unselfish, and mature man. What credit is that to you? If you serve your husband, expecting to be served in return, what spiritual rewards can you hope to gain? In that case, you're merely trading personal favors. But when you give and *don't* receive; when you love those who *don't* know how to love or who *refuse* to love; when, indeed, you can love even the wicked and the ungrateful — well, at that moment you exhibit the same love that God showed to us when he loved us in our sin and rebellion. And Jesus promises that he will richly reward you.

If your husband is spiritually weaker than you are, your job is to bear with his failings in such a way that you build him up, not tear him down. Instead of assuming the worst, call him to his best. Some women, rather than building up their spiritually weaker husbands, expend their verbal energy discouraging their husbands and tearing them down, berating them for their perceived lack of spiritual leadership.

This exactly reverses the counsel of the apostle Paul in Romans 15:1–2: "We who are strong ought to bear with the failings of the weak and not to please ourselves. Each of us should please his neighbor for his good, to build him up."

The time to obsess over your husband's character is *before* you get married, not after. Once you exchange vows, you should focus only on your obligation to love.

To love well, you have to be honest and ask some tough questions: "How do I love an emotionally distant man?" "How do I love a guy who never seems to pray?" "How do I love a man who doesn't even know how to spell 'spiritual leader,' much less be one?" "How do I love a man who loves his congregation more than he loves me?" But ask such questions in a spirit of humble and prayerful inquiry, not resentful complaint.

If you find yourself in a spiritually imbalanced marriage, expect pride to become your greatest temptation. You may forget that God is working on both of you, and that in the light of God's perfect holiness, the difference in righteousness between you and your husband wouldn't buy a vowel on *Wheel of Fortune*. Philippians 2:3 tells us, "In humility consider others better than yourselves."

Later in the same chapter, Paul urges believers to "continue to work out your salvation with fear and trembling, for it is God who works in you to will and to act according to his good purpose" (verses 12–13). Just as God may use you to move your husband toward rebirth and salvation, so he may use *even your unsaved spouse* to move you toward greater holiness. A big part of that holiness includes developing a Christlike attitude. Christ always maintained a tender heart toward the weak and immature.

Please don't get me wrong; I don't want to minimize the real loneliness and legitimate heartache of living with a person who doesn't share your faith. But I do want to open your eyes to the incredible opportunity for growth that such a marriage offers. I know of no better way to do that than to tell the story of a remarkable woman who spent more than two decades praying for her nonbelieving husband.

John and Catherine

"John" and "Catherine"* were both twenty-one when they entered what many might have considered a surprise marriage in

*This story is true, and all the quotes factual, but the names have been changed to protect the children.

1968. Catherine had seriously considered becoming a nun and had even spent seven months in the novitiate, but in the end she dropped out of the novitiate and married John, whom she had dated in high school.

John never shared Catherine's religious inclinations. Though early on, John attended church services on special days, shortly after they married, John made his intentions as clear as possible. "Going to church doesn't mean anything to me," he told Catherine, "and I'm not going to go anymore."

For the next couple of years, Catherine didn't go much either; but that changed when she had a baby at the age of twenty-three. Two years later, Catherine underwent what she calls a born-again experience. She told John that she had received Jesus Christ as her Lord and Savior and that life would be much different from now on.

"We'll see how long this lasts," John replied. "You do a lot of impetuous things, so we'll just see."

John flew for the navy, so for twenty of the next twenty-four months he lived away from home. During that time, Catherine expressed her newfound faith by going to church "continuously." When John returned home, Catherine recalls, "God began to train me to become a Christian wife." For the previous two years, Catherine had focused on being a Christian mother; now she had to add "wife" to her résumé.

Catherine admits she made many mistakes early on. "I marvel at the grace and mercy of God," she says. "Without him, I think I would have destroyed our marriage single-handedly. I did lots of things wrong."

For starters, she went to church too often, leaving her husband to fend for himself. "I was at church every Sunday morning and Sunday evening, Tuesday morning, Wednesday evening, and Thursday morning. I was neglecting my husband, which was wrong, especially since he had just returned from deployment."

John's salvation became a focal point of Catherine's prayers. Early on, God gave Catherine assurance through the book of Acts that, just like Cornelius, she "and all [her] household" would be saved (Acts 11:14).

Catherine occasionally asked John to come to church, and though John always responded graciously (he never ridiculed her faith or told her not to go), he made it clear that when it came to "religion," he wanted to be left alone. "Don't let it cloud our relationship," he said.

One time, John agreed to come to a children's program in which his kids had a part, but in addition to the program, he heard a lot of singing and praying and a short but pointed evangelistic message. John felt as though he had been tricked into coming. "Don't you ever, *ever* do that to me again," he told Catherine.

During the long season of John's eventual march to faith, Catherine had to learn a number of personal lessons. Chief among them, she said, came from Jesus' words about how the kernel of wheat must fall to the ground and die (see John 12:24).

"The main premise for me in applying that verse to my life was that my needs were not the most important needs; his had to come before my own. If I were willing to put my emotional needs aside and trust God to meet those, there would be a harvest."

Catherine freely admits that her "emotional neediness" ("I was very needy; *nobody* could meet those needs") caused tension in their marriage. Catherine came from an emotionally expressive home, and while John's home also enjoyed deep affection, feelings seldom got expressed in the same way.

John cites Catherine's patience as a primary reason why he finally became willing to reconsider the faith. "Catherine's patience was the key, especially the way she trusted in God and his timing. She did her best to live her life as God wanted her to and to quietly demonstrate those values."

It's not as though Catherine was perfect. "She had periods of impatience when I wouldn't listen," John admits. "But she never tried to push it on me when I told her I just wasn't interested."

Releasing John

A turning point came after Catherine gave birth to her third child. She and John had moved back to Denver, and Catherine felt lonely. John was gone most of the time, trying to find a new job. Catherine faced the hormonal readjustment that follows every birth;

and she had just landed in a new community. "I told the Lord how I was feeling. I knew that I was building up resentment and that my marriage was kind of on shaky ground."

God spoke very clearly to Catherine, telling her that as long as she expected John to do things for her that he couldn't do, she was setting him up for failure and herself up for resentment. God challenged her with the words, "If you will release him through forgiveness, then you will open up the door for me to work in his life."

For the next several years (no short journey!), whenever Catherine's feelings got hurt, she said out loud, "Lord, I forgive him, and I release him to you and ask you to work in his life."

One day, Catherine got tired of praying this prayer. "That's great for John," she confessed to God, "but who will meet *my* needs? What about me, God?"

She heard God reply, "Catherine, I will *always* meet your needs."

Catherine explains that surrendering to God's care and provision was "like a miracle." Each time she spoke forgiveness into John's life, she could walk back into a room without playing mind games or punishing John for any perceived slights.

John understood how much his lack of faith hurt Catherine. One time, he dropped her off for church, and Catherine walked into a service that had been prepared by husbands to honor their wives. As Catherine saw husbands giving roses to their spouses, she just lost it. She wasn't prepared for the emphasis on couples worshiping together, and she grieved over not having her husband by her side. She felt so distraught that she skipped Sunday school and cried during most of the worship service.

When John picked up Catherine and the kids, he could tell she felt sad, and he said, "I'm sorry I can't do this for you." Though Catherine still hurt, it meant a lot that John somehow was able to plug into the pain she was feeling over his absence.

Catherine occasionally shared the gospel message with her husband, but sparingly — maybe ten times in twenty-three years, "when something came up." For instance, when Continental Airlines went through difficult times, John, one of their pilots, lost his job for three years. John and Catherine finally exhausted all their savings.

"John," Catherine said, "this is a perfect opportunity to trust God. I know God is faithful, and he *will* meet our needs. Will you watch with me and see what he will do? Will you acknowledge it when he answers our prayers?"

Over the next three days, three families independently gave John and Catherine over a thousand dollars combined.

Still, John didn't give in. "I can't believe like you do," he told Catherine. "I just can't."

Then God unleashed the plan that would ultimately bring John to faith.

A Family Crisis

John and Catherine's two girls sailed through youth group "without a problem," but their son, Brian, had a difficult time connecting with the new youth pastor. To make matters worse, Brian got beat up at a church camp; and what's more, he began identifying with his same-gender parent who had absolutely no interest in faith.

As Catherine watched her son make some dangerous choices, she grew angry at her husband. She told John, "To see our children serving God is the most important thing in the world to me. Our son looks up to you; you're a hero to him, and the two of you have a very good relationship. If anything happens to his Christian faith, I'm holding you personally responsible, and I will never forgive you" — this was the first and only time Catherine ever threatened John.

"Are you saying this will affect our relationship?" he asked.

"Yes," Catherine answered.

The conversation took place as John and Catherine were on a bike ride, and as John surged ahead, Catherine thought, "That was too harsh." She started to peddle harder in an effort to catch up and apologize, but Catherine believes God quieted her down and told her not to say anything more. "Maybe I shouldn't have said it, but I may well have made things worse by talking about it more," she speculates.

As Brian began to experience disciplinary and drug problems, Catherine sensed the Lord saying something to her in prayer that at first made no sense: "You're no longer to be the spiritual head of the home."

"Well, if not me, then who will it be?"

"I'm going to lay the mantle of spiritual headship on John, and I want you to tell him that."

"How can that be? He isn't even born again!"

But Catherine eventually gave in and told John what she perceived that God had told her in prayer. John felt just as aghast as Catherine had felt. "I can't do that, Catherine! How can I do that?"

"I don't know, but that's what God said, so that's all I can tell you."

Later, the Lord directed Catherine to pray for John every day, specifically that he would learn to walk in spiritual headship as God himself came alongside to teach him. None of it seemed to make any sense, but Catherine chose to follow along.

Today, she's very glad she did.

After Brian got caught smoking marijuana, John and Catherine went to see a counselor. While praying about this visit, Catherine once again sensed that God was speaking to her: "You are no longer to discipline Brian; John is to do so. I want you to pray every day for John's disciplining process."

John had *no* problem with this! In fact, he was glad to hear it, fearing that Catherine would be too soft. For once, he thought God had a great idea.

As Catherine looks back, she realizes that "this was one of the most important pieces for God to set in place; what John did not know was that he was assuming spiritual headship."

A very difficult year and a half went by. Brian continued to abuse drugs, and he got suspended from school in his senior year of high school. John and Catherine pursued more serious counseling, but Catherine had became busier than ever after having just started nursing school. About this time, Catherine sensed that God was directing her to pray earnestly for John's salvation. Catherine had prayed for John for most of their marriage, but it often went in spurts. For a time, she would contend strongly for her husband but then get discouraged and pull back; after a time of healing, she would again enter another season of fervent prayer. Catherine remembers telling a friend, "I'm entering a new season of praying for John to become a Christian."

"Who Is in Bed with Me?"

Back at home, Brian's troubles became topic number one.

"Catherine, what are we going to do?" John asked one night.

"Honey," Catherine answered, "you have to figure that out. I'm struggling to keep my head above water with my studies at school, but I know God will help you."

John checked out two videos on drug abuse from Brian's school and watched them. He came to bed late that night and started talking about them. "This police officer talked about how we're losing kids because we are made of spirit, mind, and body. While we are touching our kids intellectually, we're not touching them spiritually. What do you think of that?"

Catherine felt as amazed as she did pleased. She admits thinking, "Who is in bed with me?"

John went on. "Do you think we could talk to Brian about this? About how he's vulnerable to drugs because we're not appealing to teens as whole persons, about how his spiritual side is being ignored?"

Catherine got very direct: "John, why would Brian listen to you when you've ignored that part of your own life?"

"Yes, that *does* worry me," John confessed.

"I'd be worried about that too. Do you want to pray together about it?"

There was a slight pause.

"Yeah," John said.

Catherine's heart started beating so hard and so fast that she felt half afraid the fire department would somehow take notice and pay an emergency visit. For the first time, she was going to be praying with her husband of more than twenty years!

Thankfully, God kept her calm. "I don't think John sensed that my excitement was for him as much as it was for Brian. I think he felt the responsibility that dated back six years when I said I would hold him responsible if Brian rejected God."

The very next day, John had a long talk with Brian about the importance of spirituality, even though — he admitted — it had not been important to him in his own life.

Born Again

In retrospect, Catherine considers it a blessing that her studies kept her so busy, or she might have gotten more involved and possibly frustrated God's plans. God seemed very stern in his warnings to Catherine: "You are not to put your hand to this; this is *my* sovereign hand at work!"

Catherine did suggest a book that, based on her husband's political interest, she thought John might like — Chuck Colson's *Born Again* (Old Tappan, N.J.: Chosen, 1976).

John looked at it and said, "I think I'd like to read that."

Catherine went — in her words — "nuts." "I was *so* excited; we had been married for over twenty years, and I had never seen him show interest like this."

Catherine called her pastor and asked him to pray; then she kept her mouth shut. "I *did* sneak a peek now and then to see if the bookmark was moving," she confesses, "and though it moved slowly, it *did* move."

John started reading the book in October 1994. In December of that same year, when Catherine noticed that Christmas was going to fall on Sunday, she asked John, "Would you like to come with us to Christmas services this year? If it's not the time, I understand."

John's answer shocked her. "I'm so sorry you had to ask me, because I've been meaning to tell you I want to come."

The ever-emotional Catherine broke down on the spot and cried. "Thank you," she said. "This means so much to me."

For the first time ever, all five members of Catherine's family attended church together on a Sunday. Catherine felt a bit like a spectacle. She had helped to pioneer this church, so she knew everybody was watching them, as well as sharing in Catherine's excitement and joy. For Catherine, it seemed almost surreal. "I felt like it was somebody else's life that I was watching in a movie. I had waited so long; I just couldn't believe it was happening."

Catherine was absolutely amazed at how God had orchestrated everything: God's call for her to pull back and stop being the spiritual head of the house; God's directives to let John handle the discipline; Catherine's renewed season of prayer; John's viewing of the videos; the way John related to Chuck Colson — even if Catherine had *tried* to orchestrate each element, there was no way she could have.

"It was an amazing thing to watch," Catherine confesses. "I still marvel at God's faithfulness."

John returned to church the following Sunday and then every Sunday after that. Catherine gave him a book containing a portion of Scripture from the New Testament and a devotional, which John read almost every day. He asked Catherine lots and lots of questions. Together, they attended a new believer class, and it thrilled Catherine that John seemed to hit it off with and eventually become friends with the teacher.

Finally, during a church service in March, the pastor asked at the end of a sermon if anyone wanted to make a profession of faith in Christ. Catherine saw John's hand go up. When the pastor prayed with John, John explained that he wanted a specific date for his conversion, though John believes he may have come to faith earlier, as he read about Chuck Colson's salvation experience.

Lessons to Be Learned

I spoke with John and Catherine about some of the lessons they learned along the way — in particular, about how other "unequally yoked" wives might gently move their husbands toward faith.

Building Bridges

Catherine often wondered how two people who shared so little in common could ever make it. Sometimes she even asked John, "Are we going to make it? We have so little in common. My faith is so important to me, but you don't even share it!"

John would say, "Catherine, where our relationship is good, it's very good. Let's concentrate on that." John wanted Catherine to concentrate on the good places in her marriage rather than become consumed by her disappointments.

Catherine honestly admits she endured a very trying and difficult season that went on for decades. "Being unequally yoked is extremely lonely. You're guiding your children by yourself; you try to stave off resentment and build a good marriage — it's just very, very difficult."

Most women in such a situation will, like Catherine, find themselves tempted by self-pity. Philippians 2:14 gives some help here: "Do everything without complaining or arguing." The word "everything" includes marriage, even marriage to a nonbeliever. Resentment and bitterness will only keep you from being spiritually productive in that relationship.

Catherine realized that since she and her husband didn't share a faith in Christ, she would have to work extra hard to find other things to share. Unfortunately, John felt most excited about things in which Catherine had little or no interest — like riding bikes, for example.

"I had to make the decision: would I start riding bikes with him, or would I sit home by myself and let the gap between us widen?"

Catherine's initial attempts didn't encourage her. "It was ridiculous! I was so out of shape. But you know what, a year and a half later, I loved it more than he did! We did 'Ride the Rockies' together — that was four hundred miles through the Rocky Mountains, a seven-day bike ride with two thousand other people. It was a blast, and we spent hundreds of hours together training for the ride."

Catherine just kept focusing on the positive. "We didn't have a family together at church," she admits, "but we did have a family together on bicycles."

Some wives might feel tempted to punish their non-Christian husband by becoming even less accommodating: "If you won't share my faith, I won't share any of your interests." But such pettiness, while understandable, does nothing except widen the gap. Catherine adamantly counsels other women married to nonbelievers, "You must find out what he loves doing and learn to do it with him."

That's not a bad lesson for wives in general!

John also loved fishing, another activity that held no magic for Catherine. Early on, when the kids were little, Catherine stayed by the campsite with the kids while John went fishing. As the kids got older, they started going fishing with John. One year, Catherine realized that she could either stay at the campsite by herself or join her family for an activity that didn't hold much interest for her.

She grabbed a pole and joined them.

Now, years later, she loves going fly-fishing with John; in fact, it's become one of her favorite things. "It's funny," she says. "What was once something I did only out of obligation is now one of the greatest delights of my life."

It took years for Catherine to learn this valuable lesson. "I'm as selfish and reticent as anybody," she confesses, "but I know that the Holy Spirit was leading me. Once in a while, I still say, 'Are we going to be OK?' We'll *never* be two people who like to do the same things. We have some areas of mutual likes, but there are many strong differences. Marriage is about choosing to allow the strong points of your marriage to be the dominant points, the areas you *choose* to focus on. Where you absolutely can't meet, you find a way to detour."

In other words, Catherine learned contentment. "Instead of spending my whole life complaining about what I wanted, I started enjoying what I already had."

You can begin this process today. If you find yourself mentally rehashing your spouse's weaknesses, counter this tendency by meditating on what you like about him. Instead of obsessing over your differences, think about the one or two things that you truly enjoy doing together.

Being Realistic

Catherine warns, "Wives can be so dominated by thoughts of 'this won't work; we're too different. We have different ideologies, different passions, even different ways of looking at things.' Ultimately, we have to learn that we'll never have some of the things we've yearned for, but God will give you ways to develop strengths already there — strengths you may not be recognizing. Along the way, we slowly mature and figure out that Jesus is the one we delight in. My greatest pleasure is my relationship with God."

Catherine had to realize that God never intended John to meet all of her needs. Even if John had been a Christian for their entire marriage, some needs would still go unmet. No husband, Christian or not, is God — yet wives tend to feel disappointed when their imperfect husbands act imperfectly!

How will you face disappointment with your husband? Will you allow a toxic mixture of bitterness, resentment, and anger to slowly poison your home, or will you choose to walk in forgiveness and in reliance on God and focus on loving your husband instead of worrying about whether you're being adequately loved?

Changing with John

Catherine eventually realized that "this waiting period for John to become a Christian was about me too." She wasn't waiting just for John. "The whole process was as integral to *my* growth in Jesus as it was for him. God made it very clear that I was not to consider myself a spectator or a martyr or someone who was just waiting. God had lessons for me to learn too."

Even if you're further along than your husband, spiritually speaking, you still haven't fully arrived. None of us have. Your own character and maturity must continue to grow. Paul told Timothy, "Be diligent in these matters; give yourself wholly to them, *so that everyone may see your progress*" (1 Timothy 4:15, emphasis added). Perfection lies beyond us in this world, but every maturing believer should be showing some positive spiritual movement.

God used Catherine's marriage to teach her how to better handle fear — in her case, the fear of a failed marriage — and how to be less controlling. As Catherine grew in these areas, God did something wonderful not only in her life but in her family as well, testifying to the truth of 1 Timothy 4:16: "Watch your life and doctrine closely.

Persevere in them, because if you do, you will save both yourself and your hearers."

Being Honest

Catherine found it extremely difficult to learn how to, in her words, "live two lives": "You have two things that are passionately important to you — your relationship with God and your deep desire that your marriage be viable and strong. It's very difficult when you can't merge the two. You feel divided."

Giving presented a particularly thorny issue. Catherine wanted to give money to God's church, but she didn't work outside the home, and initially she feared what John might say. So she began saving the change from the grocery money and giving that as a contribution — something she now regrets.

"Finally, I just had to tell John how important giving was for me. I'd tell young wives to be honest about the things that are important to you instead of hiding them." Once Catherine explained why she wanted to give and how much it meant to her to be able to do so, he agreed that she could donate a hundred dollars a month. Catherine wishes she had been more up-front all along. As the book of Proverbs observes, "An honest answer is like a kiss on the lips" (24:26).

Being Patient

Some foolish women greatly wounded Catherine when they told her, "Your husband should have been saved long ago. What are you doing wrong?"

Yet when you talk to John, he keeps coming back to how much he appreciates Catherine's patient spirit. If she had tried too hard, if she had kept pushing, she most likely would have moved John further away from the faith rather than closer to it.

Keep in mind that a cosmic spiritual battle rages inside your husband. Eternity is at stake. In the light of eternity, one or two decades aren't all that long (even though twenty years can seem like forever). John remembers times when he saw Catherine and the kids getting ready for church and then pulling out of the driveway, and something inside of him would be saying, "Go after them" — but he didn't know how. It took time. If Catherine had tried to force the issue, she would have made things worse, not better. Jesus tells us in Luke 8:15 that "by *persevering* [we] produce a crop" (emphasis added).

The Ultimate Surrender

Few things present more difficulty for a bride of Christ than being the wife of a man who is outside the faith. Catherine admits to feeling pulled hard in two directions. She loved her man and wanted her marriage to work — but she also loved God and wanted to put him first. It hurt deeply when she couldn't immediately bring the two together.

The reality is, no easy answers exist. I can't give you an iron-clad recipe that will guarantee your husband's conversion — and anybody who tells you differently, frankly, is lying. But a gentle and quiet heart, mixed with a patient spirit, in a woman who keeps praying and who finds ways to connect with her husband greatly increases the possibility that she will one day pray to the God of her dreams *with* the man of her dreams.

I can tell you this: 2 Peter 3:9 makes it abundantly clear that God does not desire anyone to perish, and 1 Timothy 2:4 declares that our Savior "wants all men to be saved and to come to a knowledge of the truth." When you combine the favor of God, the guidance and conviction of the Holy Spirit, and the persevering love of a believing wife, I *like* that man's chances.

God bless you in this glorious task! The most important place you can ever move your husband toward is *God*. When you consider the eternal benefits and your husband's spiritual health, nothing else comes close. It's not an easy battle, nor is there a guaranteed victory — but in the end, it's a fight worth fighting.

Epilogue:
Everlasting Beauty

As a new country began to take shape, a new child began to form in Abigail Adams's womb. The year was 1776. The colonies had declared their independence from England, and their breakaway leaders were working hard to create a new nation.

It's a wonder that Abigail and her husband, John, ever had time to conceive a child, given that John had to be away from home so frequently. But they did, although shortly after the conception took place in the early weeks of 1777, John had to leave once again, to attend yet another session of the new congress.

The pregnant Abigail knew she could have persuaded John to remain home. She said as much in a letter to a friend: "I had it in my heart to dissuade him from going and I know I could have prevailed, but our public affairs at the time wore so gloomy an aspect that I thought if ever his assistance was wanted, it must be at such a time. I therefore resigned myself to suffer some anxiety and many melancholy hours for this year to come."[1]

Though Abigail knew she needed her husband nearby, she also believed their new country needed him even more. She willingly inconvenienced herself for the sake of her land.

John appreciated his wife's sacrifice. He recognized her unselfishness, and he respected it. Abigail had a legitimate claim, and no caring husband could deny the hardship of a pregnant wife left alone during the winter. A famous pamphlet had called the revolutionary period a time "that tried men's souls," to which John responded that they were "times that tried women's souls as well as men's."[2]

And it's not as though this inconvenience remained limited to a single season. In another letter, Abigail confides, "'Tis almost fourteen years since we were united, but not more than half that time have we had the happiness of living together. The unfeeling world may consider it in what light they please, I consider it a sacrifice to my country and one of my greatest misfortunes."[3]

Abigail paid a heavy price for her love and devotion. Not only did she have to share her husband with his country, but she also endured many vicious attacks leveled against government officials, telling one friend, "When [my husband] is wounded, I bleed." Later in life, Abigail referred to their public life as "splendid misery."

The couple also suffered their share of marital disagreements. John could be obstinate; though he sought his wife's counsel, he didn't always follow it. In fact, early in their marriage, the couple had an opportunity to prosper financially. Unlike today, succeeding in government back then held no guarantee of financial security. John Adams believed that land would make the best investment for their savings. When the opportunity arose for the couple to invest in newly available government securities, Abigail urged her husband to take advantage of them. But John remained suspicious of investing in "coin and commerce." He understood land, the value of agriculture, and the importance of food, but he didn't trust banks. As it turned out, "had the Adamses invested in government securities as Abigail wished, they would, almost certainly, have wound up quite wealthy."[4]

Yet there appeared to be no lasting bitterness over this lost opportunity. Abigail was a realist, as well as a passionate partner in her husband's pursuits. She recognized that, though her husband excelled at diplomacy, his investment acumen fell far short of genius. Like all men, he had his limits. Abigail had made her choice, and she continued to support John in his strengths while remaining magnanimous about his weaknesses.

Abigail's unswerving devotion cemented her husband's heart to hers. When John became the second president of the United States, he wrote a long letter, begging Abigail to join him without delay:

> I must go to you or you must come to me. I cannot live with-out you.... I must entreat you to lose not a moment's time in preparing to come on, that you may take off from me every care of life but that of my public duty, assist me with your councils, and console me with your conversation. The times are critical and dangerous, and I must have you here to as-sist me. I must now repeat this with zeal and earnestness. I can do nothing without you.[5]

John Adams felt *desperate* for his wife's presence. He needed her conversation and her counsel so much so that he asserted, "I can do nothing without you."

I've spent a couple of hundred pages talking about how a woman can influence a man, but Abigail obviously cornered this market over two centuries ago.

When Abigail lay mortally ill in October of 1818, her husband remained constantly by her side. In her last few days, she awoke from a delirious haze, saw John next to her, and gently confessed that she knew she was dying, and that if it were God's will for it to be so, she was ready. She desired to keep living, she said, only for John's sake.

When John heard that even death's door hadn't dampened her devotion, he became an emotional wreck, stumbling out of the room in a stupor. Downstairs, he told a friend, "I wish I could lie down beside her and die too."

Two days later, Abigail did die; but John's respect, loyalty, and remembrance lived on. Years later, when people complimented John about his son's rise to the presidency and the pride he must feel about the role he had played as a father, Adams forcefully responded, "My son had a mother!"[6]

The Romance behind the Labor

By now, some of you may be thinking, "This entire approach Gary's been talking about seems like so much work! Where's the romance? Where's the fun?" I've retold the Adams's story because I believe their marriage had the best of romance encased within the reality of sacrifice and personal struggle.

I believe in marriage — with all of its work, obligations, and sacrifice, along with all of its joy, pleasures, laughter, and romance — because it's what God calls most of us to do. If you're reading this book, I suspect you're not called to celibacy. Physically, emotionally, and spiritually, God designed you to live in a lifelong, committed relationship with one radically imperfect man. Can you trust God enough to believe that surrendering to this life — both the good and the seemingly negative or difficult — will, in the end, produce the most satisfying life possible: a love based in faith and built on a lifetime of memories, esteem from your children for holding your home together, and rewards from your heavenly Father for creating a family that testifies to his redemptive and reconciling love?

A lifetime of romance lies hidden in the work of marriage. In your own relationship, you may occasionally feel tempted to "lie down" and get lost in romantic comedies instead of studying how to love a real man. It may seem easier to withdraw from love, to get lazy in your affections, to coast in your marriage — but such an indulgent, soft way of life will ultimately steal your sense of well-being and even your happiness. You'll lose any romantic feelings you once had for your husband, and you'll eventually despise the person you've become.

God built us in such a way that, early on in a relationship, romance is unearned and often unappreciated. Intimacy is immediate and electric. In a mature marriage, romance is maintained only through hard work, deliberate choices, and concrete actions. You can't force feelings, but you can choose to act so that feelings usually follow. If we act like we're in love, we'll keep falling in love. It's a process of growth — toward God, toward each other, and toward personal holiness.

I look at it this way: everything that God asks of me is what I ultimately want to become — a loyal, loving spouse; a sacrificing, affectionate, and involved parent; an enthusiastic worker for the gospel; a faithful and loving friend. Everything I see resulting from

the world's view of romantic relationships is what I most despise —
people getting hurt by betrayal and divorce; children being devastated by the destruction of their homes; individuals becoming more
selfish and more hedonistic as they age.

If wisdom is known by her fruit, the Bible is the sweetest teaching that has ever been told yet is somehow strangely in competition
with the most bitter of fruits, which appears ripe and ready to eat but
which makes the stomach sick and sour as soon as it's consumed.

Biblical love is a Christ-centered love that seeks to perfect holiness out of reverence for God. As we end this journey together, I ask
you to pause and try to imagine the pleasure you give God by loving
his son well. Your husband probably will, at times, take your love
and devotion for granted. He may act in harsh and critical ways.
He may be selfish and inconsiderate. But he's not the only one living in your home! An all-seeing God receives great pleasure when
his daughters love his sons, and he showers his spiritual blessings
in the form of a soul-filling intimacy that is unlike any other: "How
wonderful, how beautiful, when brothers and sisters get along! It's
like costly anointing oil.... It's like the dew on Mount Hermon....
Yes, that's where GOD commands the blessing, ordains eternal life"
(Psalm 133 MSG).

Someday, in the not too distant future, a young woman will
have the opportunity to make me one of the happiest fathers-in-law
who has ever lived, simply by loving my son well — by being generous, kind, and encouraging; by helping him to become all that God
intends for him to become; by forgiving him when he sins, lifting
him up when he's discouraged, comforting him when he's sad, and
sharing in his glory when he succeeds.

If I, a sinful man, can still feel this way about my son, just imagine how your heavenly Father-in-law will smile on you when you
love his son!

I know that relationships can be difficult and hurtful. I know
that being married to a man who "stumbles in many ways" (James
3:2) can grow tiresome and exhausting. But I also know that God
is real, that his Son has made a mighty sacrifice for our sins, that

his Holy Spirit will empower us, that his living Word will guide us, and that his promise of heavenly rewards is more secure and more certain than anything this world offers.

You have not chosen an easy life, but you are living a rich one, with unimaginable potential. God has gifted some women to build companies, some to write books, some to start ministries — but even here, I believe women still feel most fulfilled (and will be most rewarded) by loving and being loved and by exercising faith, growing in godliness, and sharing this life in intimate union.

As you continue on this life journey, seek the Lord for guidance on how to build the type of marriage he desires. Call on him to give you his wisdom in developing the "sacred art" of loving an imperfect partner so that your husband can become all that God wants him to be.

As you begin to influence your man, you will see the Lord influence you as well — to draw closer to him.

Notes

Chapter 1: The Glory of a Godly Woman

1. C. F. Keil and F. Delitzsch, *Commentary on the Old Testament: The Pentateuch* (Grand Rapids: Eerdmans, 1956), 103.
2. Ibid., 102.
3. I'm simply restating the words of Friedrich Hauck, cited in William Lane, *Mark* (New International Commentary on the New Testament; Grand Rapids: Eerdmans, 1974), 357.
4. Lane, *Mark*, 356, 357.

Chapter 2: The Strength of a Godly Woman

1. D. Elton Trueblood, *The Life We Prize* (New York: Harper & Brothers, 1951), 158.
2. Cited in Del Jones, "FedEx Chief Takes Cue from Leaders in History," *USA Today* (June 20, 2005), 7B.

Chapter 3: "Be Worthy of Me"

1. David MuCullough, "Knowing History and Knowing Who We Are," *Imprimis* (April 2005), 5.
2. Cited in André Castelot, *Josephine* (New York: Harper & Row, 1967).
3. I thank my friend Dina Horne for this great insight.

Chapter 4: The Widow at Zarephath

1. "The GQ Poll: The State of Man," *GQ* (December 2004), 224.
2. This and other comments from Leslie Vernick resulted from our discussion of the ideas in this book.
3. Lysa TerKeurst, *Capture His Heart* (Chicago: Moody Press, 2002), 12–13.
4. Dan Allender, *How Children Raise Parents* (Colorado Springs: WaterBrook, 2003), 196.
5. Ibid.
6. Ibid., 197.

Chapter 5: The Zarephath Legacy

1. The speaker is Henry Belafonte, who told the story to Bono (see Michka Assayas, *Bono: In Conversation with Michka Assayas* [New York: Riverhead, 2005], 86).
2. Ibid., emphasis added.
3. Ibid., 87.
4. Norma Smalley, "Differences Can Strengthen a Marriage," in *The Joy of a Promise Kept* (Sisters, Ore.: Multnomah, 1996), 39.
5. Elyse Fitzpatrick, *Helper by Design: God's Perfect Plan for Women in Marriage* (Chicago: Moody Press, 2003), 54–55.
6. Patricia Palau, "Influencing Our World for Christ," in *The Joy of a Promise Kept*, 148.
7. Ibid.
8. Ibid., 149.
9. Ibid., 152.
10. Martie Stowell, "When He Doesn't Keep His Promises," in *The Joy of a Promise Kept*, 164–68.
11. Ruth Bell Graham, *It's My Turn* (Old Tappan, N.J.: Revell, 1982), 74.
12. Cited in Ginny Graves, "As Women Rise in Society, Many Married Couples Still Don't Do 'Equal,'" *USA Today* (June 30, 2005), 13A. Interestingly enough, this figure has risen from 14 percent in 1987.
13. Ibid.

14. Linda Dillow, *Creative Counterpart* (Nashville: Nelson, 2003), 178.

15. This is an account from Eastern European folklore, which also states that the attacking emperor — Konrad — allowed the Duke of Bavaria and his men to live, so moved was he by the wives' actions.

Chapter 6: The Helper

1. Linda Dillow, *Creative Counterpart* (Nashville: Nelson, 2003), 138.

2. Derek Kidner, *Genesis* (Downers Grove, Ill.: InterVarsity, 1967), 65.

3. Carolyn Mahaney, *Feminine Appeal* (Wheaton, Ill.: Crossway, 2003), 34.

Chapter 7: A Claim, a Call, and a Commitment

1. Gordon Fee, *1 and 2 Timothy, Titus* (Peabody, Mass.: Hendrickson, 1995), 187.

2. Linda Dillow, *Creative Counterpart* (Nashville: Nelson, 2003), 155.

3. Desiderius Erasmus, "Marriage," in *The Book of Marriage*, ed. Dana Mack and David Blankenhorn (Grand Rapids: Eerdmans, 2001), 101.

4. Ibid., 103.

5. Ibid., 106.

6. Ibid., 108.

Chapter 8: Understanding the Male Mind

1. This anecdote and the preceding one are based on an account in David Leon Moore, Thomas O'Toole, and Kelly Whiteside, "Coaches Have Plenty of Tales to Tell," *USA Today* (February 4, 2003), 10C.

2. Michael Gurian's book, *What Could He Be Thinking? How a Man's Mind Really Works* (New York: St. Martin's, 2003), discusses this in much greater detail.

3. Gurian, *What Could He Be Thinking?* 12.

4. Ibid., 15.

5. Ibid., 16.

6. Ibid., 86.

7. Ibid., 82–84.

8. Ibid., 475.

9. John Gottman, "The Seven Principles for Making Marriage Work," in *The Book of Marriage*, ed. Dana Mack and David Blankenhorn (Grand Rapids: Eerdmans, 2001), 472.

10. Ibid.

11. Ibid.

12. Gurian, *What Could He Be Thinking?* 227.

13. Cited in Shaunti Feldhahn, *For Women Only: What You Need to Know About the Inner Lives of Men* (Sisters, Ore.: Multnomah, 2004), 146.

14. Linda Weber, "Building a Strong Marriage," in *The Joy of a Promise Kept* (Sisters, Ore.: Multnomah, 1998), 97.

Chapter 9: Jeanne-Antoinette

1. Evelyne Lever, *Madame de Pompadour: A Life* (New York: Farrar, Straus and Giroux, 2002), 11.

2. Christine Pevitt Algrant, *Madame de Pompadour: Mistress of France* (New York: Grove, 2002), 46.

3. Ibid., 55.

4. Lever, *Madame de Pompadour*, 116.

5. Ibid., 80.

6. Algrant, *Madame de Pompadour*, 76.

7. Ibid.

8. Carolyn Mahaney discusses this challenge in "True Beauty," in *Biblical Womanhood in the Home*, ed. Nancy Leigh DeMoss (Wheaton, Ill.: Crossway, 2002), 35.

9. C. F. Keil and F. Delitzsch, *Commentary on the Old Testament: Proverbs, Ecclesiastes, Song of Solomon* (Grand Rapids: Eerdmans, 1973), 131.

10. Lever, *Madame de Pompadour*, 131.

11. Ibid., 262.

12. John Stott, *The Message of 1 Timothy and Titus* (Downers Grove, Ill.: InterVarsity, 1996), 188.
13. Lever, *Madame de Pompadour*, 126.
14. Algrant, *Madame de Pompadour*, 288.

Chapter 10: Ray and Jo: Taming the Temper, Part 1

1. Jo has her own writing and speaking ministry. You can contact her through her website at www.jofranz.com.

Chapter 11: Taming the Temper, Part 2

1. Shaunti Feldhahn, *For Women Only: What You Need to Know About the Inner Lives of Men* (Sisters, Ore.: Multnomah, 2004), 24.
2. Ibid.
3. Ibid., 25.
4. Thanks to Leslie Vernick for offering helpful suggestions for this paragraph.
5. I'm indebted to Elton Trueblood for this insight.
6. I love Andrew Murray's book titled *Humility*. I've written chapters on this "queen of the virtues" in several of my books, including *Seeking the Face of God*, *The Glorious Pursuit*, and *Authentic Faith*. There's also a chapter on humility as it pertains to marriage in my book *Sacred Marriage*. If you like to listen to teaching tapes, C. J. Mahaney preached an excellent sermon on pride in March 2002 at what was then called the "PDI Leadership Conference" (main session #1). You can access C. J.'s sermons by visiting www.sovereigngraceministries.org.
7. Cited in Amy Patterson-Neubert, "Get Serious: Domestic Violence Is Not a Joke," *Purdue News* (October 16, 2003). Arriaga's article, "Joking Violence Among Highly Committed Individuals," was originally published in the June 2002 issue of the *Journal of Interpersonal Violence*.
8. Ibid.

Chapter 13: The Biology of a Busy Man

1. Stanley Weintraub, *Charlotte and Lionel: A Rothschild Love Story* (New York: Free Press, 2003), 17.

2. Ibid., 53.
3. Ibid., 64.
4. Ibid.
5. Ibid., 189.
6. Ibid., 293.
7. Michael Gurian, *What Could He Be Thinking? How a Man's Mind Really Works* (New York: St. Martin's, 2003), 36, 39.
8. Ibid., 63.
9. Ibid., 47.
10. Ibid., 48.
11. Ibid., 62.
12. Quotes and information for this story come from John Feinstein, "The Punch," *Sports Illustrated* (October 21, 2002), 68ff. The article was adapted from a book by the same name.
13. Dr. Steve Stephens and Alice Gray, *The Walk Out Woman* (Sisters, Ore.: Multnomah), 147.
14. Cited in Judith Martin, *Miss Manners' Guide to Excruciatingly Correct Behavior* (New York: Atheneum, 1982), 7.

Chapter 14: Pure Passion

1. "Christians and Sex: Sexual Issues in the Church," Church Research Report, Christianity Today International (2004), 3.
2. Michael Gurian, *What Could He Be Thinking? How a Man's Mind Really Works* (New York: St. Martin's, 2003), 109–10.
3. Ibid., 113.
4. Shaunti Feldhahn, *For Women Only: What You Need to Know About the Inner Lives of Men* (Sisters, Ore.: Multnomah, 2004), 100.
5. Ibid.
6. Ibid., 95.
7. These statistics are cited in Jerry Grimes, "Fighting the Battle against Pornography" (January 2005); on the Web at www.ciu.edu/seminary/resources/articles/life/dealing-w-pornography_grimes.pdf.
8. This and other comments from Mitch Whitman resulted from our discussion of the ideas in this book.

Chapter 16: John and Catherine: Finding Faith

1. Account and quotes taken from George and Karen Grant, *Best Friends: The Extraordinary Relationships of Ordinary People* (Nashville: Cumberland, 1998).
2. Ibid.,113.

Epilogue: Everlasting Beauty

1. Cited in David McCullough, *John Adams* (New York: Simon and Schuster, 2001), 168.
2. Ibid., 172.
3. Ibid.
4. Ibid., 429.
5. Ibid., 479.
6. Ibid., 626.

Questions for Discussion and Reflection

Chapter 1: The Glory of a Godly Woman
1. What is the difference between trying to *change* a man and trying to *influence* him?
2. Do you think it's true that women tend to be more invested in their marriages than men? If so, why do you think this may be the case? What are the challenges of such a reality?
3. If you "caught" your husband bragging about you, what do you think he would be saying? What would you like to hear him say in the future? Identify some things you can start doing to build on this.
4. On a scale of one to ten, one being, "I feel best about myself when men like me and pay attention to me," and ten being, "I believe I'm worthy because I'm made in the image of God and am loved by God," where would you fall? What can women do—for themselves and to encourage other women—to move up that scale?
5. How does your image of yourself as a woman compare with the Scriptures Gary shared in this chapter? What was compatible? What was different?
6. What are the marks of a woman who has turned her marriage into idolatry? How would doing this undercut a woman's power to positively influence her husband in a godly way?

Chapter 2: The Strength of a Godly Woman
1. Have you ever encountered "functional fixedness" in your own marriage? What did it look like? What *didn't* work as you tried to address it? Based on what Gary shared, what might be a more effective approach in the future?
2. What do you think represents the greater danger to a marriage—a husband's momentary anger, or a wife's perceived weakness? If you chose the latter, why do you think women often suppress their frustration instead of addressing it?
3. What is an appropriate way for a woman who is committed to a biblical view of marriage—"till death do us part"—to stand up and say, "If this doesn't change, our relationship *will* be affected?" What might be the dangers of such an exchange? What might be some of the benefits, for the wife as well as for the husband?
4. Do you agree with Gary that "the most damaging thing you can do in an unhealthy relationship is nothing"? What keeps some

women from acting boldly? What will help them act more courageously?

5. Have you ever "given up" on an issue in your marriage? In what way? What do you wish you would have done differently, in hindsight? How might this experience affect your future actions?

6. In what area of your marriage is it most difficult for you to be active and to show courage? How can women encourage each other to be less passive and more active in their marriages?

7. List the top two areas of your marriage that need positive, God-honoring influencing. Begin praying for God to show you appropriate, active, love-affirming responses.

Chapter 3: "Be Worthy of Me"

1. If it's true that your husband's faults may be God's tools to trans form you, what do you think God is trying to work on in your life today?

2. Why is it important for wives to maintain a healthy, biblical attitude of "becoming worthy" while seeking to influence their husbands' growth?

3. How is God using your marriage—as it is right now—to teach you how to love?

4. How has being married to an imperfect man made you stronger and wiser?

5. What is the difference between "dreaming" things for your husband and demanding that he change?

6. How does the notion that God is with you in your marriage help you face your current marital frustrations and struggles?

7. In what ways will an active and courageous addressing of the issues in your marriage prepare you to influence and transform the world?

Chapter 4: The Widow at Zarephath

1. List the three main positive traits that first attracted you to your husband. When was the last time you complimented your husband for these traits?

2. If your husband were to die, apart from his companionship, what two or three things would you miss most? How can you affirm these qualities now?

3. Does James 3:2 ("we all stumble in many ways") help you look at your husband—and your marriage—in a new light? How so?

4. What kind of expression is usually on your face when your husband returns home? What are some realistic expectations for con-

sistently greeting him in an edifying and influence-producing way? What can you do to stay sensitive to this over the long haul?

5. How would your husband's friends describe the way you look at your husband? Does this need to change? How so?

6. Where is your man most likely to fail, character-wise? How can you—following Becky Allender's example—call your husband to his best with affirmation, while still saying "no" to the sin?

Chapter 5: The Zarephath Legacy

1. What is at least one redeeming quality about your husband that provides a possible avenue for sacred influence?

2. What practical things can wives do to apply Philippians 4:8 to the way they think about their husbands? "Whatever is true, whatever is noble, whatever is right, whatever is pure, whatever is lovely, whatever is admirable—if anything is excellent or praiseworthy—think about such things."

3. Do you define your husband more by his bad days than by his good ones? How can women develop realistic expectations—accepting the fact that their husbands will have off days—while still working toward positively influencing their husbands?

4. What wounds did your husband bring into your marriage? How would you rate your current attitude toward these wounds—redemptively nurturing, or critically judgmental? How can a woman grow in this area?

5. Are you ever guilty of assuming that your husband somehow just intuitively knows what you want? In what area will you be more direct in asking for his help or support?

6. Take some time to consider the grace that God has shown to you. Think of all the impure thoughts, ugly attitudes, and immoral acts for which God has forgiven you. Then ask yourself, How can I offer the same grace to my husband that God has shown to me?

7. What percentage of your needs have you been asking your husband to meet? Do you think you have been asking of marriage more than God designed it to provide? If so, in what way? If an apology is necessary in this regard, will you be courageous enough to offer it to your husband?

8. Which relational and spiritual needs aren't being met in your marriage that might be met by cultivating other friendships at church? Do you see this as a compromise, settling for second best, or as a healthy benefit of Christian community? In addition to making sure these are same-gender friendships, what are some basic guidelines for forming these relationships?

9. If, during your engagement, someone had asked your husband how pleased you were with him on a scale of one to ten, what do you think he would have said? What do you think he would say if someone were to ask him that question now? What has changed?

10. Does your husband receive more affirmation outside the home or inside the home? What are some practical things you can do to correct this (or keep it going in the right direction)?

Chapter 6: The Helper

1. Think of a time when your husband was feeling discouraged or vulnerable. How did you react? Was there something else you might have said or done? If so, what?

2. What are at least three things older women should teach younger women (according to Titus 2:3–4) about how to love and help their husbands?

3. Discuss Gary's comment, "He [your husband] won't hear you if he doesn't feel as though you support him." Have you found this to be true? How can wives be supportive of their husbands while also disagreeing with them?

4. Identify and talk over with a friend the spiritual benefits of a woman understanding and applying her God-ordained role in marriage.

5. List three things you can start doing that would really help your husband physically, emotionally, or spiritually.

6. How might helping your husband pave the way for you to influence your husband?

7. What two or three changes can you make in your life that will move you toward becoming a better helper?

Chapter 7: A Claim, a Call, and a Commitment

1. If Titus 2:4 may be teaching that older women need to "wise up" younger women regarding their responsibilities as wives, what do you see as some of the most commonly needed aspects of this "wising up?"

2. Gary argues that "families crumble because we've lost our respect for responsibility." In what ways do you see this happening these days?

3. Do most women today value the thought of becoming more and more responsible? What *do* wives tend to value most?

4. What is most difficult about acting responsibly in the face of your husband's irresponsibility? What counsel did this chapter offer that will help you respond appropriately?

5. Is there any way in which your attitudes, words, or actions are tempting your husband to act even *more* irresponsibly than he would have otherwise? What may be more profitable alternative approaches for you to consider or pursue?
6. How can women encourage other women who are patiently laying the groundwork for long-term change in their husbands' lives? How can a wife's impatience hinder her husband's long-term character development?
7. What positive trait can you develop in response to one of your husband's weaknesses? (For example, making home a more pleasant place to be for a husband who goes out too frequently.)
8. In what area do you most need to grow in order to become a more responsible wife?

Chapter 8: Understanding the Male Mind
1. Which one of the "brain differences" between genders surprised you—or enlightened you—the most? Why?
2. In what ways has *not* understanding the male mind created conflict in your marriage?
3. Are there any ways in which you've expected your husband to act more like a woman than a man? Do you ever resent your husband's male pattern of thinking? In what way? What are some healthier responses?
4. How can future emotionally charged discussions take into account that some men take up to seven hours longer than their wives to process complex emotional data?
5. Does your husband ever "stonewall"? If so, have you contributed to this response by "flooding" him? What advice would you give to a wife who notices a pattern of withdrawing in her husband?
6. Given that talking through difficulties tends to soothe the wife but can be neurologically painful for the husband, how can couples find a healthy balance?
7. Are there ways in which you may be "crowding" your husband emotionally? What do you need to change in this regard?
8. Do you need to demonstrate love to your husband—the kind of love Jesus showed to his disciples—by encouraging him to experience something fun or relaxing? What would most meet your husband's needs in this regard?
9. Can you think of a trait in your husband that isn't sinful but that really annoys you? What's the healthiest and most God-honoring response to such a situation?

Chapter 9: Jeanne-Antoinette

1. Spend some time "studying" your husband. What would make his life more comfortable, enjoyable, fulfilling, and profitable?
2. Do you put less effort into trying to please your husband now than you did when you were dating? What are some realistic expectations in this regard for a married woman with her own vocation and/or with children at home?
3. Have you started coasting—taking physical intimacy for granted, not putting much thought into being a generous and creative lover? What one or two things can you do to turn this around?
4. Picture your marriage as a garden. Would it look neglected and full of weeds, or would it be well maintained and healthy? What two things can you do over the next six months to begin growing a healthier marriage?
5. What is the most effective way for you to "captivate" your husband? When is the last time you put this into practice?
6. List three ways that *phileō*—friendship love—can bind a man's heart to his wife in ways that *eros* love can't.
7. Has your love for your husband been marked more by a persistent pursuit or a scattered effort? What can you do to remain more persistent in your efforts? How can reverence for Christ recharge a woman's motivation?
8. How might persistently loving your husband and building him up positively affect your own life in the long run?

Chapter 10: Ray and Jo: Taming the Temper, Part 1

1. Did you notice any increase in the level of your husband's anger after the two of you were married? Did this surprise you? Looking back, can you see any seeds of that anger?
2. Why do women sometimes blame themselves for their husbands' anger?
3. Jo discovered that, because Ray was raised in an alcoholic family, she "needed to tutor him on how to talk to a woman." Discuss effective ways you've found to teach your husband how to express his anger in appropriate ways.
4. Gary writes that "Jo went to God, understood her value as his daughter, and approached Ray from a position of being spiritually loved instead of desperately empty." Have you ever approached your husband out of need instead of out of being loved by God? Talk about the difference it makes when wives first cultivate a satisfying relationship with God before they seek to influence their husbands.

5. Gary shares that "angry men sometimes tell me something they rarely tell their wives: they feel ashamed of how they've acted … In most cases, when you help your husband tame his temper, you're helping him to become the kind of man he wants to be." How might this insight help motivate you to finally take a stand against your husband's anger—or to persevere if your stand isn't immediately met with gratitude?

6. Have you, like Jo, ever held back from sharing your needs out of fear of seeming selfish? What do you think of Gary's contention that patiently teaching your husband to love you is providing your husband with a valuable spiritual service?

7. How might being motivated by your husband's spiritual welfare—rather than your own comfort—transform the issue of what you address with your husband and how you address it?

8. Why do you think so many women provide indirect clues or hints about their needs but rarely state them in a concrete manner? Why do you think it was so difficult for Jo to just tell Ray that going shopping wasn't merely about buying something but, even more, about being together?

Chapter 11: Taming the Temper, Part 2

1. How difficult is it for you to accept Gary's conclusion that "at times, you must allow your husband to feel legitimately angry with you?" Do you believe that anger can be an appropriate response to a sin you've committed?

2. Were you surprised to find out that talking about a problem can soothe you but actually increase your husband's stress? What are some ways you can give your husband space as he processes his anger?

3. How can you show respect—verbally and nonverbally—as a strategy for defusing your husband's anger? Discuss how some women act or speak disrespectfully in such a way that they inadvertently create a "frustration bomb."

4. Gary writes, "For years, men have been told to be more sensitive to women; perhaps it's time to help women understand how to become more sensitive to men." Talk about some of the ways you need to be more sensitive toward your husband—particularly as it relates to respect.

5. In light of Elton Trueblood's insight that "there are a hundred ways to miss a target but only one way to hit it," how can you maintain an attitude of humility while disagreeing with your husband? How might remembering that just because he's wrong

doesn't guarantee you are right affect the way you talk through an issue?

6. How can the church do a better job of helping women who are in physically abusive relationships?

Chapter 12: Rich and Pat: The Magic Question

1. Gary notes that men have a tendency to avoid battles that they can't win or that make them feel incompetent. How can wives support their husbands so that they'll feel just as competent at home as they do at work?

2. Pat confesses that when Rich came home, "I greeted him with a list, was in a chronically bad mood, and was usually either depressed or angry." Identify and talk about some realistic expectations for wives so that they can do a better job of getting their husbands to become more involved at home.

3. Discuss the "magic question": "What things would you like me to do that I'm not doing?" Are you comfortable asking this of your husband? Why or why not?

4. Pat entered Rich's world of fishing even though she initially had no natural interest in it. What are some of your husband's favorite hobbies or activities, and how can you build intimacy by joining in with him?

5. Pat says, "God gives you your spouse as the person who can fix those things in you that you really don't want to fix." This might be a hard lesson to accept, but what are one or two things God is using your husband to "fix" in your own life?

6. How can small groups in particular, or churches in general, help challenge "underinvolved" husbands?

Chapter 13: The Biology of a Busy Man

1. Was there a "romance adjustment" after your honeymoon, in which your husband started focusing more on his vocation and less on you? How did you handle it?

2. How can women resist becoming disappointed in their husbands and instead work to become part of an "indissoluble team," like Lionel and Charlotte?

3. Michael Gurian asserts that "there is a biological tendency in men to seek self-worth through personal, independent performance," while women tend to achieve a greater sense of self-worth through relationship. How can understanding these biological tendencies encourage a couple to work together and complement each other?

Are you willing to allow your husband the same zeal to pursue performance as you pursue intimacy?

4. Gary warns about the tendency for women to seek a quest-oriented man and then try to turn him into a "sedate shepherd" after the wedding. What advice would you give a young bride who faces this temptation?

5. Do you agree that the psychological cost of a frustrating job debilitates and discourages men? If so, how can women support their husbands who face such a situation?

6. Gary talks about "the gift of laughter." Can women who aren't naturally enthusiastic still offer this? If so, how?

7. Discuss with the group (or with God or a close friend) what you think it's like for your husband to be married to you.

Chapter 14: Pure Passion

1. What do you think of Gary's claim that "sex represents one of the most effective ways by which you can care for—and motivate—your husband"?

2. Do you believe that husbands experience sex more personally than do wives? How might this affect the relational dynamics in the bedroom?

3. Does Michael Gurian's assertion that a man's "self-worth is linked, to a great extent, to how often and how well he engages in the sex act" surprise you? How does it affect the way you might look at your husband's advances in the future?

4. Gary suggests that a sexually fulfilled husband "is far more likely to be more heavily involved and invested in the home," and that by making an effort at physical intimacy, wives "open the door to the emotional intimacy you so rightly desire." Do you think this is a manipulative use of sex, or a God-ordained function of sex?

5. Discuss how sexual promiscuity is affecting the spiritual integrity of men; then suggest ways that wives can help their husbands avoid this trap.

6. Were you surprised by Gary's comment that "many wives simply don't understand how much effort it takes for some men to remain sexually faithful to one wife"? Do you think this is true of *your* husband? Have you ever thought about how you can make it easier for him? Or thanked him for remaining faithful?

7. How can wives support other wives whose husbands are struggling with pornography? Based on Gary's teaching in this chapter, what advice would you give a woman who just discovered something inappropriate on their home computer?

8. How can wives say "no" to improper sexual demands while still being generous with regard to pure expressions of physical intimacy?
9. Gary ends this chapter by saying that a mutually satisfying sex life knits a man's heart to his wife, helps protect his spiritual integrity, and helps a wife learn how to live in a godly and selfless way. How has God used the sexual relationship in your marriage to teach you how to love?

Chapter 15: Ken and Diana: Affair on the Internet

1. To what extent are you and your husband cultivating *shared* interests? What are some practical ways couples can grow in this area?
2. How can wives help husbands take an interest in *their* hobbies?
3. How did Diana's solid faith help her to maintain the right attitude while confronting Ken?
4. How can couples guard against Satan taking advantage of a natural lull in a relationship and trying to turn it into a permanent break?
5. Discuss practical ways in which you can engage in "winning [your husband's] heart so that you can influence his soul."
6. Are you and husband currently growing together, or are you slowly growing apart? How can you reinforce the former, or if you are growing apart, how can you reverse this?

Chapter 16: John and Catherine: Finding Faith

1. Discuss the impact of Jesus' words in Luke 6:32–36 about loving those who aren't always easy to love, specifically as they relate to a woman married to a nonbeliever or a nominal Christian.
2. How can Christian wives who are married to nonbelieving or spiritually immature husbands follow Paul's directive in Philippians 2:3 to "in humility consider others better than yourselves"?
3. How might God use an unsaved spouse to help a Christian wife grow in godliness?
4. Do you agree with Catherine that it's possible for a Christian wife married to a nonbeliever to err by going to church functions too often? What might be some other common errors of Christian wives in such marriages?
5. How might Christian wives be setting up their nonbelieving or spiritually immature husbands for failure, expecting them to do things they just can't do?
6. Catherine urges wives, "You must find out what he loves doing and learn to do it with him." How can wives move past the frustra-

tion of having different faith expressions while still being open to sharing other activities?

7. What are some of the practical issues—such as money management or time at church—that are likely to be problematic in an unequally yoked marriage? How can a believing wife act and speak in such a way to promote redemption instead of contention?

8. How can wives balance patient perseverance—waiting for the right time—with direct sharing of the gospel?

Gary Thomas

Feel free to contact Gary at glt3@aol.com. Though he cannot respond personally to all correspondence, he would love to get your feedback. Please understand, however, that he is neither qualified nor able to provide counsel via e-mail.

For information about Gary's speaking schedule, visit his website (www.garythomas.com). Follow him on Twitter (garyLthomas) or connect with him on Facebook. To inquire about inviting Gary to your church, please e-mail his assistant: laura@garythomas.com.

From Gary

Dear Readers,

Thank you so much for joining me on this journey. I hope you found it helpful. My sincere prayer is that you will have gained both significant insight into your husband's heart and mind and renewed spiritual fervor for God.

Some of you might be wondering, "What should I do now?" I'd like to offer two suggestions. First, if you haven't read *Sacred Marriage*, I encourage you and your husband to do so, as this book provides the foundational thought for what you've just read. In addition to providing stories of how women have learned to draw nearer to their God as they learned to love their husbands, *Sacred Marriage* can introduce your husband to some of these same concepts in a context that will challenge *him*.

Second, consider reading *Devotions for a Sacred Marriage*. By reading one devotional entry a week (preferably with your spouse), and doing so faithfully for a year, you can begin training your heart and mind to look at marriage through the perspective of how God is challenging you spiritually and personally. It takes time to retrain our minds to think biblically; I've worked hard to create a very practical tool for just this purpose. You'll find a sample entry right after this letter.

May God bless you as you seek to serve him by becoming the woman he created you to be; and may God continue to make your marriage a truly sacred, soul-shaping union that reflects Christ's love for the church.

The peace of Christ,
Gary Thomas

27

Marriage Is Movement

Behold, I am coming soon!
Revelation 22:12

Lisa and I went to see the movie *Seabiscuit* with Rob and Jill, two of our closest friends. At the start of the movie, I sat by Rob and Lisa sat by Jill, so that Lisa and Jill could share the unbuttered popcorn and Rob and I could assault our arteries with the buttered kind. But halfway through the movie, Lisa had to get up for a moment, and Rob slipped over to sit by his wife.

There was something wonderfully refreshing in seeing a man who has been married for eighteen years still eager to sit by his wife for the last hour of a movie. That simple movement said a great deal about Rob and Jill's marriage, and it personifies a biblical truth.

I heard of one wedding in which the *bridegroom* actually walked down the aisle instead of the bride, in order to capture the biblical picture of Christ — *the* bridegroom — going to his bride, the church. As Christ pursues the church, so the husband is to pursue his wife. (Note to future husbands: it's the rare woman indeed who would even *consider* giving up that famous walk down the aisle; I wouldn't recommend trying this at home!)

Marriage is more than a commitment; it is a movement toward someone. Husbands, are you still moving toward your wife? Or have you settled in, assuming you know her as well as she can be known, and thus turning your sights to other discoveries and challenges? Even worse, are you violating your vows with the "silent treatment" or a refusal to communicate?

Wives, are you moving toward your husband? Are you still pursuing him, seeking to get to know him, trying to draw closer to him? Have you considered new ways to please and pleasure him, or have you become stagnant in judgment, falling back to see if he'll come after *you*?

Jesus moves toward us even in our sin; will we move toward our spouses even in theirs?

Movement is about more than communication; it's about the force of our wills. Are we choosing to pursue greater intimacy in our relationship? Do we seek to resolve conflict, or do we push it aside, assuming it's "not worth the hassle" while letting our love grow colder? Are we still trying to understand our spouses' worlds — their temptations and trials, their frustrations and challenges — or are we too consumed with our own? Are we praying for our spouses, encouraging them to grow in grace and holiness, or are we tearing them down behind their backs, gossiping about them so that everyone will feel sorry for how difficult we have it?

Honestly ask yourself, "Do I know my spouse any better today than I did three years ago?" If not, maybe you've stopped moving toward your spouse. And if you've stopped moving toward your spouse, you've stopped being married in the fully biblical sense of the word.

This week, why not launch yourself on a new exploration — your spouse? Why not see what new things you can learn — how you can grow even closer to each other, how you can give up a little more independence and embrace a little more interdependence? Why not make a renewed attempt to study your spouse every bit as much as a biology student studies the movement of cells under a microscope or a seminary student pores over thick reference books late into the night?

So many people say the "excitement" has left their marriage. Well, exploration is one of the most exciting journeys known to humankind. Most of the globe has been mapped, many times over — but that person who wears your ring? There are still secrets yet unknown and yet to be explored on that side of the bed.

Get busy.

Sacred Marriage

Gary Thomas

Scores of books have been written that offer guidance for building the marriage of your dreams. But what if God's primary intent for your marriage isn't to make you happy . . . but holy? And what if your relationship isn't as much about you and your spouse as it is about you and God?

This book may alter profoundly the contours of your marriage. It will certainly change you. Because whether it is delightful or difficult, your marriage can become a doorway to a closer walk with God.

Devotions for a Sacred Marriage

A Year of Weekly Devotions for Couples

Gary Thomas

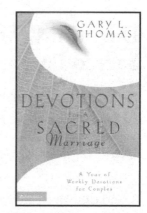

The author of *Sacred Marriage* returns to the topic of how God uses marriage to expand our souls and make us holy. With all new material, *Devotions for a Sacred Marriage* explores how God can reveal himself through your marriage and help you grow closer to him as well as to your spouse.

Fifty-two devotions encourage you to build your marriage around God's priorities. From learning to live with a fellow sinner to sharing our lives as brothers and sisters in Christ, *Devotions for a Sacred Marriage* challenges couples to embrace the profound and soul-stretching reality of Christian marriage.

Sacred Parenting

Gary L. Thomas

Many books have been written about how to parent a child effectively, how to become a better parent, and how effective parenting produces better kids. But *Sacred Parenting* delves into a different reality: how parenting affects the parent. It explores the spiritual dynamics of parenting, and why caring for children is such an effective discipline in shaping our souls and forming the character of Christ within us. Parents of all children will be encouraged by seeing how others have successfully handled the challenges of parenting and will be inspired by stories that reaffirm the spiritual value of being a parent.

Devotions for Sacred Parenting

A Year of Weekly Devotions for Parents

Gary L. Thomas

Spend time once a week for an entire year contemplating the soul-transforming journey of parenting.

Devotions for Sacred Parenting continues this journey with fifty-two short devotions, containing all new material. The life-related devotions are creative and fresh, and readers will be inspired, challenged, and encouraged as they explore the spiritual joys and challenges of raising children. Each devotion will point them to opportunities for spiritual growth—and help them become more effective parents at the same time.

Sacred Pathways

Gary Thomas

In *Sacred Pathways*, Gary Thomas strips away the frustration of a one-size-fits-all spirituality and guides you toward a path of worship that frees you to be you. If your devotional times have hit a snag, perhaps it's because you're trying to follow someone else's path. This book demolishes the barriers that keep Christians locked into rigid methods of worship and praise.

Sacred Pathways unfolds nine distinct spiritual temperaments—their traits, strengths, and pitfalls. Illustrated with examples from the Bible and from the author's life experience, each one suggests an approach to loving God, a distinctive journey of adoration. In one or more, you will see yourself and the ways you most naturally express your relationship with Jesus Christ. You'll also discover other temperaments that are not necessarily "you" but that you may wish to explore for the way they can stretch and invigorate your spiritual life.

Authentic Faith

Gary Thomas

Bestselling author Gary Thomas helps us sharpen our spiritual vision and fortify our commitment by examining ten disciplines God uses to forge a fire-tested faith. A biblical view of these disciplines can safeguard us from disillusionment when—not if—difficulties surface in our lives. How we respond will determine the depth and vitality of our walk with God.

Authentic Faith reveals the rich benefits that derive from embracing the harder truths of Scripture. This eye-opening look at what it means to be a true disciple of Jesus will encourage you, bolster your faith, and help you rise above shallow attachments to fix your heart on things of eternal worth.